Dear Reader:

The book you are about to r̶e̶a̶d̶ [is a] St.
Martin's True Crime Library [book] — Your Guide to
"the leader in true crime!" Each month, we offer a fresh
account of the latest, most s̶e̶n̶s̶a̶t̶i̶o̶n̶a̶l̶ crime that has captured
national attention. St. Martin's is the publisher of bestselling true
crime author and crime journalist Kieran Crowley, who explores
the dark, deadly links between a prominent Manhattan surgeon
and the disappearance of his wife fifteen years earlier in THE SUR-
GEON'S WIFE. Suzy Spencer's BREAKING POINT guides readers
through the tortuous twists and turns in the case of Andrea Yates,
the Houston mother who drowned her five young children in the
family's bathtub. In Edgar Award-nominated DARK DREAMS, leg-
endary FBI profiler Roy Hazelwood and bestselling crime author
Stephen G. Michaud shine light on the inner workings of
America's most violent and depraved murderers. In the book you
now hold, VANISHED AT SEA, acclaimed author Tina Dirmann
takes a closer look at the mysterious disappearance of a couple
after they sell their boat to a former childhood actor.

St. Martin's True Crime Library gives you the stories behind the
headlines. Our authors take you right to the scene of the crime and
into the minds of the most notorious murderers to show you what
really makes them tick. St. Martin's True Crime Library paperbacks are better than the most terrifying thriller, because it's all
true! The next time you want a crackling good read, make sure it's
got the St. Martin's True Crime Library logo on the spine—you'll
be up all night!

Charles E. Spicer

Charles E. Spicer, Jr.
Executive Editor, St. Martin's True Crime Library

Other True Crime Library titles
by Tina Dirmann

Such Good Boys

VANISHED AT SEA

The true story
of a child TV actor and
double murder

Tina Dirmann

St. Martin's Paperbacks

VANISHED AT SEA

Copyright © 2008 by Tina Dirmann.

Cover photos of Skylar Deleon and Jennifer Deleon © Newport Beach Police Department. Cover photo of the *Well Deserved* © Chuck Silvers. Cover photo of boat © Jack E. Hancock / Orange County Register.

ISBN: 0-312-94197-8
EAN: 978-0-312-94197-0

Printed in the United States of America

St. Martin's Paperbacks edition / January 2008

St. Martin's Paperbacks are published by St. Martin's Press, 175 Fifth Avenue, New York, NY 10010.

10 9 8 7 6 5 4 3 2 1

ACKNOWLEDGMENTS

It's never easy to tell a story like this. One filled with so much inexplicable tragedy. It requires the time, patience and trust of so many people, often at the most terrible time of their lives.

And so, I have a long list of "thank yous" to people who invited me into their lives, and allowed me to tell one of the most chilling, and most riveting, crime stories of my journalism career.

First, thank you to Dave Byington, Evan Sailor and the entire team of stellar investigators at the Newport Police Department. I feel privileged to have written about the hard work you all put in to bring the Hawks family the justice they deserved. Thank you for inviting me in to witness all your work and dedication.

Matt Murphy, prosecutor extraordinaire. Where do I begin? You'll never know how much I appreciated your endless patience with answering all of my endless questions. Thank you for your trust, your time and your friendship. There's nobody better in the prosecuting business. Keep putting away the bad guys!

Thank you to my editors at St. Martin's Press, Michael Homler and Charlie Spicer, for your support and very kind words about this book.

My wonderful agent, Jane Dystel, thank you for pushing me to write another true crime, when you know I didn't want to! You were right . . . it was so worth it!

To Eliza Gano . . . I couldn't have asked for a more dependable and hard-working research assistant. I don't think you ever complained, not even once, no matter how tedious the task. I couldn't have done this without you.

The Alvarez Family (Fred, Tracy, Apple and Alex)! How can I thank you guys for opening the Ojai compound to me, giving me a safe haven to do all this writing. You listened to me talk about this story until your ears must have been weary and bleeding. Is that why we ended up drinking so much wine each evening? And Fred, I couldn't have asked for a better second set of eyes. Thank you for never saying no as I tossed every new page your way. I love my Ojai family so very much.

And finally, the Hawks and O'Neill families. Matt, Ryan, Jim, Jack, Gayle and all those who loved Tom and Jackie so. It was an incredible honor to write about these fine people. Thank you for letting me in close enough and sharing all of your memories—the ones that made you laugh and the ones that made you cry. I know one thing as I've concluded my reporting—Tom and Jackie were indeed wonderful people. And I want you to know I struggled every day on this project to present a story that did right by them. I honestly wish I could have known them.

I also want to offer a special note of remembrance to someone who played a very key part in helping me tell this story. Dixie Hawks, a woman of style, class and intellect. Dixie lost a battle with lung cancer just before this book was published. Dixie, you will be missed.

VANISHED
AT SEA

CHAPTER ONE

The name of the boat said it all—*Well Deserved*. And it was.

Standing on the deck of their 55-foot yacht, taking in deep breaths of the salty sea breeze brushing their skin, Thomas Hawks and his wife, Jackie, knew life didn't get any better than this.

They weren't rich. He was a retired probation officer. She was a stay-at-home mom. But they scrimped, they saved, they invested. And they retired early. By the time they sold their Prescott, Arizona home, they had earned enough to fulfill a lifelong dream—live life on the ocean blue. They fought hard to get there. And it was well deserved.

"We have been told that God doesn't count time on the water towards your lifespan," Thomas said of his life at sea, "so I'm sure Jackie and I have many more cruising years ahead of us."

But even when life's rewards are earned, there's no guarantee fate won't turn against you. Even the best of luck can go bad. Even the brightest fortune can be washed away by storms. Even the most promising horizon, appearing so blindingly brilliant, can be hiding the dark squall gaining strength just beyond your sight.

And so, there's no way Tom and Jackie could know what lay ahead for them. The past two years had been so good. The couple spent their days traveling up the Mexican coast—Puerto

Vallarta, San Carlos, La Paz, Guadalajara. If a patch of beach looked appealing, they simply stopped and dropped anchor. Sometimes their wanderlust brought them to the tiniest Mexican fishing villages, ones so small, locals didn't bother naming them. But Thomas and Jackie had the kind of easygoing, fun-loving presence that never left them strangers in a strange town for long. They made fast friends and typically found themselves mingling with the locals, sharing their fish, indulging in a few beers. How long they stayed at each spot could depend on the flip of a coin.

"Do we leave today or stay another night?" Thomas might ask Jackie. "Or maybe we'll just flip for it."

Tom couldn't imagine having spent the past twenty-four months doing anything else—though he had come dangerously close to postponing it all.

After nearly two decades of service as a probation officer for Yavapai County, Arizona, 56-year-old Tom was itching to start his new life at sea.

Shortly after turning in his notice to retire, bosses at the Yavapai County Probation Department weren't ready to let Tom go. He had worked for two decades as a probation officer and it would be hard to find someone who would work as hard as Tom did.

Or care as much.

Twice a year he organized a ten-kilometer run to raise money for the sheriff's office's D.A.R.E. (Drug Abuse Resistance Education) program. As a volunteer Search and Rescue officer, he scoured his county's rugged backlands in search of lost hikers. And he rode with the sheriff's Jeep Posse, where he'd once helped comb the woods of Prescott for a little deaf boy who'd gotten himself lost. The team ultimately found him, scared but healthy, hiding beneath a clump of bushes.

He was the kind of guy even the probationers on his case load looked up to.

"The way my dad looked at it," Ryan Hawks said of his dad's job, "he thought he was helping someone who went down the wrong path in life get back on the right path. He thought this was his way of giving back to his community."

One probationer, an artist, in thanks for all the guidance Tom provided, presented him with a portrait—of Tom himself, an avid bodybuilder, lifting weights. "That's how much these guys loved him," Ryan said. "They always wanted to give him things to show how much they appreciated his help."

Desperate to keep Tom on the job a little longer, the county offered him another $500 a month on his retirement pay if he'd put in one more year. Initially, Tom said yes. Even though he'd already sold his home. Even though he'd already bought the *Well Deserved*. He said yes.

Then a close friend, Judge Robert Kuebler, the man who'd married Tom and Jackie so many years before, retired at age 53. He'd been a judge and educator for better than thirty years. Three months later, the father of five was vacationing in Deer Valley with his wife and one of their sons when his car careened out of control. His wife and son were airlifted to the nearest ER, and survived. Robert did not.

Tom took the news hard. Thirty days later, in August 2001, he put in his notice once again. And this time, he meant it.

"You know what," he told Jackie. "Life's too short. Let's go."

Later, Tom would write about his decision in a nautical magazine, explaining, "The sea was calling us and we couldn't wait any longer. Life is just too short to put things off, and one cannot discover new oceans unless they have the courage to lose sight of the shore."

Jackie was overjoyed. The 47-year-old homemaker was Tom's second wife, but they had already spent twelve blissful years of marriage together. She had overcome her own challenges in life, too—like beating a brush with death over fifteen years ago, before she'd ever met Tom. She'd gone on to lead a happy life, finding joy in the simple tasks of keeping a tidy home for herself and her husband. And she doted on Tom's sons from a previous marriage, Ryan and Matt, whom she'd helped raise. Though she was only their stepmother, they grew to love her so, they simply called her "Mom."

But Tom was her best friend, and she couldn't wait to spend days at sea with him. She dreamed of weeks with nothing more stressful on their minds than catching their dinner—until they could become so unaffected by time, they wouldn't know if it was Tuesday or Saturday.

"Every day's a weekend for me," Tom liked to joke to his sons, especially when the boys complained about work deadlines, early morning meetings, and unreasonable bosses.

But as good as life at sea was for Tom and Jackie, something changed in the winter of 2004. Young Matt Hawks, an Arizona firefighter, and his fiancée had just had their first baby, a boy named Jace. And suddenly, Jackie longed for something more than her carefree, nomadic life at sea. She wanted to watch her first grandchild grow up. Tom, a fiercely loyal family man, couldn't argue with that.

So the *Well Deserved* went up for sale. The plan was to buy a house their grandbaby could visit, probably in the Mexican resort town of San Carlos, along the Sea of Cortez—a spot where abundant sea life and mild temperatures made it ideal for cruising any time of the year. Of course, they'd pick up a smaller boat, so whenever the urge hit, they could take excursions up the Mexican Gulf.

In November 2004, Tom placed an ad in *Yachting World* magazine:

1980 LIEN HWA TRAWLER
55' × 15'8". 1350 fuel, outstanding condition, cruise ready, everything imaginable. $435,000. Moored in Newport Beach, CA. By owner.

The ad had been running several days before they got a call from a prospective buyer. His name was Skylar Deleon.

CHAPTER TWO

The *Well Deserved* was exactly what Skylar was looking for. He'd been scouring "for sale" ads in newspapers and nautical magazines since late summer. So far, he'd called on a few ads showcasing large cabin cruisers. But nothing felt just right. So he waited. This would be no spur-of-the-moment decision. He knew what he wanted. Something big. Really big. And worth a lot of cash.

Not that he had the cash to buy the two-bedroom, two-bath, double-decked luxury craft, boasting a hand-carved teak interior. At 25, he was unemployed, uneducated, and recently dishonorably discharged from the Marines. He had a 1-year-old toddler and his wife Jennifer was pregnant with baby number two. The pair currently called home the converted garage attached to his in-laws' middle-class home in Long Beach, California. And they were $87,500 in debt.

Life couldn't be more bleak.

Jennifer put the pressure on.

"She has a very strong personality," Skylar would say of her. "But she's really smart."

Indeed, Jennifer was a woman with big plans. She was never going to be satisfied with her meager state. She made it clear to her husband—he needed to bring home money. She wanted a home for herself, for her kids. And her job cutting hair at Little John's Family Hairstyling was never going to get her there. Already, she'd borrowed $32,000 from her father, an instrument technician for British Petroleum, always promising they'd pay him back soon. But soon never came.

"Don't worry," Skylar began telling her as she approached her sixth month of pregnancy. "I have a plan. Everything's going to work out just fine."

But that was hard to believe. So far, nothing in Skylar's life had worked out "just fine."

The son of a convicted drug dealer, Skylar never had an easy life. He'd squeaked through high school. But he was a handsome enough boy—with dark hair, an angled chin, and a charming smile. He'd tried his hand at acting as a kid. A poor memory, however, meant he could never quite remember his lines during the auditions. He managed to score a few bit parts in commercials. But his biggest claim to fame was a non-speaking role in two episodes of the children's television show *Power Rangers*. That was in 1993, and Skylar was just 14 years old. As an adult, he kept in contact with his old showbiz manager, but he'd never have a paying gig again.

He floundered for more than a year after high school graduation before joining the Marines at 20. For a guy with no money, no education, and little family support, the military could have been a lifeline, as it has been for so many young men and women starting out with few options before them. A regular paycheck, job training, and access to the best health and retirement benefits. But after fifteen months in service, Skylar went AWOL. In response, the Marine Corps kicked him out. Still, he was lucky. Such an offense could have brought a court-martial and time behind bars. Instead, as so many others had, the military simply decided to wash its hands of him. And just like that, another option slipped through his fingers.

For a guy living a life so distinctly different from Thomas and Jackie Hawks, Skylar did share one thing in common with them—a love of the ocean. He took scuba diving lessons, spending hours at sea in pursuit of his dive certificate, then continued on, hoping to snag an advanced dive master's license.

Along the way, he poured thousands of dollars into a beat-up boat his grandfather owned, hoping to earn a living by chartering the thing out for dive trips. He toyed with the idea of starting a business cleaning boat hulls, too.

But in the end, nothing panned out. He was never the kind of guy who had more than a few dollars in his pocket. And now he was married, the father of two, and desperately broke. As his obligations grew, so did Skylar's desperation. To survive, he developed dark secrets. Some say Jennifer was the driving force behind those secrets. She was a young wife with high expectations, and letting her down wasn't an option. It wasn't just that he wanted to provide for her. It was a more complicated, frightening push to show her—just watch, he could do it, he'd succeed. A blackness developed over Skylar, who became obsessed with a single thought: money. He wanted it. He needed it. And there was nothing he wouldn't do to get it.

It's hard to believe Jennifer didn't know that about her husband. Didn't know something bad had happened when, in December of 2003, her unemployed spouse dumped $21,000 into their bank account. He spent another $2,200 to buy her a platinum-and-diamond wedding band. Then handed out $18,000 in new hundred-dollar bills to a boat repair yard to fix up his old boat in hopes of jump-starting his chartering and boat-cleaning business.

And in the fall of 2004, it was Jennifer who made no secret of their next purchase plans. Boasting of a large influx of cash about to come their way, she contacted a realtor, asking to be shown waterfront homes in the 2-million-dollar range. She eagerly made plans to move from her parents' 19×19 foot garage into a multi-million-dollar estate.

Their luxury purchases raised eyebrows. Where could a man like Skylar get so much money all of a sudden, acquaintances wondered. Inheritance from distant relatives, he told some. Old acting royalties, he sometimes said. Drug money, he confided to others.

And by the time he spotted the ad for the $435,000 *Well Deserved* that first week of November, he was ready to make her his own.

On the afternoon of November 6, Skylar and friend Alonso Machain met Tom and Jackie on the deck of their boat as it was moored in the well-to-do beachside community of Newport Beach, California. Tom took one look at Skylar and was immediately skeptical. How could a guy so young have the cash to buy such a luxury item?

"I was a child actor and made some pretty good money," Skylar told him, overstating his stint on the *Power Rangers* show. "I invested that money. So I've done pretty well for myself."

Skylar put all his charm into play for his first meeting with the Hawkses. He joked with the couple, and threw in just enough nautical terminology that Tom was convinced the kid knew his way around a boat. Eventually, Skylar earned Tom's trust. Jackie's, too. And when he asked to come back with a couple of friends to take the boat out for a test ride, Tom agreed.

They met again late in the afternoon of Monday, November 15, 2004. As they pulled out of Newport Harbor, Jackie used her cell phone to call her dear friend and Lido Isle Yacht Club port captain, Carter Ford. When he didn't answer, she left a simple message at 4:07 p.m.: "We are out to sea."

CHAPTER THREE

"Have you heard from your dad?"

Family friend Donny Treffen called 28-year-old Ryan Hawks on a Tuesday afternoon, less than twenty-four hours after Skylar's group and the Hawkses had left for the test run at sea. Just the weekend before, during dinner with friends and family along California's Santa Catalina Island, Tom mentioned that they might, at last, have found a buyer for the boat. If so, they'd need a trailer to move all of their things off the ship. After two years of life onboard, they had accumulated a lot of personal effects to move—clothing, pictures, mementos, equipment. Donny offered his pickup truck for the job.

"Hey, if you feed me, I'll help you load up the truck," Donny teased.

"Deal," Tom said. The plan was for Donny to meet the Hawkses on their boat Tuesday morning and begin unloading. But by that afternoon, there was no word from Tom or Jackie.

"Last I talked to him, he was almost positive he was going to sell the boat and would need my help moving back to Arizona," Donny told Ryan. "But I can't reach your dad. The phone just keeps going straight to voicemail. It's not like him to stand me up."

Already, Ryan felt it. Something wasn't right. His father, the

most responsible man he'd ever known, standing up a friend offering help? And on top of that, not answering his cell phone?
Ryan struggled to make sense of it.

"His phone is never off," he said. "That's just strange. Let
me try calling them and I'll get back to you."

He called Tom. And sure enough, the line on the other end
never rang, instead rolling right into voicemail. Ryan called
Jackie's phone. Again, straight to voicemail.

Ryan called his uncle for help. Jim Hawks was a carbon
copy of Tom, his younger brother. Tough, self-reliant, as dependable as the sunrise, Jim was the recently retired chief of
police for the Carlsbad Police Department in neighboring San
Diego County. If anything was wrong, Jim would sniff it out.
Really, Ryan was hoping his uncle would put his mind at ease.

Jim listened to his nephew and promised, if Jackie and Tom
didn't turn up soon, he'd drive out to the Newport Harbor himself and track down the *Well Deserved*.

"Okay," Ryan told him. "You know, they probably sold that
boat and are out celebrating somewhere. Their phones are just
out of range or something."

That's what Ryan said. But it's not what he was thinking.

"I knew this man," he would say later. "I lived with this man.
So much just seemed wrong. It was bizarre."

On November 23, still with no word, Jim and Donny met
Carter Ford in Newport. Immediately, Carter spotted the 11-foot
dinghy Tom and Jackie used to cruise between their yacht and
the Balboa Peninsula. Tom would never leave the dinghy's mo-
tor to sit in the water overnight. And yet, there it was, left carelessly floating in the ocean. Not to mention the dinghy's
condition. So dirty. There was a rope, securing the dinghy to the
dock. But it was a sloppy knot. The men knew—Tom and Jackie
Hawks were not the last people on this boat.

Jim glanced out to sea and caught sight of the *Well Deserved*,
anchored and still just a short distance away. Using Carter's 21-
foot cruiser, they made the five-minute ride out to the yacht the
Hawks called home. They yelled out, but no one answered.
Ford circled the craft. An uneasiness fell over the men. The

deck was dirty. A towel was tossed unthinkingly out of a port-hole. And a green tarp used to cover the ship's nautical equipment was slipping off. The instrument panel was left uncovered, exposed to the elements.

With each observation, Jim's alarm grew. His brother loved this boat. His sister-in-law used tender loving care to clean it every day. Obviously, someone else was now in charge of the *Well Deserved*. But who?

"It's like looking at your grandmother's kitchen, where she keeps it tidy and immaculate," Carter Ford explained. "Then, all of a sudden, it's not like that anymore. It's a complete mess. The visual effect was the same for me. Clearly, someone else had taken control."

Then there were other signs. Peeking into the cabin, Jim could see that his brother's prized plaques, awards won for his exemplary service as a probation officer, were no longer on the wall. But he left behind his beloved surfboard, the one he'd had customized with his name, HAWKS, airbrushed in bold letters along the top. Even if he'd gone off to Mexico, he'd want that board with him, in case he got the urge to catch some waves. It wasn't right.

Jim pulled out one of his old cards from the police department and jotted a note on the back: "I'm a retired police officer looking for my brother. Please call." He left a number.

It took an entire day, around 7 in the evening, before Jim's phone rang. Jennifer Deleon was on the line.

"Look, I'm pregnant and at work, so I don't have a lot of time to talk," she blurted out in a rush, "but a friend of mine found your card on the boat."

Jim thought she sounded odd. Nervous? And he didn't know why she was telling him she was pregnant. Now Jim was nervous. Especially when she hesitated answering even the simplest questions, like her full name. And her husband's.

"Um," she paused, "I'm . . . I'm Jennifer. My husband is Skylar."

"And what's your last name?" he coaxed.

"Deleon," she said.

"And you guys just bought the boat, right?"

"Yes," she said.

"Well, she's a very fine boat," he said, trying to ease her into some small talk, hoping she'd open up. "I hope you enjoy it."

"Yes, I'm sure we will," she said.

"My brother said your husband was a Power Ranger," he tried, still prodding for information, and hoping to put her at ease.

"Yes, yes, he was," she said.

"Well, we're just trying to find out where my brother and his wife went after your purchase, because we haven't heard from them."

She paused a moment, then answered, "Yeah, we haven't heard from them either, unfortunately. But they talked about going to Mexico, so maybe they're still there."

"Did they say where in Mexico? Or why they were going there?" he asked.

"I'm not sure," she said. "But they mentioned buying some property, I think."

At least that much was true, he knew. Tom and Jackie were hoping to buy a home either in Mexico or back in Arizona, near Jace.

"Well, if you hear from them . . ." Jim began.

"Of course," she said. "I'm sorry. I've just got to get back to work. But I have your number."

"Sure," Jim said. "Thanks for calling me back."

Jim felt sick with alarm. After all his years in police work, the signs were pointing in directions he didn't like. There was no way Tom and Jackie would have hopped off to Mexico without telling a soul in the family. His mind turned to their last trip out to sea. What happened out there on the *Well Deserved*, he wondered. What happened to his capable, caring brother and beautiful sister-in-law?

Two days later, on November 26, Jim was shocked when his phone rang again, and Jennifer was back on the line.

"I just wanted to see if you've heard from your brother," she said, this time sounding much more at ease.

"No," he told her. "We haven't."

"Okay, because we've been trying to reach them. They were

supposed to come back and show us how to change the fuel tanks."

"No, we haven't heard anything yet," he said.

"Well, I also wanted to apologize for being so short with you last time I called," she said. "I was just really tired and busy at work."

"Sure," said Jim, acting with caution. He didn't trust this woman. "Can I just ask you a few more questions? We're a little worried here. You said they talked about going down to Mexico?"

"Yes, to buy property in the San Carlos area, if I remember correctly," she said. "My husband has Mexican citizenship, so, he offered to help them with that."

"You know, when I was out at the boat," Jim said, "I could see they left a lot of their personal belongings behind."

"Yes, they did," Jennifer said. "They seemed anxious to be on their way, so we just told them to come back whenever they wanted and pick up their things. That's another reason we're waiting for their call!"

"Uh-huh," he said. "And how did you guys pay, if you don't mind telling me? Did you all go to a bank or hand him a cashier's check?"

At this, Jennifer paused. Jim thought he heard a muffled voice in the background. A male voice maybe? He couldn't tell. Jennifer came back on the line.

"Right, um, we paid cash," she said. "We just met them in the parking lot by the pier and we gave them cash for the boat."

"Well, this just isn't like them," Jim told her frankly. "We're filing a missing persons report. I think we need the police to step in."

"Oh no," she said, sympathy filling her voice. "I'm so sorry. Well, if we hear from them, we'll certainly have them call you right away. And will you do the same? When you hear from them, have them call us? Like I said, we have a lot of questions for them."

"Of course," said Jim. But he already suspected the worst. He was terrified that, in fact, no one would ever be hearing from his brother and sister-in-law again.

CHAPTER FOUR

Just eleven days earlier, late in the afternoon of November 15, Thomas Hawks had been enjoying one of the last afternoons he'd ever spend on the deck of his boat when he got the call. It was Skylar.

"We're here," he told Tom.

Tom made his way down to the dock along 15th Street at the Newport Harbor. As he walked, he braced himself for the bittersweet decision to let go of his pride and joy, the *Well Deserved*. Once again, life was about to change for him in a big way. But he was ready for it. He looked forward to living in a house once again, to being settled enough that he could embrace being a first-time grandfather.

Skylar stood there with his sidekick, 21-year-old Alonso Machain, a slightly framed man with long, thin limbs, gawky features, and pale skin. Thomas already knew Alonso from their previous meeting, so he put out his hand and greeted the men warmly. But a third person stood alongside Skylar. The man, CJ, said nothing as Tom approached. The newcomer must have made an odd first impression on Tom. The hulking 39-year-old black man stood 6 feet tall and packed 240 pounds of muscle. At that size, with that build, he would have cut an intimidating picture. However, per Skylar's instructions, CJ dressed as conservatively as a choirboy on his way to Sunday school, wearing pressed slacks and a green sweater. Skylar introduced him as his accountant.

"He won't be saying much," Skylar told Tom. "He doesn't speak much English."

Tom surely found that explanation strange—Skylar's trusted accountant couldn't speak English? How did they communicate? But he accepted it anyway, and took the trio aboard the dinghy, bound for the *Well Deserved.*

Jackie waited on deck, smiling warmly as she always did when new arrivals came aboard her home. As it was already late in the afternoon, Tom wasted no time firing up the ship's engine and slowly guiding her out of the harbor. They weren't out to sea long when CJ reached for his stomach.

"I think he's seasick," Skylar told Tom. "Maybe he should go lay down for a few minutes."

Tom stopped the boat and helped CJ make his way down below, out of sight from the ever-tilting seascape. Skylar took the moment to announce he'd like to go for a dive.

"I'd like to go down and check out the hull under the water," he announced. The Hawkses didn't argue. Seemed like a reasonable request from a prospective buyer. And since their boat was in tip-top shape, they had nothing to hide. Generally, they loved showing off how well they had taken care of their home. Skylar slipped on a wet suit and jumped in. As he disappeared underwater, Jackie stood on deck chatting with Alonso. By now, she was used to making small talk with strangers, after all the traveling to foreign ports with her husband. Tom chimed in now and again. But Skylar wasn't gone long. There wasn't a lot to inspect. As promised, everything looked great.

Skylar climbed back onboard and headed down below to get out of his dive gear and check on the ailing CJ. Tom followed. Alonso made his way into the kitchen with Jackie, distracting her with chatter, asking questions about her travels.

But when a violent crash caught Jackie's ear, she jumped with fright. "What the hell is going on?" she said in alarm, trying to push past Alonso and look in on her husband.

But Alonso couldn't let her get through. "It's on," he thought.

They were taking Tom down. He had to act fast. Grabbing Jackie, he pushed her back, hard, and thrust a black, pistol-sized stun gun into her thigh. He tried feverishly to zap her with enough electricity that she'd fall to her knees. But he missed. Or the damn thing just wasn't working. She was still charging against him. So he tackled her slight, 110-pound body, bringing her down by force before pulling out a pair of handcuffs and tightening them around her wrists.

Jackie probably knew that in the next room, her husband was also in the battle of his life. A bodybuilder all of his life, Tom would not go down easily. He was 57 years old, and stood just 5'8", but he was 185 pounds of solid muscle. This was a man who taught others how to lift weights while at sea, who won trophies for arm-wrestling competitions, who, as a young man, had more wrestling championship titles than he could remember. So, as CJ and Skylar rushed toward him, he surely used every ounce of strength to push them off. CJ tried in vain to get Tom in a chokehold. Tom was too strong. He couldn't get a grip on him. But armed with a stun gun of their own, CJ and Skylar had the advantage. As Tom buckled, CJ delivered a crushing blow to Tom's face, leaving him with a bloody nose.

Alonso gathered himself enough to peek out as Tom's hands were forced behind his back and into handcuffs. He brought a nearly hysterical Jackie into the bedroom and sat her on the bed next to her husband.

"Go to the engine room and see if you can find some duct tape," Skylar instructed Alonso.

Alonso returned, tape in hand, and on Skylar's direction, ripped off strips to settle over Tom's eyes and mouth. Jackie was next.

With his victims safely bound, Skylar reached for his cell phone. Alonso thought it was odd that Skylar would be making a call at such a moment. But it was only the first of more than a dozen calls he'd make from the boat that day.

After his call, Skylar marched Jackie and Tom, one at a time, into the kitchen and presented a stack of papers.

"I'm going to need your signatures," he told them. "And thumbprints." As he spoke, he gripped a 12-inch heavy metal

Maglite. It would strike a vicious blow if anyone got out of hand.

"I'll uncuff your right hand so you can sign. But don't cause trouble. Just sign where you're supposed to, initial where I tell you to. Cooperate and you'll live," Skylar said.

A terrified and trembling Jackie Hawks finally spoke, hoping to reason with her tormentors.

"I don't care about the boat, I don't care about the money," she told them, fighting for calm despite the tears tumbling down her cheeks. "You can have whatever you want. We won't call the police. Just let us go. Please—just don't hurt us."

As she made her plea for mercy, Skylar handed her the first document—a bill of sale for the boat. Then another stack of papers.

"Just sign and you'll be okay," he told her.

She shook uncontrollably as she took the pen. Her hand trembled so fiercely, she struggled to scrawl out her signature.

Tom probably guessed as he saw the documents authorizing Skylar Deleon as their power of attorney—giving him open access to every bank account, savings account, and asset the Hawkses owned—that he and Jackie would never make it back to shore alive. Not only that, but Skylar was demanding to know their birth dates, mailing address, Social Security numbers, banking information. Tom eyed the Maglite as the cuffs came away from his wrist.

"If you try anything," Skylar reminded him, "I'll smash you over the head with it."

"No," Tom said, "I won't try anything. I'll do whatever you want."

He signed, as instructed. Then dipped his thumb over the ink pad Skylar provided and dotted the paper in front of him. But with every move, his mind must have been reeling, mulling over his options. Tom had never been a man to give up when life got hard. And he wouldn't start now.

Instructing Alonso to take the Hawkses back to the bedroom, Skylar punched in another call. There was a brief conversation before Skylar snapped the phone shut and jabbed a series of coordinates into the boat's Global Positioning System.

Now operating on automatic pilot, the boat turned around, heading deeper into the ocean. Skylar made another call.

The boat chugged slowly toward an area Skylar knew well—a patch of ocean between Santa Catalina and San Clemente Islands. Skylar was a regular at the popular dive spot, known for ocean floors with such severe drop-off points, divers allege some dips reach into eternity. Sadly, Catalina Island was also a favorite stop for the Hawkses—it was where they'd had dinner with Jim, Donny, and other friends just days before. For nearly two hours, the Hawkses sat below deck, restrained, but next to each other on the master bed they'd shared for so many months at sea. Alonso, charged with babysitting the captives, hated the sound of Jackie's terrified sobs. Her mouth was taped, but he could still make out her muffled words.

"Why?" she kept saying. "Why are you doing this?"

Alonso said nothing.

"Please, I'm too young to die!" she screamed. "We have a grandson. I just want to see my grandson again. Please."

Tom strained against his cuffs to reach Jackie's hand. Alonso didn't interfere when he saw Tom reach his wife and gently stroke her fingers. Tom ached to calm her. But for now, a faint touch was all he could offer. What could be worse than helplessly sitting still for two hours, waiting for your inevitable end to come? Maybe knowing that your life partner, the woman you love more than anything in the world, is awaiting her death, too.

As the boat slowed to a stop, Skylar and CJ made their way to the fore and slowly unhooked an anchor. Together, they hauled the 66-pound weight to the boat's rear.

"Alonso, bring them up!" Skylar barked from the deck above. "I want them with us."

As he had the entire trip, Alonso did what he was told. By the time he was settling Jackie and Tom on the rear deck, Skylar and CJ began wrapping ropes around the couple's waists. Skylar looked at the duct tape loosely placed over their eyes and mouths.

"Let's tighten this up," he told CJ. He tore at the tape on their faces.

"Skylar!" Jackie cried out, her mouth free for a moment from the tape. "How could you do this to us? We've been so kind to you. So why? How could you?"

Skylar had no response for Jackie. What could he say? Instead, he wrapped the tape in a complete circle around her head, covering her eyes. He looped the tape again, this time over her mouth.

Skylar picked up the rope once more, now securing one end of it to the ship's heavy anchor. Though he couldn't see it, no doubt, Tom knew what was coming. Facing his last moments, he waited until he felt Skylar within reach, and then, with everything he had, he kicked backward. Skylar was hit squarely in the groin. The force of Tom's blow was so fierce, it lifted Skylar off the deck before he fell into a heap on his back. He moaned and cursed for a moment, working to regain composure. CJ reacted, punching Tom in the face, forcing him to reel back. He surely would have fallen if his body hadn't been braced by his wife, tied against him.

Skylar laughed. And he was still chuckling when he reached for the anchor and hurled it into the ocean.

CJ stepped up to push Tom backwards. And this time, the couple lost their footing and crashed onto the deck. From a standing position, they might have had a fighting chance to brace themselves against the wood flooring, resisting the anchor as it fell overboard and rushed to the ocean's bottom. But on their backs, they slid across the deck, slipping toward a small open door along the boat's edge. They could hear the clink of the anchor's chain as it unwound. And as the last links gave out, the rope went taut and slammed their bodies against an open portside door. Jackie's head and shoulder struck the ship's ledge, hard, causing a gruesome thump before her body tumbled over and into the water, her husband beside her. The bodies plunged beneath the ocean's surface, and then, in an instant, disappeared completely. Ripples broke along the water. And from above, Skylar leaned over the ship's railing to watch until the water became still once more.

With his adrenaline racing, Skylar reached for his cell phone and made another call.

Alonso looked up and gazed to the right of the boat, where
Catalina Island lay in the distance. He didn't know his eyes
rested on the spot where, just days before, the Hawkses had
dined with loved ones, proclaiming themselves happier than
ever and looking forward to selling their boat to the young man
who'd earned all that money as a child actor.

With the murder behind them, the men set about scouring
the boat. Alonso found $3,000 in a briefcase in the main cabin,
and a few more dollars tucked into an envelope in the master
bedroom. He handed it all to Skylar, who divided the cash three
ways.

After, Skylar flipped through a leather-bound captain's log,
where Tom had meticulously recorded ports of call, weather
conditions, and unforgettable adventures—like the swim he'd
taken alongside a school of humpback whales. Skylar skimmed
the pages, then snapped it shut and hurled the book of memories overboard. He returned downstairs to stand before a wall of
plaques and certificates of appreciation, all from Tom's department, thanking him for outstanding service. Tom had been so
proud of them. Now, Skylar picked them off the wall and, like a
kid tossing Frisbees in the park, flung them into the ocean. The
stun guns followed behind.

It was late by the time CJ found the fishing rods and cold
beer stashed onboard. It was dark now, and the *Well Deserved*
was making its way back to Newport Beach. With a nearly two-
hour ride home ahead of him, he popped a few of those cold
ones, gingerly tossed his line into the ocean, and sat back for
the ride.

CHAPTER FIVE

After twenty-six years of looking into the worst that humanity had to offer, Newport Beach Police Sergeant Dave Byington knew when he was listening to a crime unfolding. And after investigating literally hundreds of missing persons cases, he was pretty good at sensing when a missing family member was just getting away from it all, eager to escape marital problems, work stresses, or financial woes. And when there was reason to worry.

James Hawks had reason to worry.

"We can't reach him," Jim told Dave during a phone call to the detective, "or Jackie. It's been too long now. It's not like them."

It was November 29. Fourteen days of silence.

"I'm extremely close to my brother," Jim said. "He's a good family man. Always in touch with us, even when he and Jackie are out to sea. They have everything on that boat, cell phones, satellite phones, email, just so they could stay in touch."

And now, Thanksgiving had come and gone, without even a call.

Every call to Tom and Jackie's phone still rolled to voicemail. But most chilling for Jim was the fact that the couple hadn't used their phones or credit cards in fifteen days.

"They aren't vacationing somewhere. They're missing," Jim said.

Sergeant Byington's dark eyes filled with concern.

He was an attractive man—the definition of tall, dark, and handsome, with thick black hair and lightly browned skin. As a young man, he was trouble. Lots of partying. Lots of girls. But he grew up fast when one of his girlfriends ended up pregnant. He would marry her, divorce her, and then marry her again. They are still married today, with two kids.

But he still talks about the time before all that, before he settled down completely, when he'd landed on the wrong side of a badge during a wild night out. He was just 15, growing up in the predominantly poor, predominantly Hispanic neighborhoods of East LA. A group of buddies drove him out to ritzy Newport Beach for a night of drinking when the very young and inebriated Dave Byington paused to urinate on a white car parked at a nearby curb. Unfortunately, the car turned out to be a Newport Beach police car.

"I didn't know it was a cop car," the detective says now about the incident, a chagrined smile on his face. "I told the officer, 'Hey, in East LA, all the cop cars are black and white!' That was my defense!"

They arrested him anyway and called his parents to come pick him up. But years later, as he was being sworn in as a newbie officer for Newport, he thought of that time.

"Hey," he warned his superiors after the new badge was firmly on his chest, "I came back to seek my revenge, that's all!"

By the time Tom and Jackie went missing, he had been a dogged investigator for more than two decades. As a long-time member of his department's narcotics team, he was aggressive, tireless. Around the halls of the Newport Beach Police Department, the name Sergeant Dave Byington was synonymous with the word *respect*.

Now, as head of his department's Economic Crime and Robbery/Homicide Units, he found himself sitting with Jim Hawks and easily relating to the former career cop. He didn't take Jim's case more seriously than others out of some vague notion of lawman loyalty. But he realized Jim knew his way around a criminal case. Jim had already done some basic cop work—looking into his brother's phone and credit records, even making a trip out to the boat. By now, it wasn't just gut instinct telling Jim something was wrong. Early evidence pointed to it, too.

But Jim was retired. And this wasn't his jurisdiction. He filed a missing persons report with his old department in Carlsbad the day after Thanksgiving 2004. Maybe Jim had started there because he knew the men and women who made up that department—and they cared about him. But he understood they'd have to transfer the report to Newport Beach authorities. Ultimately, Jim needed Sergeant Byington's help.

As the sergeant listened to Jim's story, he found himself drawn to something else during that first interview, something more basic and human. He understood the way Jim described his brother's love of family. Sergeant Byington was also a husband and father. His was a closely knit Latino family, and he knew what it would say to his loved ones if he just didn't show up for Thanksgiving dinner one year.

"Tell me more about the couple that bought your brother's yacht," the sergeant said.

Jim recounted his last dinner with Jackie and Tom on Catalina Island, when they'd mentioned the young actor offering to buy the *Well Deserved*. And he told the detective about the odd phone call from Jennifer Deleon, who explained that she and her husband, Skylar, had bought the vessel from them on November 15, but hadn't heard from the Hawkses since.

Sergeant Byington looked down at the name scrawled in his notebook: *Skylar Deleon.*

That's where his investigation would begin.

CHAPTER SIX

Skylar Deleon almost didn't make it into this world.

In November 1978, Lynette Birchett was pregnant, unmarried, and scared to death of her baby's father.

She sat, fidgeting nervously, in the waiting room of a Van Nuys, California, abortion clinic. This was no way for a girl to spend her 18th birthday.

If they had called her name just a few minutes earlier, she would have missed him. Instead, she was there, alone, when John Jacobson burst into the clinic and marched to her side.

"If you do this," he told her, "if you kill my kid, I'll kill you. Simple as that. I've got a shotgun. And I swear, I'll kill you."

Lynette never saw a gun that day. But she believed him.

"I was so scared of John in those days," Lynette said of her early years with him. "He had a lot of power."

Lynette met John at a friend's party when she was just 16 years old. John was 21, handsome, with deep brown hair, and skin tanned from his days outside laboring in construction.

"He was such a hard worker, that's what I liked about him," Lynette said. "When I first met John, I thought that he was someone who could really take care of me."

Though she was just a junior in high school, when John suggested they get an apartment together, Lynette jumped at his offer, fleeing what she described as an abusive, unloving home. They moved into a tiny one-bedroom in a low-rent district along Woodman Avenue in the Valley of Los Angeles. And life for the new couple was good. Happy.

"Then I remember someone stole our rent money," Lynette said. "Everything seemed to just change after that."

Hoping to make up the shortfall, Lynette said her husband tried selling some pot for a friend. "It was easy and he made so much money so fast," Lynette said. "And that was it. He started selling drugs full-time to make money. It started out with just pot, but then he turned around so much money, that turned into coke, then PCP, then pills—anything he could." The dealing became so good, the couple moved from their apartment into a modest home.

Eventually, John became not just a seller, but a user of his product, his former wife recalled. His moods altered wildly, between life of the party, and a man with dark demons.

"He was abusive," Lynette said. "He started hitting me. God, he'd hit me all the time."

So when Lynette found herself pregnant, she didn't want her baby. Raising a child with John Jacobson meant a life of more abuse, more drugs. She should have run then. But she didn't.

On December 4, 1978, Lynette drove for four hours across the Nevada state line. In Las Vegas, she married her baby's father.

Their son was born at Sierra Memorial Hospital in Sun Valley, California, on August 12, 1979. But this was long before the infant would ever be known as Skylar Deleon. On his birth certificate, he is listed as John Julius Jacobson, after his daddy.

After recovering from the birth of her son, Lynette longed for a legitimate way to make a living. John was adamant. He wouldn't give up dope sales. But he fronted enough cash to Lynette so that she was able to open up a small business, Backyard BBQ.

"I ran that business," Lynette said. "I stayed working the whole time I was with John. I didn't want anything to do with selling drugs. I just ran the business. And John liked the idea of having the business because it made him look legal. But he took all the profits I ever earned. God forbid we ever saved a dime."

Relatives close to John at this time say he had a fateful meeting with major drug runners at a party one night in LA. These were men boasting big contacts with Colombian suppliers. That's where the real money was, they told John.

"All I can tell you is that suddenly, there wasn't just small amounts of coke coming out of our house back then," Lynette said. "I'm talking kilos. It was major."

And the Jacobson family began living the very high life. They moved from a three-bedroom, middle-class home on Chase Street in Panorama City to a huge estate in Woodland Hills, California. It had an Olympic-size swimming pool and four bedrooms, filled with the latest electronics and expensive oak furniture. They traveled in limousines and rented high-end luxury cars.

"Back then, I never even did laundry," Lynette said. "If I ran out of clothes, I just bought new ones."

John had so much cash, he launched a music business, promoting a rock band called Pretty Poison. He booked them into major clubs along the famous Sunset Boulevard Strip in Hollywood.

"He used all the money he was making to get them a big record deal," Lynette said.

Meanwhile, life at home became a constant party, with huge bashes at the pool, and strangers sleeping over. Once, guitarist Eddie Van Halen even stopped by, hoping to buy an expensive Stratocaster guitar that John owned.

"I remember, [Eddie] was such a nice guy," Lynette said. "He had just broken up with his girlfriend, so he was really down. This was just before he started dating Valerie Bertinelli."

From the outside looking in, theirs was a life to envy.

"But I was dying inside," Lynette said. "It was hell. Little John never saw what real life was like. He saw crazy coke whores drifting in and out of his home."

Worse still, Jon Jon, as his mother took to calling him, began having seizures. Doctors couldn't figure out an exact cause, but put him on phenobarbitol—a heavy sedative and anticonvulsant medication. The seizures slowed, but wouldn't completely go away until he was 15 years old.

"It's probably all the coke in the air," an angry Lynette remembers telling her husband. "He's probably inhaling it!"

Jon Jon was just 16 months old when Lynette left John for the first time, tired of the drugs, tired of the other women her husband brought home. A furious John filed for divorce, and it became final in March 1982. A judge awarded custody of Little John to his dad.

But Lynette still longed to be near her son. She kept coming back, often under threats from John, who alternately claimed to love her and promise to see her dead if she didn't return. And John promised she'd never walk away with his boy.

As Jon Jon aged, his seizures raged on. At night, he wet the bed.

Lynette hoped her estranged husband would see how their son was suffering, and would give up his drugs and become a good father. So she stayed—until John flew into one of the worst drug-enhanced rages she'd ever seen. Lynette can't even remember now why he was so mad. It took so little to set him off. But he grabbed a pistol, she recalled, and shot out the windows of their multimillion-dollar home. When he finally calmed down, passed out, Lynette scooped up her toddler and ran. This time, she made a vow to herself, and Jon Jon, never to return.

She struggled to make a new life for herself, now that she was alone and no longer had her business—she'd lost Backyard BBQ in their original divorce settlement.

But she'd lose one more thing before earning her freedom.

Lynette was home, alone with Jon Jon, when a man she recognized as one of John's associates paid her a visit. "You know, he'll never let you have that baby," he told her calmly. "I think you better let John raise his son. Or you're out, you understand?"

Lynette understood. He had just told her that she'd lose her son, or her life.

After that, Lynette rarely saw her boy. He would only live with her once more, when he was 8 years old and his dad was serving a 3-year prison sentence.

According to court documents, a federal task force busted John in May 1987 for transporting methamphetamine and cocaine on a run from Redding, California, to Oklahoma. He was charged with conspiracy to manufacture a controlled substance, distribution of a controlled substance, and interstate travel in aid of racketeering. On November 20, 1987, John struck a deal with prosecutors, pleading guilty to the cocaine charge in exchange for dropping the manufacturing and racketeering charges. He began serving his sentence on January 25, 1988, at the Federal Correctional Institution in Lompoc, California.

Skylar flourished while away from his dad.

"His grades went up, he stopped wetting the bed," Lynette said. "I was remarried then, too. He was doing so much better. And then John was paroled early, about two years later. And he came back for Little John."

Maybe Lynette should have fought to keep her son. But once again, fear kept her from doing so. She had two other children to think about by then, another son and a daughter. And so, she thought of them as she let Jon Jon go back to his dad. Still, today, knowing how her boy's life turned out, she acknowledges regret.

"If he had stayed with me, I know he would have turned out so differently," Lynette says. "If you talk to his dad, he thinks he did the best he could for Skylar, bought him everything he needed. But he didn't see what he was doing to him. That's why I had to get out. Skylar was a great baby. Bottle-broke at one, potty-trained at two. And I stayed until I could take no more. But I wish Skylar could've stayed with me. He would have had a normal life. I know it."

CHAPTER SEVEN

"My life growing up was hell," Skylar said as an adult, looking back on the time he spent with his dad. "My life sucked. I can remember praying that I wouldn't wake up in the morning."

He remembered the time his father took him away from his mom, right after John left Lompoc prison in Santa Barbara County. Skylar was 10 years old. He didn't want to go. He pleaded with his father to let him stay with Lynette and his new stepfamily. But John wouldn't have it. He'd never let Lynette and, more pointedly, Lynette's new husband, raise his boy.

"Forget it," he told him. "You're my kid."

It didn't even matter that John had moved on from his life with Lynette. He now had someone new in his life, too. Before going to prison, John met and married Melissa Lisa Wildin. The couple made their home in Redding, California. Lisa moved to Lompoc so she could visit her husband while he served his time.

John intended to move back in with his wife, who gave birth to the couple's daughter on May 11, 1987, just days after John was arrested. And while he was out on bail, days before he started his prison term, she got pregnant again. She gave birth to John Sr.'s second son while her husband was behind bars.

But now that he was out, a joyous family reconciliation wouldn't be that simple.

First, there were problems with John Jr. He was terrified to see his dad again. And to see the scary cast of characters his dad called friends. One pal in particular, a 25-year-old party buddy of his father's, who sometimes crept into Jon Jon's nightmares, had been molesting the boy for months before his dad was arrested.

John Sr. dumped his son at his estranged wife's doorstep shortly after picking him up from Lynette, telling her to take care of the boy while John settled some business in LA. But Jon Jon knew it was only a matter of time until his dad came back and he would be forced to spend time with his dad's buddy again. So he finally broke down, telling his stepmom everything. It was the first time he'd ever said anything to anyone.

John and his second wife, who went by her middle name, Lisa, alerted the Santa Barbara Sheriff's Department about the molestation in January 1989. The case was turned over to Los Angeles County authorities, since the molestation had occurred in the city of Van Nuys. But it's not clear what happened to the complaint from there. No record of an arrest for the man Jon Jon accused is on file in LA County.

At any rate, the man never saw Jon Jon again, Lynette said. But still, she noticed a difference in her son.

"You could tell he was just changed," Lynette said. "He was so withdrawn after that. He was always looking down. It's like he was trying not to think about it all this time. It just really changed him."

Maybe if Jon Jon's home life had been stable, he could have recovered from the damage caused by such a violation. But as the molestation charges were filed, John and Lisa's marriage crumbled.

While John served his time in prison, Lisa met someone else. She told John she had fallen in love and he couldn't move back in.

John Sr. didn't take the news lightly.

"I love you, and our kids," he always began. But as Lisa held firm to her decision to divorce him, John's tone turned menacing. "Then I will kill you. I will kill you both."

Just like Jon Jon's mother before her, Lisa feared for her life.

Her husband, she came to believe, could put a contract out on her life. He had those kinds of connections, she told friends. She was so convinced he'd have her killed, or kill her himself, that on September 13, 1989, she turned to the sheriff's department for help.

"He can be violent," she told a Santa Barbara County Sheriff's Department deputy. "Before he went to prison, sometimes he carried guns."

The deputy took a report and told Lisa to get a restraining order.

On September 18, 1989, as John called to say he now had a car and a gun and was on his way to kill her, he was in violation of that restraining order—and of his parole terms. A warrant was issued for his arrest.

But John didn't care. He was losing his grip on reality. He called a federal marshal involved in his drug-running case and began rambling.

"I have a gun," he said. "But all I want to do is see my children. If I have to, I'll take care of my wife to do it. Cops will have to shoot me to stop me."

To the marshal, John sounded like a desperate man, like someone who would do harm to himself or his family. He pleaded with John to turn himself in before he did something he'd regret.

"I don't know what to do," John said in response. "I just want to see my kids."

On September 24, 1989, as John drove through Santa Maria en route to Lompoc, deputies finally re-arrested him. He went back to Lompoc prison to finish his sentence, finally ending his time at a halfway house in Los Angeles on June 22, 1990.

This time, while John was in prison, Lisa filed for a divorce. It became final in July 1990.

Through the entire drama, Lisa kept Jon Jon, raising him alongside his siblings. She grew close to her stepson, whom she'd take in periodically, whenever his father's life veered out of control.

"I'm the only real mother he's ever known," Lisa said. "I sure love him a lot. He was always a sweet kid."

But as her stepson got older, Lisa couldn't stop the abuse he endured at the hands of his father.

With John unable to go back to dealing dope because of his probation, he turned to a new way to make money—his eldest son.

"He would take me to auditions in Hollywood," recalled Skylar, who lived in an apartment in Huntington Beach, California, with his father. "He'd hit me if I couldn't remember my lines. I got scared when I knew I didn't get the part, because I knew he would hit me."

Skylar says his stepmother was in the house when this took place, but she never interceded. "She was scared to death of him, too. We all were," Skylar said.

But what he lacked in memory skills, he made up for in appearance.

"Growing up, he was always a beautiful little boy," recalls his grandmother, Marlene Jacobson. "He was cute and had a great personality. As he got older, he got more handsome."

His looks landed him several commercials, roughly thirty-seven in all, Marlene recalled.

"He did something for Disneyland once, something for Buick," she said. "And then one time, he was a friend of one of the little boys on [Home Improvement] with Tim Allen."

But his big claim to fame came in 1993, when, at 14 years old, he was cast in the new hit children's action television show, Power Rangers.

"It was the first year it was on television," Skylar said. "I had a guest lead. That's what they called it. In one episode, I get zapped away to another place. That show was called 'Power Ranger Day.' Then, in another episode that season, the very last episode, I'm with a black Power Ranger and we took a karate class."

There were only two "guest lead" spots, in all. Neither was a speaking role. But a shot of Skylar was cut into the show's opening credits, and that ran all season—about seven months. It would be the closest Skylar would ever come to legitimate stardom.

It should have been a happy time for Jon and his dad. But even then, John seemed to resent his son's fledgling success.

During practice for a scene on the show, Jon learned a few moves from a karate instructor. He came home, kicking in the air at phantom bad guys and making karate-chopping sounds.

"Hiiii-ya!" he shouted, slicing into the void before him with a firm chop. "Take that!" he screamed with a kick.

Watching from afar was John Sr., who couldn't help but make fun of his boy's play. "That's not karate," he told him sarcastically. "That's just a bunch of shit."

Stung by his father's words, Jon paused a moment—then spun around and kicked skyward, his foot missing his dad's nose by a whisper.

John gripped his son's leg before it hit the ground and offered the boy a warning: "Just because you think you know karate doesn't mean I still won't take a baseball bat to you. Remember that."

Jon didn't consider it an empty threat. He was already familiar with the end of his father's fist. "He gave me black eyes, he'd hit me, kick, grab me by the hair and pull me," Skylar said. "There was always some reason. My grades were never good enough, or whatever, you name it."

What few paychecks he got went straight into his father's pocket.

"But *I* earned it, Dad," Jon managed to tell his father after one of his checks arrived in the mail. "Why do you get it all?"

"I don't 'get it all,'" John mocked his son. "It's to support you!"

By the time he was entering his teens, Jon was torn. Despite the prison time, and the abuse of his wives and his son, John Sr. was still someone the boy looked up to. He wanted to impress his dad, somehow. At the same time, he hated his father's macho man act.

During one of his infrequent visits with his mother, Jon told her he thought John Jacobson Sr. "was a no-good man."

"He knew what his father was by then," Lynette said. "Because he was smarter than his dad."

As a teenager, Jon attended Huntington Beach High School. The beachside town of Huntington is a hotbed for surfers. The top surfers in the country gather along the city's sandy shores every summer to battle it out in a series of competitions. Inevitably, Jon picked up the hobby.

To hear Skylar tell it, he was among the best surfers cruising the waves of Huntington. He said he joined the surf team in high school. He said that during the 1997–98 Huntington Beach Surf Series, he'd finished in 6th place—an amazing accomplishment in a tournament that would have been teeming with talent.

"I also won awards with the National Scholastic Surfing Association," Skylar said.

It's hard to tell how much of Skylar's story is fact and how much is fiction. As he aged, he became a talented storyteller, frequently weaving fiction into the facts of his life story.

There are no records supporting Skylar's achievements. His high school yearbook shows a snapshot of the surf team. But Skylar's not in it. And organizers for the Huntington Beach Surf Series say they don't keep records on 6th-place winners from a decade ago. The National Scholastic Surfing Association also has no record of John Jacobson, Jr.'s achievements.

But Skylar insists that as a kid, he was only really good at one thing—surfing. He desperately wanted his dad to come watch him show off on the water. Yet the more Skylar threw himself into the sport, the more his dad put him down for it.

"My dad hated me doing it," Skylar said. "I think because he knew that was the one thing I could really do. So he didn't want me to do it anymore. Waste of time, he said. So he forced me to quit and move in with Lisa. She lived in Kansas by then. Even if I wanted to, I couldn't surf out there."

Skylar begged to stay in California. He wanted to live with his grandparents in neighboring Westminster, still near Huntington's beaches. But John said no. And that was that.

"He's not someone you argued with," Skylar said. "So I moved."

Jon was at Huntington High School long enough to take a senior photo for the yearbook's Class of '98 pages. In the shot, he's wearing a neatly pressed white shirt and black tie, his dark hair cut short and tinged blond at the ends. He looks so clean-cut, he could have easily passed for an honor roll student on his way to band practice. But later that year, he left the sandy shores of California for Kansas and enrolled in Marion High School. It was a huge, picturesque campus, with well-manicured lawns and activities like baseball, football, basketball, track, wrestling, golf . . . But with no beach in sight, a surf team was out of the question.

Jon hated going to class, generally. But the lifelong California boy especially hated his new school, located in the middle of middle America. He felt trapped.

He dug in long enough to graduate, then flew back to California. It was supposed to be just a visit with his grandparents, but he stayed more than a year, hitting the beach and running across the border to take advantage of the surf spots of Ensenada, Mexico.

Despite always being something of a drifter himself, John Sr. told his son he was amounting to nothing. Only sissies surfed that much, he said. It was time the boy did something with himself that would bring home a paycheck.

Jon should have been used to those words by now. It was a regular criticism. But it stung, still. Only this time, he would strike back, going to extremes to prove his father wrong. Jon Jon joined the Marines.

"He always told me not to do it. 'You're not manly enough,' he'd say. So I did it. I did it partly just to get away from him. And partly, just to prove him wrong."

On November 21, 1998, 19-year-old Jon Jacobson Jr. began basic training with the United States Marine Corps. At the time, Jon claimed to hate his father, but in reality, his most fervent hope was that in the Marines, he'd finally become a man who would make his dad proud.

CHAPTER EIGHT

Ryan Hawks struggled to focus. It was the middle of the night, and the roadway ahead of him was dark and desolate. Still, he couldn't stop. He wasn't even halfway through his journey from Arizona to California, and he wouldn't stop until he was at his uncle's house.

Only two days earlier, Ryan left his apartment in San Diego to drive into Arizona to spend Thanksgiving with a friend and attend his engagement party. He didn't want to go. His parents had been missing for over a week. But he was going a little mad at home, waiting for the phone to ring, hoping to hear his dad's booming voice on the other end of the line. His friend convinced him that a couple days out of town might be good for him. Anyway, he could use the time to go door to door, hitting up his parents' friends and asking if anyone had heard from them yet.

At his pal's November 26 engagement party, Ryan did his best to keep his mood light.

"Any word from your parents yet?" concerned friends asked.

"No, no, but they're fine," Ryan said reassuringly. "They just sold that boat, and my dad dragged Jackie up to Cabo for a few days to look at the senoritas!"

His friends laughed at the joke and nodded in agreement, some of them knowing Ryan's parents and their zest for life.

But on the inside, Ryan was crumbling.

After the party, he got a call from his uncle. "Come home," Jim said. "There are some things I have to tell you."

No, he told his nephew, he wouldn't go into it over the phone. "Just come home," he said.

Although night had already fallen hours ago Ryan got into his car and drove as fast as he dared back to California. His shoulders ached as exhaustion and stress settled in, but his mind reeled with worst-case scenarios. Three hours into the drive, he called his brother from his cell phone.

"I think they're dead, Matt."

"Yeah," Matt answered solemnly. "I think so, too."

Ryan had four more hours of driving ahead of him. But after the call, he pulled to the side of the road and cried.

Ryan and Matt Hawks had the kind of childhood John Jacobson Jr. would have envied. There were no rock stars, no limo rides, no TV spots. But there was love.

Not that the Hawks brothers didn't have their own challenges.

"Growing up, my dad was a hard guy to live up to," Ryan says of his father.

Tom was a caring dad. And a strict one. He had high expectations for his sons. But only because he set even higher ones for himself.

Even as a kid, Tom was no stranger to tough work and big adventures. Born on a ranch in the rural town of Chino Valley, Arizona, Tom rose at 5 a.m. to work his family's farm, shucking cornstalks until it was time to catch the school bus. It was intense, backbreaking labor. But as he grew up, Tom learned to make up for that time by playing intensely, too.

Tom used to love to tell the story of how, as a young teen, after his family relocated near the beaches of San Diego County, he and a cousin bought motorcycles. With only $50 between them, they took a 360-mile road trip from California's most southern tip to its northern end—San Diego to Sequoia National Park. When they had to spend half their cash fixing a flat tire, the duo survived on nothing but beans for days.

"Cold ones for breakfast, warm ones for lunch, hot ones for dinner," Tom joked.

At 14 years old, he built his own dory. At 17, he sailed the tiny vessel, only slightly larger than your basic canoe, from Oceanside, California, to Catalina Island. The trip took eighteen hours, and he did it alone.

He spent two summers working at Catalina Island Boys Camp, serving as a sailing instructor and lifeguard.

By then, Tom was also a talented surfer. With his hair bleached dirty-blond from the sun, he earned the Best Looking Male title in his senior yearbook. He was a champion wrestler, winning a scholarship in the sport to Chapman University. And he was a Vietnam veteran, ultimately opting to join the Air Force instead of going to college.

"His dad was in the Air Force and dropped bombs over Hiroshima," Ryan recalled. "So he grew up with the idea that you defend your country. It was bred into him. He felt it was his duty to do it."

Tom served four years in the Philippines, surviving deadly combat battles. The experience would hang with him for a lifetime. Many years later, he could be in the middle of a boisterous dinner party, and Tom might fall silent, letting his mind drift back to the battlefield.

"I was pinned down once," he told a friend after a few beers one night. He was into his fifties by then, but the memory still caused tears to well in his eyes. "I couldn't move for a day, just had to lay there hiding behind nothing but this curve in the street, along the curb. I couldn't move. I couldn't even raise my head up because I'd get shot. It was awful. My buddies were out there, getting killed, and I couldn't even get up and help them."

Tom survived, escaping any physical wounds. And by the time he was finally discharged, he earned top security clearances and the rank of sergeant.

But there was more to Tom than just his scholastic and professional achievements. He would always be most proud of the tight relationship he had with his big brother, Jim. The siblings were best friends. And fierce competitors. Jim, too, was a decorated wrestler, who'd also won the Best Looking title in high school, the year before Tom. He also joined the military, choosing the Army to do his duty. After the service, Jim joined the Carlsbad Police Department in San Diego County. Tom joined the Carlsbad Fire Department and enrolled in night classes at Chapman.

"The most impressive thing about Tom back then . . ." said Dixie Hawks, who met Tom on a blind date in 1971. "Well, you'd think it'd be his looks. But it wasn't. This was an era of drugs and hippies. But not Tom. He was a straight arrow."

She was so in love with this man, who was hard-working enough to carry full-time hours at the fire department, yet earn a bachelor's degree in psychology and get his real estate license on the side. And compassionate enough to find time to volunteer at the local Boys & Girls Club.

Eight months after their first date, Tom took Dixie to his parents' home, and there, in the living room, proposed on bended knee. Without hesitation, the pretty, petite brunette said yes.

In 1976, Tom and Dixie moved to Del Mar, into a home Tom helped build. Dixie was eight months pregnant with their first son, Ryan. Two years later, they had Matt.

But not everything went well for Tom and Dixie. Tom proved to be a difficult man to live with at times.

"He gave a lot," Dixie said. "But he expected a lot, too."

Like the time she was expecting with Matt. Feeling run-down, she mentioned taking an early maternity leave from her job as a court reporter, instead of working up until delivery time, as she did with Ryan.

"Ah, you're just spoiled," Tom said in a tone that was only half teasing. The jab stung. And Dixie never took the extra time.

"He never babied me," Dixie said. "But then, I would never ask him to."

Things took a turn for the worse after Tom, bored with fire-fighting—a job that required a lot of time just sitting around the station waiting for an emergency—quit to open a restaurant. When the business collapsed, so did the marriage.

"The restaurant failing was hard on him," Dixie said. "Especially for a guy so used to succeeding. It was not a good time."

The couple divorced, but remained on such good terms, there was no need for some judge to tell them who could have the kids this weekend or that, and who would spend Christmas with whom.

"It was a hard decision, but a good decision," Dixie said of her choice to let Tom take full custody of her sons. After the divorce, Tom had moved to the mountain town of Prescott, Arizona, where he wanted a fresh start on life. His parents had already returned to Arizona years earlier. And there was an opportunity to go into business with a friend, running a local bar, Matt's Saloon. So he bought a small home and settled in.

At first, Dixie did her best to raise the boys on her own. But staying on top of her two energetic sons while juggling a job that kept her inside a courtroom all day was overwhelming. Tom saw that when Dixie brought their boys to Arizona for a visit. And he offered to take 7-year-old Ryan, and Matt, 5.

"The boys had been missing him so much," Dixie said. "Tom's a big kid. Always has been. He loved fishing and being outdoors. And they loved being with him. Anyway, who else would I want these boys to grow up emulating?"

"I had a great mom," Ryan said. "But there was no way she could raise two boys the way my dad did. And she knew that."

Tom was no pushover parent. Ryan and Matt would be the first to point that out.

"I can't tell you how strict he was," Ryan said, shaking his head for emphasis. "He believed in making us work. And we worked for free. He never paid us, but he'd say, 'You work this weekend, and next weekend I'll take you guys camping.'"

So the boys pitched in, adding rooms to their small home, building bedrooms, then a gym, then a patio, eventually tripling its size. As the boys grew older, and Tom's bar business flourished, he bought more property, fixing up run-down dwellings to sell or rent.

"We were constantly doing side jobs," said Ryan, who, as the older son, spent most of his time at his dad's side learning carpentry work. Little Matt helped when he could, but typically found himself acting as a gofer, handing over tools on demand, running for water, pulling weeds.

At home, Tom owned a small flock of chickens and it was up to Matt and Ryan to wake up at 6 a.m. every day before school and break bags of ice over the chicken coop so the fowl wouldn't overheat under the intense Arizona sun.

"It was important to him that we developed strong work habits, even when we were young," Ryan said. "We even worked for our own lunch money. I know it sounds crazy, but it's true."

Over the years, Tom would give his children money for things that came up in life—school dances, clothes, cars. When Ryan was a sophomore in high school, his dad gave him the $1,300 needed to buy a motorcycle he'd been eyeing.

But everything was a loan.

"I got a job scrubbing dishes at a steak house down the road to pay my dad back for that bike," Ryan said. "Plus interest. eighty dollars, every month until it was paid back."

But there were always rewards behind the hard work. Twice a year, the guys went on a big vacation, usually boating adventures sailing along the Mexican coast, where they fished for every dinner. The boys spent each summer with Dixie in California, but Tom would pick them up at the end, just before they had to head home for the next school year, and sail with them from the San Diego coast into Catalina. For seven days, they camped and fished, just Tom and his sons.

For the first several years after Tom's divorce, life went on like that, with just the Hawks men working like hell so they could earn time boating, fishing, camping. They were happy. But it was an earned happiness, every moment.

"It was a really good childhood," Ryan said.

"Maybe he never was one to give me money to bail me out," Matt said. "But he taught us strategies on how to do it. He'd say, 'You don't need a new TV, you don't need new clothes, make the most of what you have. Enjoy the simple things life has to offer. Your friends, your family, time together.' And he was right. Those lessons he taught me then, they are still with me today."

"I once had a girlfriend tell me, 'You're always putting your family before me,'" said Ryan. "And I told her, 'That's right. And I always will.' My dad was the best friend I ever had."

But it wouldn't always be just the boys.

It was a blistering August day in 1987 as Tom sat sipping a cold beer, hoping for relief from the unrelenting sun during the annual Fireman's Chili Cook-off in Goldwater Lake, Arizona. Dear friends Mary and Hal Slaughter talked the single dad into joining them for the day. And that's how he found her, laughing and talking animatedly as she sat within the confines of her wheelchair. Mary introduced Tom to the striking woman with a slight frame and dark, curly hair. She was so engaging, so bubbly, he couldn't imagine what tragic twist of fate must have robbed her of the ability to walk.

"Tom," Mary said simply, "I'd like you to meet my friend, Jackie."

CHAPTER NINE

It was 3 a.m. on Saturday morning when Ryan finally reached his uncle's home in Carlsbad. He braced himself for whatever Jim had to say. He respected his uncle, as much as he respected his dad. And he knew the former investigator, a graduate of the FBI Academy, could read the signs better than anyone.

"Look," he began, "we have to face some hard facts. By the bank transactions, we know they've not withdrawn any money. And if they sold that boat, they would've made a deposit. They haven't. The police have checked three different borders, and they haven't made any crossings."

"What if they drove to Mexico and had an accident?" Ryan offered, not yet willing to let go of all hope. "Maybe they ran off the road or something."

"If that happened, they would've been found in a day or two," Jim countered, gently trying to get his nephew to accept the inevitable. There was no use in pretending anymore. "Ryan, this is day twelve. They've been gone twelve days. We've checked all the hospitals, all the police stations, we've done a massive search looking for their names to come up anywhere on the grid. There's nothing."

And it wasn't just the cops searching for Tom and Jackie. An entire network of boaters who knew them, loved them, wouldn't let their absence go unnoticed. Unlike in many neighborhoods, where people may live side by side for years and barely say more than hello to the people next door, boaters know each other. They ask for advice on how to make this or that boating repair. They ask which route to take to sail to some faraway destination. Have you ever been to this diving spot? Can you watch my vessel while we go on land for a few days? They become a second family.

"If these sick people thought they could kill on a boat and get away with it," Carter Ford said, "they were wrong. People in some communities come and go. But overall, boaters need other people. I mean, when harbor patrol first started looking for them, within one minute, my cell phone rang three different times from three different people alerting me something might be wrong. People here really do look out for each other."

And so it was, for twelve days, friends and fellow boaters pulled out all the stops to spread the word: *Tom and Jackie are missing*. They worked the phones, calling friends and friends of friends. They held strategy meetings, brainstorming on what to do, where to look next. Tom's cousin, a realtor with a background in graphics, now used his skills to draw up flyers with pictures of Tom and Jackie, looking tan and happy on their boat. There was a picture of the *Well Deserved*, too. And of their silver Honda CR-V and license plate number.

HELP US! COUPLE MISSING AFTER SELLING BOAT IN NEWPORT BEACH!

Missing Since 11-15-2004

Thomas Charles Hawks 57 years, Resident of: Prescott, Arizona Male Caucasian, short brown hair, hazel eyes, 5'8", 185 pounds.

Jackie Ellen Hawks 47 years, Resident of: Prescott, Arizona Female Caucasian, brown hair, brown eyes, 5'6", 110 pounds

Anyone who may have been in touch with the couple or has seen their vehicle call Newport Beach Police.

Carter even had some flyers laminated, so winter rains wouldn't dissolve the paper.

"We tacked those flyers everywhere," Carter said. "You couldn't walk anywhere in Newport Beach without seeing them. We put it anywhere Jackie and Tom would have gone—where they got their mail, did their laundry, grocery store, where they might buy a sandwich."

Carter also took to watching the *Well Deserved* at night. One evening, he boarded a 50-foot vessel docked next to the ship. He wanted to see the people now in charge of the yacht. Word had it, the *Well Deserved* sat still during the day, but was coming and going at all hours of the night, leaving around 1 a.m. and not returning until sunrise. That started a lot of talk. More than one boater wondered out loud if the *Well Deserved* was being used for illegal activities. Maybe drug runs, some suspected.

The Carlsbad Police Officers Association put up a $1,000 reward to any hotel or motel employee who could confirm that the couple had been registered guests on the night of November 15.

On November 27, 2004, Newport Beach Officer Mario Montero first picked up the missing persons report faxed to his agency by Carlsbad Police Sergeant Jay Eppel. He decided to run a safety check onboard *Well Deserved* as it was moored in the ocean. He didn't have a search warrant, so he couldn't do much. But he could force open the lock and make a brief walkthrough, just as a precaution. For all he knew, Thomas and Jackie could be inside, hurt and unconscious. Or their bodies could be there.

As Detective Montero walked through the yacht, he found no sign of them. But he would make another disturbing discovery that day. Lying forgotten on the floor was a receipt for a November 17 purchase—a pack of bleach wipes and a box of heavy-gauge garbage bags. Must-have items for crime-scene cleanup. The detective collected the receipt and left behind his business card.

In the coming hours, investigators would issue a nationwide missing persons alert. They called the Mexican Consulate asking for help searching their hospitals and accident reports. They called the American Consulate, too, and the Office of Immigration and Customs, looking for border crossings of the silver Honda. They put out a shortwave radio broadcast, asking for sightings of the couple from any mariners at sea. And they called the National Insurance Crime Bureau, which investigates fraudulent insurance claims, in case the Hawkses, or someone using the Hawkses' car, had had an accident and tried to report it.

Everything came up empty.

Now, after recapping all that had happened in the past two weeks, the tough veneer Jim had developed as a lifetime lawman faded away and he looked at his nephew with gentleness in his eyes.

"Ryan, I want you to know, your parents lived an amazing life," he said softly.

Ryan knew it was time to let them go. But even as loss seared through him, he pushed the pain back. He had a mission now. How was it that his parents, the only two people he knew without an enemy to their name, had ended up murdered? Had they been shot, strangled, stabbed? And why?

And most important of all—Who was responsible? Was it this so-called buyer, Skylar Deleon? This wouldn't be one of those unsolved murders. If Skylar Deleon had taken Ryan's mom and dad from him, he would not get away with it. Ryan vowed to work tirelessly with investigators, doing whatever they asked of him.

Words his father used to tell him when times got tough now resonated: "This is an obstacle. You can get over it, and you'll move on. And when you do, you'll be stronger."

Over the next few days, he contacted a private investigator to do a background search on Skylar. He consulted a civil attorney about putting a lien on the yacht. He called the investigators constantly, asking for updates, asking what more he could do.

It took every bit of strength and discipline his father had ever taught him to push past his sorrow and face the coming months. But a steely determination melted over him the day he met with his uncle. He'd do whatever it took to get to the bottom of his parents' murder. And as he worked, there would be no more tears—he wouldn't give his parents' killers that satisfaction.

CHAPTER TEN

Jackie was shocked when the muscular, square-jawed man her friend introduced her to appeared interested. From her wheelchair, she felt anything but desirable. But Tom was interested. He spent the rest of the day at the chili cook-off at Jackie's side, chatting her up. When he challenged her to a race, she burst out laughing.

She immediately liked Tom. And as the day ended, he asked for her phone number. She gave it to him. But not without some feelings of guilt. Was it too soon? Was she ready? After all she'd been through in the past year, this probably wasn't a good idea. She didn't think she could date someone new. Not yet. Only twenty months before, Les, her husband of eleven years, passed away. Killed, actually. She was still mourning him. So how could she possibly open her heart to someone new?

Jackie met Les Newell at the Safeway market where she was a checkout clerk, a job she had throughout high school. He was a customer who flirted with the pretty 18-year-old every time she rang up his groceries. Finally, he worked up the nerve to ask her out.

Les, an electrician at the local power company, was good to

Jackie. He adored her easygoing personality. And he thought her beautiful, with her delicate features and lean body. She went to cosmetology school, and though she never worked professionally, she used her skills to make sure she always looked her best. Les was proud to call her his wife.

The couple had been married over a decade when Les decided to build them a house in a very rural area of Dewey, Arizona.

After months of working all day, every day, on the house, Jackie and Les needed a break. They splurged, buying a motorcycle and taking a trip to the East Coast. They were on their way home from that trip, driving through the Prescott Valley on the evening of December 15, 1985. Les sat up front, Jackie wrapped tightly behind him, peeling down the road.

That's when the water-hauling truck barreled through an intersection, ignoring a stop sign. The driver pulled out in front of Les and Jackie, striking their bike. As they hurled toward the trucker, the bike sliding out of control, Les swung against the force, positioning himself between the truck and Jackie. The impact crushed him, killing him instantly. Jackie had a ruptured spleen, a shattered pelvis, her left leg was deeply severed. But she would live.

Only later would Jackie learn that the truck's driver had been drinking that evening.

"He was drunk," Jackie's mom, Gayle O'Neill, said of the driver. "Very drunk."

At the hospital, Jackie lingered in a coma. When she awoke days later, she learned of her husband's fate. And her own: doctors said her pelvis had been so badly damaged, she'd never be able to have children. And the leg, her surgeons added, was beyond repair. Amputation was a must.

"No!" a devastated Jackie cried. She'd already lost her husband, the ability to ever have children. She wouldn't lose her leg, too. "I won't let you. I don't care if it doesn't work. I want to keep it!"

And so, she did, resigned to dragging her lifeless leg with her the rest of her life.

After five months of recuperating at her parents' house in Ohio, Jackie returned to Arizona, determined to finish the home she and Les started. Her parents begged her not to go. It was too much, too soon, they said.

"I have to, Mom," she said. "I've got to finish our house."

But when she arrived back in Dewey, a stunned Jackie found her house nearly complete. There were still a few odds and ends that needed tending to. But the bathroom, master bedroom, and kitchen were done. She could move in immediately. A close friend, a contractor, and his wife finished the work for her. That's how much friends cared about Jackie Newell. An overwhelmed Jackie wept with gratitude.

She did her best to move on, filling up her days with gardening and housework. But there were hard days. Gayle remembered how her daughter sobbed after finally working up the courage to read the police report on the accident. Its graphic description of how Les was brutally crushed was too much detail for any loving wife to know.

Weeks later, Jackie was only learning to socialize again when Hal and Mary encouraged her to stop by the chili cook-off. At just 31 years old, she was ready for some fun after months of working so hard in physical therapy. Already she was preparing for the transition from her wheelchair to crutches. Could walking on her own be so far behind?

Though she may have had doubts early on about befriending the 41-year-old father of two, those fears quickly evaporated the more she got to know Tom.

"Tom was just a nice guy," Gayle O'Neill remembered of her son-in-law. "Nobody was his enemy. And Jackie thought he had to be a very caring man—he was a single dad raising two young boys on his own."

But it was the ice cream that really won her over.

On his rides home from work, Tom took to showing up at Jackie's doorstep with her favorite—a chocolate-covered Häagen-Dazs ice cream bar. Once, when Jackie got home too late from her daily errands, she arrived home to find the empty Häagen-Dazs wrapper outside her door. She giggled at the thought of him sitting on her stoop, eating her melting ice cream and waiting for her to come home. The wrapper, left behind on purpose, was his way of saying, "You missed out, honey!"

"That's just the kind of cute, fun little things he'd do for her," said Tricia Schutz, Jackie's friend of more than twenty years. Jackie confided, she was falling for Tom.

"He's so good-looking," Jackie told her friend. "And a body-builder, too!"

So it was no surprise when she moved in with Tom and his boys after several months of dating. And on July 29, 1989, they made their union official. Friend and local judge Robert Kuebler led the ceremony as they exchanged vows in a Hawaiian-themed wedding near a koi pond at the house Tom and his sons spent so many weekends building.

Already, their faces were tan with all the time they'd spent boating and fishing outdoors. Her skin looked radiant against the bright orange sundress she wore. She tucked a small clip of orange flowers into her dark curls and carried a bouquet of tropical wildflowers. Tom wore a bright multicolored Hawaiian shirt. Son Ryan stood to his right, acting as best man. Little Matt stood at Jackie's left side.

"It was supposed to be a small, intimate affair," Tricia remembered. "But they ended up having about one hundred people there! That's because with Tom and Jackie, everyone was a friend. It turned into such a party."

And by the time Jackie walked down the aisle, few could tell that only four years ago, she had nearly lost her leg. She had some scarring around her ankles and left knee. And she'd walk with a lift in her left shoe for the rest of her life. But only her closest friends knew that. Once a year, for the rest of their time together, Tom presented his wife with a new cane, which she used during their long evening walks together.

No one was happier to see Jackie marry Tom than her dear friend Tricia, who could only shake her head at the memory of Jackie fretting that she wasn't ready to love someone new.

"Tom was a great man," Tricia said. "He would walk on water for her. He was good for her. They were good for each other."

With that, Matt and Ryan became Jackie's stepsons. And she was terrified, Tricia remembered.

"It was trial and error for her at first," Tricia said. "She went from being told not too long ago she'd never have kids to raising two rambunctious little boys."

In the beginning, Ryan and Matt weren't sold on the idea of a stepmom, either.

"I actually didn't like it," Ryan remembered. "I thought she was a little too controlling. Before she moved in, we used to play every day after school, riding our BMX bikes, doing whatever we wanted. I had a good two, maybe two-and-a-half hours of fun until he got home. Then they got married, and she made me come home right after school every day and do chores. That ruined all my playtime!"

But, in the end, the boys saw how happy Jackie made their dad. And that was enough to make her family.

"She was a wonderful, wonderful mother to those kids," Tricia added. "I knew she always wanted to have children. And I think that was part of the draw to Tom, his kids. They really worked as a team to raise those boys. If you spent any time around that family, you never would have known Jackie wasn't their real mom. She couldn't have loved them any more."

Dixie could see how good Jackie was to her sons, and she was grateful to have another person around to love them.

"It was a group effort to raise them," Dixie said. "We made a point of never talking badly about one another. The boys always saw us as friends. In fact, I remember Matt once saying to me, 'Mommy, why don't you just come over and live with us?' That's how well we all got along."

Jackie fit in easily with her new family's domestic routines. She cooked dinner for the group every night, while Ryan and Matt set up the dining room table so everyone could eat together. Except on Friday nights.

"That was movie night and eat-out night, for as long as I can remember," Matt said. "We'd order pizza or Taco Bell and then rent movies, every single Friday night. Then on Saturday and Sunday, we'd do chores or go to the lake. We were always together. My dad wasn't somebody who'd go take vacations by himself with his wife. We were their priority. Everything we did, we did as a family."

Over the years, Jackie's role in the family became that of

mediator, acting as a calming voice to her husband's sometimes overly high expectations of his sons.

In high school, when Ryan joined his school's wrestling team, hoping to follow in his father's championship footsteps, Tom was down on the mat next to his son, telling him how he'd handled the last opponent all wrong and how he should handle his next one. Having a former state wrestling champ as your dad and coach was not easy.

"I saw that one coming," he might say if a match didn't turn out in Ryan's favor. "With that frame of mind, that attitude, you had that lost when you walked out on the mat. You lost before you started."

But it was Jackie, sitting in the stands, filming every match, who kept the peace in those moments. She would come down from her seat to stand next to her husband and soothe his competitive spirit.

"I really relied on her to calm him down and relieve him," said Ryan, who did, in fact, end up winning plenty of wrestling trophies of his own. "She knew how to handle him."

And when Ryan, just before entering Northern Arizona University, opted to take out a loan to buy a used Mustang 5.0, his dad looked on disapprovingly. "How are you going to pay for that, your insurance, and the university?" Tom asked, shaking his head.

Of course, in the weeks before college began, Ryan drove the car all over town, racking up speeding tickets. And every time, old family friend Judge Kuebler ratted Ryan out, calling up Jackie and Tom to tell them everything.

"I couldn't get away with shit in that town," Ryan recalled with a grin.

It was a time like that when Tom could really lose his temper. But it was Jackie, always Jackie, reminding her husband that Ryan was already a young man, ready to make his own mistakes in life. And Tom had to let him.

It wasn't too long before Ryan sold the car and spent the next two years riding a mountain bike around campus. His junior year, Tom spent $1,000 on an old truck and drove it up to his son. "I drove that truck until the end of college," Ryan said.

"Of course, I also paid my dad back for it. I would never not think about paying him back."

But by far, the happiest times for the Hawks family were when they were out boating together. By the time Matt reached 8 years of age and Ryan, 10, the family picked up a small pontoon boat. It only had room for about six people, but whenever it was warm, they hauled the boat up to the lake for swimming and fishing on weekends.

They soon upgraded to a 17-foot Boston Whaler Montauk, which they used to sail into Catalina Island. By the time their sons were in high school, Tom and Jackie bought the 22-foot Cabo Yacht, perfect for deep-sea fishing and ocean-diving trips. As they upgraded again, spending $40,000 on a 28-foot Skipjack, they were already thinking of the future. During crossings into San Carlos, they talked about a retirement at sea.

But until then, they loved nothing more than to invite close friends to join the family's nautical outings. Tricia and her husband tagged along on excursions into Lake Havasu. She remembered how carefree the Hawks family looked. Tom might splash into the water after his family, emerging with his wife sitting on one shoulder, one of his boys propped up on the other, flexing his carefully sculpted muscles. As long as they were near the water, playing like that on the waves, they didn't have a worry in the world.

"Every chance they could get," Tricia remembered, "they were always camping and boating. That was Tom and Jackie. They were always on the go."

And even though by the end of their lives, Tom and Jackie were looking for a more stable existence, they still had an eye out for adventures to come. Ten days after his death, Tom's captain's license arrived in the mail. Tom didn't technically need it—he knew the *Well Deserved* like the back of his hand, and he'd been a boater his entire life. But it meant something to him to be a certified captain. So while he and Jackie sat docked in Newport Beach, waiting to sell the *Well Deserved*, Tom signed up for a Coast Guard class, where he studied more nautical books, and took the test for certification. On November 25, 2004, he could have officially called himself Captain Hawks.

CHAPTER ELEVEN

It was time to talk to the Deleons.

Sergeant Byington surmised from the brief call Jennifer made to Jim that she and her husband were the last people to see the Hawkses before they disappeared. At minimum, Skylar, and maybe Jennifer, were witnesses in the case. At worst, they were murder suspects.

On November 29, 2004, after hanging up with Tom's brother, Sergeant Byington asked two detectives to do surveillance on the Deleons. A quick criminal background search turned up nothing too interesting. Jennifer had a clean record. Her husband had a burglary arrest two years ago. But nothing indicated they were violent. Or killers.

That afternoon, the surveillance team spotted the couple leaving the Grand Avenue home they shared with her parents in Long Beach and climbing into a car with their daughter, 1-year-old Hailey. They drove to a business complex and disappeared inside Hope Chapel. An investigator alerted Sergeant Byington, who decided it was time to make contact.

The sergeant's resources were thin. Just about every man in the Crimes Against Persons Unit was busy working other cases. So he'd go out on this one himself. But with two people to interview, he'd need a second set of hands. Sergeant Byington looked over his sparse office and spotted Detective Evan Sailor, sitting quietly, poring over paperwork at his desk. Detective Sailor was technically in the Economic Crimes Division, working mostly fraud cases, but he was a good detective, meticulous with detail. He'd been with the department seventeen years, and could get to the bottom of the most complicated financial scam.

Plus, Sergeant Byington was his boss. So, he dropped the missing persons report on Sailor's desk.

"This came in over the weekend," Sergeant Byington said. "We've already made a few calls on it and been out to the boat. But we need some follow-up. I'm short-handed today. I'll need you to pitch in."

"Sure," Detective Sailor said, already eyeing the report, taking in every word about the couple who'd put their yacht up for sale and then disappeared.

Like most cops, Detective Sailor had been a part of countless missing persons investigations over his career. Most turn out to be false alarms, with the people turning up safely in a day or two. Others disappear on purpose. Disgruntled teenagers aren't the only ones who run away from home. Adults do it all the time. As he looked over the report, Sailor didn't see anything too unusual. Certainly nothing that would hint at the investigation to come.

"Let's go out and talk to the boat-buyers and see what they have to say for themselves," the sergeant said. "Believe it or not, they're actually at church as we speak."

The makeshift chapel looked more like a business complex than a place of worship. It was housed on the second story in the middle of a strip mall. But inside, there were rows of chairs and a pulpit. The investigators watched for a moment, catching a glimpse of Jennifer and Skylar mingling among a group of volunteers. According to the chapel's pastor, Dave Pocoroba, Jennifer's parents had been members of the church for four years, attending service every Sunday morning. Her mother, Lana Henderson, taught at the Sunday school. Since the day she was born, Jennifer was raised in a God-fearing home. But as an adult, her church attendance grew erratic. She still showed up for services, sometimes. And once she married Skylar, she brought him with her. They went just often enough to appease Jennifer's overbearing mother. Volunteering for cleanup duty was probably part of that deal.

"Whenever there was a need," said Pastor Pocoroba, "Jennifer and Skylar would clean up the church, help get it ready for Sunday service."

But Skylar did like to describe himself as a Christian man. As an adult, as his life spiraled out of control, Skylar would claim there was good inside of him. And that he believed in God. That could be why, despite his sporadic church attendance, he befriended his pastor. They went fishing together, and when he learned Pastor Pocoroba was a certified diver, Skylar took the faith leader out on the water for a few dives around his favorite spot, Catalina Island.

It was during those times, however, that Skylar admitted he wasn't as devout as he'd like to be. In fact, he didn't think there could really be a God in heaven, watching over him.

"He expressed a lot of doubts," the pastor said. "He didn't understand why things had to be unfair, why God should be unfair. He had doubts about hypocrisy in religion. He believed people were hypocritical. He was new to being a Christian and was just trying to feel out the situation, trying to decide whether he truly believed. Or not."

But a shaken faith didn't keep Skylar from helping out the church—and appearing to enjoy it.

"He complained about a very rough past, so it seemed that Hope Chapel was a good place for him to develop faith in God and be with people. I'd say especially for Skylar, this was a place of healing."

The pastor simply liked Skylar and his wife. He saw them as a young couple in love, raising a family and struggling to find their way in the world. So no one was more shocked when the Newport Beach detectives walked into the church looking for the Deleons.

Recalls Pocoroba, "Neither one of them seemed like they would ever hurt a fly. Especially Skylar. He was always the perfect gentleman, always helpful, generous, pleasant to be with. You always had a good time when he was around. And always looked forward to seeing him. If he really did do [something], then he's the greatest actor in the world."

It was about 3:30 in the afternoon when the detectives arrived at Hope Chapel and spotted Jennifer and Skylar pushing a cart full of cleaning products down the church's narrow hallway. Baby Hailey sat to the side in her stroller.

It was a good show. It left the investigators unsure of what to think of the mild-mannered couple as they made their approach. Both detectives wore suits, not uniforms, but they pulled out their badges. As he began to speak, Sergeant Byington offered his card: Newport Beach Police Department, Crimes Against Persons Unit.

"Mr. and Mrs. Deleon, I'm Sergeant Byington and this is Detective Sailor. We're with the Newport Beach Police Department and we're conducting a missing persons investigation regarding Thomas and Jackie Hawks."

Skylar was nonplussed. If he was scared, he didn't show it. And if Jennifer knew her husband had done anything wrong, she didn't show it. They simply smiled and listened.

"We'd like to speak to you both, if you don't mind. We've been told that you two may have been the last people to see them before they disappeared."

Jennifer spoke first, agreeing to help in any way she could. She led the group to an upstairs office inside the chapel. As they walked, Jennifer pushed baby Hailey in a stroller. Skylar pushed a cart full of cleaning products.

"Actually," Sergeant Byington said once inside the small office, "we'd like to speak to you separately."

Detective Sailor would interview Skylar. Sergeant Byington handled Jennifer. If Skylar committed a crime, his wife likely knew about it. And likely, a heavily pregnant Jennifer would be the one more willing to talk, if only to keep herself out of trouble and home to raise Hailey and her soon-to-be-born baby.

Skylar didn't protest. He walked back out, Detective Sailor behind him, leaving Jennifer and Hailey alone in the office with Sergeant Byington. As Byington took out a notebook and launched into his questions, Jennifer busied herself cleaning the office.

"You don't mind if I tidy up in here while we talk?" she asked.

"No, no," he said. "Do what you've got to do. So, how did you know Thomas and Jackie?"

"My husband and I bought a boat from them," she said, straightening a stack of loose papers on the desk and pulling furniture polish from a cleaning cart inside the room. "No one's heard from them?"

"No, no one's been able to reach them since they sold the boat," he said.

"Well, actually, I've also been kind of worried about them," she said, emptying a small trash can into a garbage bag. "I can't get them, either. I've called a few times. We've had some questions about the boat."

"When did you and your husband buy the boat?"

"It was November fifteenth, in Newport Beach," she said. "We met them out by the dock where they kept the boat."

"Did the purchase take place on the yacht?" he asked.

"No, just on the street, around Fifteenth Street and the bay. We just gave them the money there and did all the paperwork."

"Were you and your husband the only ones present during that purchase?"

"I was there, with my daughter and my husband. We had a notary there, too. And both Tom and Jackie," she said. "Oh, and a friend of my husband's, he was with us. I don't remember his name. I don't really know him. But he said he was familiar with boats, so he came along to see what we were buying."

"So, not including Tom and Jackie, there were two other witnesses to your purchase?" Sergeant Byington asked.

"Yes, that's right," she said. Hailey, bored with the adult conversation, began to whine from her stroller. Jennifer pulled her restless toddler onto her hip and continued to clean.

"Are you and your husband employed?"

"Yes. I'm a hairdresser," she said. "I own my own business. I rent my own booth and have my own clients and then pay a set fee to the shop owner. And my husband is an electrician."

"Is he in a union or is he an apprentice or a journeyman?"

"Well, he was going to school, but then he stopped," she said. "So, now there's a job we're waiting for that would actually certify him. But that's taking forever. So we're waiting on that one. That's the one I want for him."

"And you live in Long Beach, right?"

"Yes, with my parents," she said. "They had a garage that we turned into a studio apartment for us."

"So, do you mind if I ask how much you paid for the boat?" Sergeant Byington asked.

"We gave them two-hundred and sixty-five thousand dollars for the boat," she said. "In cash."

"Really, two-hundred and sixty-five thousand dollars?" the detective questioned. "Are you sure?"

"Yes, I believe so."

"Because I know the Hawkses were advertising it for four-hundred and thirty-five thousand dollars," he said.

"Well, we paid two-hundred and sixty-five thousand dollars. I'm not sure how my husband negotiated that price. I wasn't in on all their previous conversations. But I've got a notarized bill of sale to prove it," she said.

"Okay," he said, making a note of her claim. "What did the Hawkses do after the sale was finalized?"

"After they took the money? Well, they just got into their car and drove off. I think they said something about going to Mexico."

"You saw them drive away?"

"Yes, I did."

"And that was the last you saw of them? You haven't seen or spoken to them since?"

"No."

"And then after you bought the yacht and the Hawkses drove away," Sergeant Byington said, "what happened?"

"We went to look at it," she said. "The sale included a dinghy, so we rowed out to see our new yacht. We went onboard and just walked around for a little while, checking it out. Then we got back into the dinghy and left."

"Did you go anywhere after that?"

"No," Jennifer said. "We just drove home."

"I see," he said. "Okay, just stay here for a few more minutes. I'll be right back."

He made his way outside the chapel to find Detective Sailor, interviewing Skylar in the church's hallway. The two investigators took a moment to compare notes, out of earshot of the Deleons.

Their stories matched, mostly. Yes, his wife had been present for the purchase, Skylar told Detective Sailor. Along with a notary. And a friend of his, Alonso Machain. And yes, they watched the Hawkses drive away in their car, a silver Honda. They'd mentioned going to Mexico, Skylar said. He didn't even put up a fight when Detective Sailor asked if they could go on-board to look at the *Well Deserved*'s Global Positioning System, which the investigator said could show where the couple had traveled to earlier that day or in the recent past. Of course, Skylar said, signing a consent form that would allow crime-scene investigators onboard.

But Skylar's story had one pretty wild twist.

"I asked him, 'Hey, obviously you're a young couple, living with Mom and Dad, you don't have a steady job—how can you afford to buy a yacht?'" Sailor said. "And he tells me it's dirty money. He said he did buy the boat, it was a legal purchase and all. But the cash he gave them to buy the boat was dirty."

"Dirty how?" Byington asked.

"Sounds like drug money," said Sailor. The fraud investigator wanted to zero in on ways the money could be traced. But if it was drug money, that would be damn near impossible. "He said it was drug money, brought up from Mexico. It had something to do with his dad, who apparently is some big drug runner up there."

"We'll have to get more on that story," said Byington, his narcotics background kicking in. "How about the price of the yacht? How much did he say they paid for it?" Sergeant Byington asked.

"First he said two-hundred and sixty-five thousand dollars," Detective Sailor said. "But I didn't believe him. I told him, 'I'm not the IRS, I don't care about any tax evasion plan you have, I'm just trying to find some missing people.' So then he changed his story and said it was actually four hundred thousand dollars."

It was enough of a discrepancy that the detectives decided to see the bill of sale for that boat.

Back in the office with Jennifer, Sergeant Byington asked why she and her husband were trying to hide how much they paid for the boat.

"My partner just told me that Skylar admitted you paid over four hundred thousand dollars for the boat."

She didn't mean to lie, she told the detective. She wanted to cooperate in their search for the Hawkses, if she could. She just didn't want her husband to get in trouble for tax evasion. Apparently, they had decided to report the sale price of the *Well Deserved* as $265,000 instead of $400,000 to cut down on the luxury taxes they'd have to pay to the IRS.

"Well, I think we need to go now," Jennifer said. "We're done cleaning."

"Sure," the sergeant said, grabbing a large bag of trash out of her hands, offering to carry it downstairs for her so she could handle Hailey. "Obviously, if you hear from them? Our number is on the card there."

"Of course," she said. "I already told James Hawks, as soon as we hear, we'd call, but so far . . ."

"I know, I know," Sergeant Byington said. "It's just that the other end of the family is real concerned."

"Oh, I understand," Jennifer said in her most sympathetic voice. "It concerns me! It doesn't make me look very good. And it makes me uncomfortable. But I would feel the same way. If that happened to someone in my family, I would be in everybody's business."

"Just one more thing," the sergeant said. "We'd like to see that bill of sale, anyway. You never know when it's going to help with something."

Jennifer said it was back at a hotel where they were temporarily living. Several days earlier, an extension cord connected to a large saltwater aquarium in her parents' living room burned up, causing a small fire. The family had to move into the Extended Stay America hotel while repairs were made.

They'd follow them to the hotel, Sergeant Byington told her.

After rejoining Detective Sailor and Skylar, all four walked outside and into the church's parking lot. Sergeant Byington made small talk.

"Thanks for being honest with us about where that money came from," he told Skylar. "Drug money, right? What kind of drugs?"

"Cocaine," Skylar said. "My dad's this big drug runner up in Mexico."

"So, it was your dad's money?" he asked.

"No, it was mine," said Skylar, who just kept on talking, offering more details than were asked of him. Perhaps by talking so much he thought he'd give the impression of being cooperative—and, therefore, less suspicious. But the more he talked, the more lies he told. Nevertheless, as with most of Skylar's lies, he skillfully weaved just enough fact into his fiction to make everything he said sound believable.

According to Skylar, the cocaine came from a dope rip-off. He said he'd busted into the home of a former co-worker back in 2002 because the guy, Ted Wangsanutr, was sitting on 100 kilos of cocaine. Skylar broke into the house, stole the cocaine, and moved it to Mexico. Across the border, his associates sold the dope. Friends in Mexico had been holding the cash all this time and just brought it over the border recently, so he could buy the *Well Deserved*.

"I got busted for the burglary," Skylar said. "That's why I'm on probation right now. But I still had the cocaine."

"You're pretty lucky to have found drug dealers in Mexico who could be trusted enough to sit on all that cash for you, all this time," Byington said. "And then just drop it off to you in the United States when you were ready. You're lucky the whole damn thing wasn't stolen."

"Well," Skylar said, "it's my dad. He's a very powerful guy down there. Nobody crosses him."

As his partner chatted up Skylar, Detective Sailor distracted Jennifer with talk of her impending delivery.

"Do you know what you're having?"

"A boy. Then I'm done," she said, laughing. "People have been joking I might be having twins, because, you know, it's common in my family. And I got really big, really fast! But, thank goodness, it's only one big boy! So, no more, I'm done being pregnant."

"Yeah, I have two little ones myself," he said. "I have a two-and-a-half-year-old girl and just had a little boy two months ago."

"Oh, how fun, how fun!" she gushed.

"So, I'm curious," Detective Sailor said. "What was the purpose in buying the boat? Because most people come into some kind of money and they buy a house. Did you think this was someplace you could live?"

"Possibly, as an option," she said. "And also, we always talked about doing a business on a boat. Because we have another boat now, but that's way not big enough." She giggled again. "But I like this one. And I want to keep it."

"How did you guys find the boat?" Detective Sailor asked.

"Oh, it was in a magazine," she said. "I think magazines get sent to him because he has a boat. He sees things in them all the time and will say, 'Oh, let's buy this!' And I'm usually like, 'Nope, you can't buy this!' " Again, she broke into a giggle.

"Skylar made it sound like there was a dad who gave him some money," Detective Sailor said. "He said his dad acts like he just has money from God."

"We talked to him," she said. "But I don't know. Personally, I'd rather buy my own house than have to deal with that man."

"So, is any of this money from the dad, or is this all your money?" he asked.

"No," she said, raising her voice a few octaves to sound more like a teenager trying to explain why her homework assignment is missing. "From what I understand, um, this is all from his acting royalties. Because money from his dad is kind of shady. And I'd rather just do this all on my own than deal with that man."

"Did the Hawkses tell you what they wanted to do with the money you gave them?" Detective Sailor said.

"Well, I know they talked about buying property," Jennifer said. "My husband also talked about possibly helping them do that, but that's as far as it went."

At the same time, Skylar tried explaining his generous attempt to help the Hawkses to Sergeant Byington.

"I told them I could help them set up a bank account and some things so they'd look like they were already established in Mexico, and that would help them save on taxes when they bought property," Skylar said.

"And what did they say?" Byington asked.

"They were for it," he said. "They were like, 'Sure, go ahead, set it up!' So while we were in Mexico, we called their bank about setting up an account for them."

"Why were you in Mexico?"

"To set up an account for them real quick," he said.

"Were they with you?" Sergeant Byington asked.

"No, just me and my wife went down, strictly to open an account for them in Ensenada," he said.

"But they had the cash for the boat already?" the sergeant questioned.

"Oh, yes, they had the cash," he said.

"So did you open the account?"

"No, because the bank said we needed them with us and we didn't know where they were," he said.

It was a confusing story. But for now, they let it go until they could check out Skylar's tale on their own.

At the hotel, the detectives walked into a disaster area. The one bedroom with kitchenette was a complete mess. Clothes were on the bed, on the floor, hanging out of drawers in a nearby dresser. On top of the dresser, a stack of papers lay in disarray. Jennifer glanced through the stack and pulled out a manila envelope containing several documents.

"Now, where is that bill of sale?" she said out loud, scouring through papers. "I know I have it somewhere. I just can't find it at the moment. Can I get it to you later? Here's what I've got so far."

Sergeant Byington took the envelope from her, containing some paperwork on the transfer of the boat title, and some documents from the Coast Guard, registering the Deleons as the new owners of the *Well Deserved*—though Jennifer and Skylar had listed a new name for her, *Pure Luck*.

Another stack of legal papers looked like they authorized Skylar Deleon to have power of attorney over Jackie and Thomas Hawkses' assets.

Each set of documents held the Hawkses' signatures. The power of attorney papers even showed their fingerprints.

"Let's go make copies of this stuff at the hotel's office," said Sergeant Byington, who decided to hold back his questions on the paperwork, especially the power of attorney records, until tomorrow, when a tape recorder would be running. "And then, when you find that bill of sale, maybe you wouldn't mind just dropping that off to us at the station?"

"Sure, no problem," she said cheerfully.

"By the way," Jennifer asked the detectives before they left, "did you have anyone following us today?"

"No," Sergeant Byington lied, not willing to confirm anything for Jennifer, especially since the surveillance team would remain on them for a while, "we sure didn't."

"Okay," she said. "I just could have sworn there were two guys following us around today."

"Huh, isn't that strange?" the detective said.

As they drove back to the station, the detectives couldn't help but note what an odd meeting it had been.

"It was unreal," Sergeant Byington said of the moment. "Here we are, about to interview them about a murder, and they're doing volunteer work, cleaning a church with their baby? I felt like saying, 'Wait a minute, did you need me to polish your halo a bit before we get started?' "

The next morning, Jennifer and Skylar arrived at the Newport Beach Police Department to drop off that bill of sale. It was dated November 15, 2004, listed the sale price as $460,000, and was sealed with a stamp by notary K. Harris. But unlike the previous documents, this one didn't have the Hawkses' signatures on it. Only Skylar's, signing in their place under his power-of-attorney authorization.

"Thanks, Mrs. Deleon," said Sergeant Byington, who decided to use the opportunity to re-interview Skylar about his drug story, and the last time he saw the Hawkses—this time with a tape recorder running.

"I wanted him married to that story," Sergeant Byington

would say later of his decision to talk to Skylar again. So he casually asked Skylar for a few more minutes of his time.

"I just wanted to go over a few things from our conversation yesterday. Would you mind helping me out one more time?"

"Sure," Skylar said, following the sergeant to a back office.

He led Skylar, alone, into an interview room. And as a tape recorder rolled, Byington asked him to explain, once again, how he bought the *Well Deserved*. And again, Skylar launched into the story of his "drug rip," how he'd stolen the coke during a burglary in 2002, sold it over the border for $350,000, then had associates of his father's sit on the money there until he could figure out a way to launder the cash. When he saw the ad for the *Well Deserved*, he figured that was his answer. He spoke of giving the Hawkses $400,000 in cash for the yacht, which Tom said he was going to use to buy some property in Mexico. The last time he'd heard from the couple was when they were driving away from Newport Beach in their silver Honda, bound for south of the border.

"You mentioned selling the coke for three hundred and fifty thousand dollars," Sergeant Byington said. "If you paid four hundred thousand dollars for the yacht, where'd the rest of the cash come from?"

"I do have some money," Skylar told the detective, "from child acting royalties. I did commercials and was in the show *Power Rangers*. I've got the tapes, if you want to see."

Sergeant Byington declined.

In all, Skylar rambled on for over an hour, going into great detail for the sergeant, who tried not to interrupt too many times.

"I wanted it all on tape," Detective Byington said. "So I just let him talk. I let him think I was accepting everything he was telling me. But it stunk like a fart in church."

The detective hoped Skylar still believed he was just a cooperating witness in their missing persons case. Not a suspect. Not someone who should probably shut up and grab an attorney. Still, Byington had to ask about the power of attorney papers—and, somehow, not sound accusatory.

"You know, I noticed there were some papers in the stuff your wife gave me listing you as power of attorney for the Hawkses.

How come Mr. and Mrs. Hawks decided to do that?" Byington asked, trying to come off more curious than suspicious.

"Oh, that stuff. Well, Tom said he wanted to invest in some property in Mexico, but he wasn't comfortable dealing with real estate and banking matters over there. So I volunteered to help him out. I've spent a lot of time down there, I lived there for a while, and I'm real familiar with their banking system. But in order to help him, I needed to be able to access their accounts here."

At first glance, that story didn't seem too far-fetched. The family did say the Hawkses wanted to buy property in the San Carlos area. And the signatures on the paperwork looked legitimate, when compared to the signatures on their drivers' licenses.

With every response, Skylar was smooth, answering without the slightest pause or stutter. And his manner, so polite he came off more timid than intimidating.

"In my mind, he seemed like such a docile, almost effeminate guy," the detective said. "He was just this real mousy character. When he left that day, I actually thought he probably didn't have the balls enough to do it himself. Only later I'd learn he was the most accomplished liar I've ever known. Now that I think back, I know I was talking to a complete sociopath."

As Sergeant Byington ended his interview with Skylar, Detective Sailor stood onboard the *Well Deserved*. With Skylar's written consent to search the yacht, the detective joined a group of crime-scene investigators scouring it, looking for any evidence that would help tell the story behind Jackie and Tom's disappearance. Divers searched the waters below and around the *Well Deserved*, in case they weren't on it, but under it. They found nothing. Dogs sniffed the decks looking for drug residue, in case Skylar was using the boat to hold narcotics. Or the Hawkses used the boat to transport them. They found nothing.

So far, Detective Montero's brief walk onto the *Well Deserved* three days before yielded the only startling find—a receipt for trash bags and bleach. Perhaps more telling this time, for a boat that a couple had lived on over two years, was what wasn't found: not a single fingerprint for Tom or Jackie. In fact, investigators didn't find a single fingerprint at all, from anyone. That boat had been wiped clean.

Despite Skylar's timid performance for investigators, they increasingly believed he was lying about something. Maybe he wasn't the mastermind behind the Hawkses' disappearance. Maybe he was too mild-mannered for that. But he knew more than he was telling.

And so did his pregnant wife.

CHAPTER TWELVE

Hello, Bajaskylar. I like your picture! Jennifer.

With that simple email message, Skylar Deleon met his future wife.

In September 2001, Skylar opened an email account with Yahoo and filled out a voluntary profile. He listed his name, his age, boasted of his military experience, posted his picture, and called himself BajaSkylar. "Baja" was a nod to his favorite surfing spot, "Skylar" was the new moniker he used while hiding out in Mexico for the past six months, on the run from United States Marine Corps authorities.

Within days, Jennifer emailed. The assertive move was entirely in her character. No one would ever describe Jennifer Lynn Henderson as a shy woman. She was outgoing, loud—bossy, some might even say. She was plain-looking, average build with long brown hair, pale skin, and brown eyes. Not someone who stood out easily to boys. And she was not some soft girlie-girl. In high school, she was considered more of a jock, always palling around with her teammates on the Long Beach 49ers softball team, where Jennifer played shortstop. She grew up adored by her working-class parents, who dragged her off to Sunday school every week. The message from them in her senior yearbook now seems eerily prophetic:

To our Little One. You are truly a gift from God. God has given you many gifts. Use them. Don't take them for granted. We are proud of you. Love you Always, Mom, Dad, and brother Mike.

In the three years following graduation, Jennifer had gotten her cosmetology license and worked as a hairdresser in local shops. She was a confident woman. And definitely not the kind of lady who needed to wait around for a guy to ask her out.

"How'd you get my email address?" Skylar wrote back.

"I found it in the Yahoo! email directory. Do you want to talk? I'm 21, I live in Long Beach, I'm cute and very athletic."

The description sounded good to Skylar. He could use a new distraction in his life, anyway. The past year hadn't turned out the way he'd hoped.

The Marine Corps was tougher than Skylar ever imagined. For some reason, he actually believed he was going to surf for his country. As ridiculous as it sounds, Skylar swears a recruitment officer explained how it could be possible.

"They said they had extreme games in the Marines and that I could do that. They said they'd work that out for me so that I could surf for the Marine Corps," Skylar said.

Of course, that never happened. Instead, he went through basic training and then served as a desk clerk. It was boring, tedious work, but nothing he couldn't handle. What got to him was the hazing from other privates.

"I was having tons of problems in my unit," Skylar said. "Lots of hazing. A lot of it my dad was causing, because he didn't want me to join."

It became a pattern with Skylar, to blame his father for all the problems in his life. He'd wanted to become a championship surfer his senior year of high school, but couldn't, because of his dad. He wanted to excel as a Marine, but couldn't, because of his dad.

"He'd call my unit and start complaining, 'How come this is happening and how come that?' And I would end up getting a lot of hazing because, you know, 'Your daddy is always calling,' they'd say. It always made things worse for me. He was always causing trouble."

So, Skylar got into fights. Most of them verbal. But a few turned into blows. It didn't help when word got around that Skylar had thought he was going to surf his way through the service, prompting privates behind his back to tauntingly call him the Marine Corps' Gidget.

The end came when his father called the unit leader and left a message about the 1998 Ford Expedition Skylar had been driving. Apparently, John got the truck for his son, but Skylar was supposed to be paying his dad for it in monthly installments. Skylar had fallen behind.

"He owes me a payment for my truck," John said. "Tell him I'm coming to get the money or I'm taking my truck home with me."

The call frightened him, Skylar said. Not just because he feared his dad's explosive temper, as always. But he knew if his dad came to the base and started trouble, he'd never hear the end of it from the men in his unit.

"So I just left," Skylar said. "I went AWOL. I went to Ensenada, Mexico, for the next six months. I just love it there. The people are just more understanding."

While in Ensenada, he changed his name to Skylar. Relatives with the last name Deleon became the inspiration for his new surname, Skylar Deleon. The new handle not only helped him stay under the radar from the Marines, but it also helped him steer clear of any trouble his father may have gotten into during his drug-running past. Carrying his old man's name meant he'd carry his old man's debts, too.

Skylar loved Mexico, where living was cheap and surf opportunities plentiful. He began diving, too, almost daily. He even dated a woman there for several months, promising that he was done with the United States and that he wanted to renounce his citizenship and marry her. Of course, he never did.

It wasn't the first time he'd been south of the border. He made many trips there as a kid, whenever his dad had to go over to conduct business, or hide out for a while.

Still, despite what he told his girlfriend, Skylar was not ready to live across the border for the rest of his life. He knew he'd have to deal with his AWOL status eventually, or he'd be on the run forever. And really, there was no other future for a man like Skylar. He'd never be the guy who went to college, earned a degree, and then landed some office job. If the Marines would give him a second chance, he wanted it. If they could re-assign him to a new unit, he could start fresh.

It was the constant argument inside Skylar's head—wanting to do the right thing, but ultimately, choosing the easy way out.

For now, Skylar opted to do the right thing. He crossed the border into San Diego and made his way to the Camp Pendleton Marine Corps Base, where he turned himself in. Of course, he went back armed with a story, claiming that his father had been deathly ill and needed Skylar's care. It wasn't the truth, but at least he wasn't running anymore.

"I just wanted it done," Skylar said. "I wanted to stay in. My commander recommended me to stay in. They told me I'd have to be punished for going AWOL. Maybe I'd have to do some time. And I'd have a court-martial on my record. Or, in lieu of a court-martial, I could just sign myself out, wait six months, and then sign myself back in. So that's what I did. I separated in lieu of a court-martial."

Six months later, Skylar did try to sign himself back in, but the Marines rejected him. In two years, maybe, they said, he could try again. But he didn't. By then, his life would veer so far off course, he'd never regain control.

And Jennifer Henderson would play a big part in his undoing.

Emails between them led to phone calls. Then Skylar worked up the courage to ask her out.

"We met at the Westminster Mall," said Skylar, who was living in Westminster with his grandparents at the time.

He showed up on a Suzuki GSX-R750 borrowed from a friend, hoping the new motorcycle would impress her. But when blonde-haired, brown-eyed Jennifer walked up, it was Skylar who was impressed.

Recalled Skylar, "I thought, 'Wow! She's pretty cute!' She

seemed pretty nice, too. So I asked her out to a movie later. We saw *Spy Game*. That was in September 2001."

Jennifer, who'd brought a friend along with her to the meeting, in case Skylar turned out to be a dud in person, ditched her pal and caught the movie with Skylar. After that, the two were inseparable.

He fell for Jennifer right away, though he claims he was concerned about some of her "party girl" behavior. For a man who was raised by a convicted drug runner and would one day end up in prison on multiple murder counts, Skylar said he was always a clean-living man.

"I've been around more drugs in my life," Skylar said. "But I didn't use. I've never used. I've only been drunk three or four times in my whole life! But Jennifer, when I first met her, she was into some things I disagreed with. She was into smoking and drinking. She was more of a party girl."

Jennifer calmed down after they started dating, Skylar said. "I even got her to quit smoking."

They'd only been dating about six months when he bought her a ring. The couple made their way to Catalina Island for an afternoon of play, with Skylar getting in some scuba diving while Jennifer soaked up the sun on the beach. That evening, they had dinner at one of the resort town's tiny seafood restaurants, then took a walk just before sunset. As they reached Casino Point, a picturesque spot where evening lovers often pause to look out over the ocean, Skylar asked Jennifer to marry him. He was so nervous, his hands shook as he placed the ring on her finger. Jennifer looked down at the platinum band with three half-carat princess-cut stones, meant to represent the past, the present, and the future.

"She knew it was coming," Skylar said. "We'd been talking about it, looking at rings. But I was still really nervous."

She said yes and the duo set about planning their wedding. Too impatient to wait for the time it would take to plan a big service, they actually had two ceremonies. The first was on the beach. Jennifer wore a sundress, Skylar wore shorts. Pastor Pocoroba performed the ceremony. The only guests were Jen's parents and her brother, Mike. And on September 22, 2002, exactly a year since their first meeting, they held a second ceremony—a huge party on a rented yacht, the *Spirit of Newport*, in Newport Beach. This time, Jennifer wore a strapless white wedding gown and Skylar put on a tux. He held on to her tightly as they danced in front of their guests, more than 100 in all, including Skylar's parents.

"He looked so happy to be married," Lynette said. "Like he was still just a young kid, still having fun."

And it could have been a good life for Skylar. At least a happier one than he'd ever known, growing up under his father. He'd taken care of his screwup with the Marines, his in-laws had given him and Jennifer a place to live, she was making a little money with her job cutting hair, he worked side jobs and had time for surfing and scuba diving. It wasn't a rich life, but it could have been a happy one.

But that wedding would mark the end of happy times for the newlyweds. As the holiday season approached, and the temperatures turned colder in California's beach towns, everything changed.

Looking back, Senior Deputy District Attorney Matt Murphy described Skylar Deleon's marriage to Jennifer Henderson as the first in a series of fatal mistakes Skylar would make. "Individually, they probably never would have had what it takes to do anyone harm," Matt said. "But together? They were like fire and gasoline."

CHAPTER THIRTEEN

Matt Murphy was on his way to court, battling the gridlock that permanently plagues Southern California freeways, when he got the call from Sergeant Byington.

"I think you need to come in," he said. "We've been working this missing persons case. But there are some details I think you need to hear."

If Sergeant Byington was calling him, this was no longer simply a missing persons case. This was a homicide. Matt was a senior prosecutor in the Orange County district attorney's Homicide Unit.

"Okay," said Matt, already mentally juggling his daily court calendar, trying to carve out some time. "How about I come by first thing in the morning?"

"See you then."

At 38, Matt was still young in comparison to most staffers in the district attorney's office. But he was an aggressive prosecutor. A compassionate victims' advocate. And there was no place else he wanted to be.

He was a born prosecutor. Even if it had taken a silly fraternity prank to make him see it.

As a student at the University of California, Santa Barbara, Matt's combination of smarts and boyish good looks made him a popular guy. With sandy blond hair and a splash of freckles across his nose, he would always, no matter how old he got, look like a man more comfortable balancing a surfboard than the cold, hard facts of a murder case.

He was, in fact, a dedicated surfer. It was no accident that his college of choice, UCSB, was nestled near the ocean, next to some of the finest surf spots California had to offer.

He was a top-flight student. But as his fourth year in college approached, he still wasn't sure what he'd do after graduation. Until his fraternity, Phi Sigma Kappa, was accused of hazing because a pledge class was forced to streak through a neighboring sorority house. It was a typical college boy prank. A stunt that left the sorority girls giggling. And it was a Phi Sigma Kappa pledge class tradition.

But during Matt's senior year, the fraternity was hit with a formal complaint from the university. They faced penalties, maybe suspension. They could even lose their charter. Normally, the frat's president would defend the chapter's good name. But as the charge came down, the girlfriend of Phi Sigma Kappa's president dumped him. Devastated, he withdrew from college and went home. That left Vice President Matt Murphy to defend his brothers.

"And we won," Matt said. "We were cleared. It felt so good."

And when a female friend of Matt's was raped on campus, he was so outraged, he joined Greeks Against Rape. That's when he realized he was at home, championing a cause he believed in. A political science teacher saw that in him, too. The professor, who had a law degree of his own, encouraged Matt to enter law school. Just the thought of it felt right.

After graduating from UCSB, Matt took seven months off to surf the South Pacific by himself. Then he settled down to conquer University of Southern California law school. He was midway through, with thoughts of going into international law, especially after studying for a summer in Paris. But in 1991, he accepted an offer to clerk for the Orange County Office of the District Attorney.

He landed in the writs and appeals office, where his first assignment was a motion in the case of a drug dealer caught carrying $158,000 in cash. The defendant was a major runner from Colombia. That day, a hardened narcotics cop sat down with the prosecutor trainee and briefed him on the bust.

"And it was so cool," Matt said. "By the end of the first day, I knew this is what I wanted to do for the rest of my life."

As he ended law school, he was a senior clerk in the district attorney's office. And a favored son. "Just pass the bar," they told him, "and you have a job."

"I never wanted something so bad in all my life," Matt said. "I was really sweating it."

When he got word that he'd made the cut, "It was one of the most exciting days of my life," he said.

He put in his time at the DA's office and steadily rose through the ranks—handling misdemeanor and domestic violence cases, then juvenile gangs. But it was in the sexual assault unit where he built his reputation. He grew into an aggressive prosecutor, driven by a fierce devotion to the victims in his caseload. With every trial, he held on to the memory of his college friend, the woman raped on UCSB's campus by a fellow student. He never forgot the experience of standing by her side, waiting for the justice system to bring her closure.

Maybe that's why, as a prosecutor, his policy was to give out his personal cell number to the victims and their families. He wanted them to know they weren't alone.

"That's the single most important factor," Matt said. "To let them know someone cares. I'm not going to blow this off. You have an ally."

He never lost that dedication when, after four years of handling sexual assaults, he moved on to homicide cases.

Now, twelve years later, he was a seasoned prosecutor—hard on defendants, gentle with victims, endearing to jurors.

He had no children and never married, though he'd come close. "Once," he said. "Now I'm single. Very single." Mostly, his life revolves around a close group of tight-knit buddies from college, surfing, and the law. "I love to play golf," Matt says.

"But I suck at it. I love surfing, but I suck at that. And I love being a prosecutor. And it's the only thing I'm really good at."

The next morning, sitting in the conference room of the Newport Beach Police Department, Sergeant Byington and Detective Sailor recapped it all—who the Hawkses were, how they'd put their yacht up for sale, how Skylar and Jennifer claimed to have purchased the yacht. But nobody had seen the Hawkses since. That had been fifteen days ago.

"What do we know about the Hawkses? Any chance they could be on the run?"

"I really doubt it," said Byington, sketching out a bit of background on the duo—no criminal history, good family, law enforcement career. "We're still looking into them. But so far, they just seem like good people. They weren't in debt, no warrants out for their arrest. They loved each other, they loved their kids, they just had a new grandson. And now they're gone."

They pulled out their notebooks and reviewed their interviews with Jennifer and Skylar. By the time Detective Sailor got to the cocaine-stealing story, Matt understood why the detectives brought him in.

"You don't believe this guy."

"No way," Sergeant Byington said. "I think Skylar's a liar."

"And his wife? Does she know?"

"I've already caught her lying for him once," Sergeant Byington pointed out. "And she swears she was with him when he bought *Well Deserved*. I don't know how involved she was, but I think she knows something. For sure she knows her unemployed husband couldn't afford to buy a yacht using cash he legitimately earned."

"You think they were killed on that boat?" Murphy asked.

"Probably," Sergeant Byington said. "But I don't have any proof of that yet."

The detectives were already working to get Skylar's cell phone records, to see who he called in the hours before and after the sale of the *Well Deserved*. If he had any partners in crime, his outgoing and incoming call list would tell it all.

After the briefing, Matt turned the case over in his mind. It was Friday night and he was due to be in Palm Springs for the weekend. He owned a place there with his sister, and he wanted to take advantage of the area's impressive golf courses for a few days. But that evening, as he drove east toward California's desert haven, he couldn't get the story of the missing couple out of his mind. Jackie's last message had been, "We're out to sea." Then they disappeared. But there was no sign of foul play on the boat, the cops said. And Skylar's drug story—it sounded bogus to everyone.

Matt made it to Palm Springs and fell asleep that evening with the Hawkses on his mind. But at 2 a.m., his eyes flew open. Suddenly wide awake, he wrestled with sleeplessness for a while before surrendering to the thoughts weighing on his mind. He swung his legs to the floor and got out of bed, reaching for the case notes Sergeant Byington and Detective Sailor had put together for him. He pored over the details, and as he did so, a flurry of questions flooded his mind: Who are the Hawkses? Could they be shady? Could they have lived a lie in front of friends and family, only appearing to be honest, hardworking people? If so, what could they be into? Drugs? If not, why had they been killed? Just for the yacht? Detective Sailor and Sergeant Byington were skeptical of the buyer's drug rip-off/money-laundering story. But if he didn't steal a bunch of dope, why tell the police he did? And why on earth would the Hawkses ever sign over durable power of attorney to strangers buying their boat, even if they did want help buying property in Mexico?

He read the file top to bottom, then reread it, scribbling notes to himself until nearly sunrise. He only quit as the clock neared 5 a.m., because of a 6 a.m. tee time with a pal. But after that round of golf, Matt called the detectives repeatedly to brainstorm and ask more questions. The case haunted him throughout the weekend.

It took a few days of mulling the case over before an idea came to him. Matt needed to bounce this one off someone who not only knew his way around a boat, but knew a few things about the drug business. He knew just the man.

Nearly every year since college, Matt took an extended surfing vacation into Timor, Indonesia. The place was known for the kind of waves only an experienced surfer, or a man with a death wish, would take on. It was during these surfing adventures that Tom met the man nicknamed Salty Sam, a lifelong boating man who ran a charter boat business in Timor. Just a glance at Sam's weathered face, deeply lined and permanently tanned, told the story—he was a man who had seen a lot in his life. He looked hard because he lived hard. Matt suspected Sam might have known a drug smuggler or two in his life, and had probably heard firsthand the tales they had to tell. Sam never outright told his young prosecutor friend that, but Matt guessed it was the unspoken truth.

Now, with his wilder years behind him, Sam lived on a boat in Australia with his wife and little girl. If anyone knew how to tell fact from fiction in a case like this, it would be Salty Sam. Matt shot his friend an email.

"Hey, call me when you get a second. I'm working a case I think you might like to hear about," Matt wrote.

Sam didn't hesitate to call.

"Matt?" Sam said, surprise lifting his throaty voice a few octaves. "Hey, California boy! How the hell are you? You headed Down Under to see some real waves?"

"Nope," Matt said. "I wish. But I just got this case I want to run by you. Tell me what you think."

"Uh-huh . . ."

"It involves this guy, Skylar, and his wife, Jennifer. They just bought a fifty-five-foot yacht out here in Newport Beach, California. But he's this unemployed twenty-five-year-old guy living in his in-laws' converted garage with his pregnant wife and daughter. And the couple they bought the yacht from? They're missing. Been gone since the day they allegedly made the sale, over two weeks ago."

"And how is this guy telling you he bought the boat?"

"He says it was from money he made in a dope rip," Matt said. "He says he stole one hundred kilos of cocaine from some guy he used to work with, someone who had all this dope stashed away in his house up here in Orange County. Then he took it to Mexico, sold it, and friends have been holding the three-hundred and fifty thousand dollars cash he made over there for the past two years. Until just two weeks ago. Basically, he's trying to launder the money by buying the yacht."

"Yeah, that's a bunch of bullshit," Sam said, not waiting for Matt to ask a question. "There's no way a drug deal would go down like that. No way. First of all, this guy's co-worker is just going to have one hundred kilos of coke laying around his house in the suburbs, totally unguarded? And then your man says he takes it to Mexico and sells it there? Bullshit. Listen, last I checked, all the dope comes *from* Mexico and gets sold *here*. No one's growing coca plants in the U.S. and smuggling them over the border. It's the other way around."

A lot of what Sam said echoed Sergeant Byington and Detective Sailor's doubts. He knew his friend's take on the case was, so far, right on the money.

"So let me ask you," Matt said, "if these people were killed on a boat, what should I be looking for? We've searched that entire boat and come up with no evidence of foul play. What am I missing?"

"The anchor," Sam said. "If you're ever going to throw a body off a boat, you're going to attach it to an anchor. A yacht that size should have two anchors on it. If I were you, I'd look to see if one of them isn't missing. If they were killed onboard, they were chained to the anchor and thrown off."

A chill ran through Matt. As soon as his friend said it, he knew it was true. And he couldn't imagine a more terrifying way to die. He thought about this couple's last moments together, sitting there, tied to an anchor. Tom would be helpless to save Jackie. She was probably crying, begging for her life. Matt imagined her gulping sobs as she hit the ocean, now taking in water with each gasp for air. If these people were truly innocent victims—not drug dealers or gang members, as so many murder victims are—just honest people trying to sell a boat, then this was the most cold-blooded case he'd ever prosecute. Already, he itched to put away the people responsible.

"Sam," he said, "thanks. I owe you several beers next time I see you."

When he met with Byington and Sailor again, Matt asked about the anchor.

"When you guys searched the boat, you took an inventory of everything onboard, right?"

"Yep, we did," Detective Sailor said.

"Was there an anchor onboard?"

"Yeah, there was an anchor," he said.

"Just one?"

"That's right," he said. "But I think there were supposed to be two onboard. That boat has an opening on it where you'd store another anchor. And pictures the Hawkses posted when they put the yacht up for sale shows it with two."

He didn't have any solid evidence yet telling him what had happened out there. But Matt was convinced. The *Well Deserved* had left Newport Beach harbor with two anchors, and come back with one onboard and the other at the bottom of the ocean.

CHAPTER FOURTEEN

Skylar sat behind the driver's seat of the Ford pickup staring out at the house along 1040 North Baxter in the city of Anaheim. Because it was already after 9 p.m., he had to squint through the darkness, searching for signs that someone might be home. He sat there a long time, gripping the steering wheel of the truck that belonged to his in-laws. Since marrying Jennifer, he mostly drove the truck now. The wet suits he used for surfing excursions typically lay scattered in the pickup's extended cab, as they did now.

It was December 9, 2002. He'd only been married to Jennifer a handful of months, but he was already feeling the pressure to prove he was a provider. He bragged to Jennifer's parents that his job at Ditech.com, where he worked as a loan officer, was going so well, his bonus check this Christmas would certainly be a fat one. If things kept going this way, he'd have enough for a small deposit on a home for him and Jennifer in no time.

In truth, Skylar was not a loan officer at one of America's largest mortgage companies, owned by the prestigious General Motors Corporation. Instead, he was a clerk in the appraisals department. Just a paper pusher, really. He did start off doing loans. But in the fast-paced, nonstop competitive business of mortgage lending, Skylar had struggled to stay on top at the company that promised customers online service twenty-four hours a day, seven days a week.

"I wasn't smart enough to do loans," Skylar recalls of the reason he was demoted. "I tried, but sales stuff wasn't for me. There was too much pressure. The bottom ten percent of the company got fired every month."

But Skylar didn't want his new in-laws to know of his failings. So he lied. And promised a big bonus was coming.

As December began, Skylar asked his co-worker, Wade Lohn, if he'd help him collect a debt from someone he knew. Wade and Skylar were more co-workers than friends, but Skylar's sense of humor made him an entertaining character at work. Wade was a well-built man, muscular, who'd actually been called on by friends in the past to stand by as they collected money owed to them. Usually, he just stood in the background and looked intimidating. He didn't see why he couldn't do that now, for Skylar.

Just days later, as Skylar sat in his truck, he called Wade.

"I'm at the house now," he said. "Come on over."

David Ramos, another Ditech co-worker, sat in the truck's passenger seat.

"Let's go in," Skylar said.

By the time Wade got to the house, Skylar and David were already inside. Skylar opened the front door to let in Wade, who stood gripping a green backpack in his hands. Skylar handed him a semi-automatic handgun and a pair of handcuffs.

"What are these for?" Wade asked.

"Just in case we need to detain someone," Skylar said.

Wade shoved the items into his backpack. Skylar began throwing other things in the bag—a pearl necklace, a silver pocket watch, keys to a Yamaha motorcycle, keys to a Lexus.

It was sometime after 10 p.m. when Skylar noticed a figure standing on the lawn making a call.

"That's not Ted!" yelled Skylar, who thought someone was outside calling the police. "We've got to run!"

The three men bolted from the house, Skylar and David heading to the Ford. Wade ran in the opposite direction.

But it was homeowner Ted Wangsanutr standing on his front lawn that evening. It wasn't, however, the police he was calling.

He'd come home to find someone had latched the top bolt on his door—a lock he didn't even have a key for. His uncle was the only other person with a set of keys to his house, so he called to ask if he'd been by and accidentally locked the top lock.

But as he made the call, shock swept over him as he caught a glimpse of the three men in black hooded sweatshirts, hoods pushed up over their heads, charging out of his house. Two jumped into a pickup truck. A third tossed a green backpack to the truck's driver before running on foot in the opposite direction. Ted dashed to his own car, intent on following that truck. He didn't know what was going on, but whatever it was, he damn sure wasn't going to let these guys get away with it.

As he drove, Ted punched 911 into his cell. He followed them down side streets and eventually into the city of Buena Park. By then, officers from the Anaheim Police Department caught up to the chase and jumped on their tail. Ted, relieved, slowed and let the cops take over.

It only took minutes before cops forced the duo to a stop and hauled them out of the truck, onto the street, and into handcuffs.

"You recognize these guys?" Officer Clifford Pratt asked Ted. With their sweatshirt hoods pulled back, Ted took a good look at his burglars. He couldn't have been more stunned as he looked over their faces. At least one of them was a friend—or so he thought.

"Yeah," he said, "I do. That's Skylar Deleon. We work together."

Ted was a successful loan officer at Ditech. After hours, he often hung out with Skylar. And when Skylar took to admiring a motorcycle Ted owned, even tossed his co-worker the keys, and would let him borrow the thing whenever he wanted. Ted had considered him a friend. Skylar, however, was just feeling out his co-worker, trying to see how much money the man had. He came to believe Ted was pulling in a lot of cash at his job. He figured Ted was pretty well off. In actuality, he was not. But he owned his own home, drove a nice car, and had enough left over for luxuries like vacations, nice clothes, the motorcycle. To Skylar, that was rich enough.

Police pulled the stolen items from Skylar's borrowed pickup, including the string of pearls that once belonged to Ted's grandmother. On the truck's floorboard, they also found a photocopy of a driver's license belonging to Wade Lohn.

Police seized the handgun, shoved into the glove compartment, a clip for the gun under the driver's seat, the handcuffs, and a pair of latex gloves. Looking over those items, investigators surmised that if Ted had actually made it inside that house and surprised the burglars, he might very well have ended up hurt, if not dead. These weren't the type of items used by simple burglars looking for a quick and easy score. Gun, latex gloves, handcuffs—only criminals who weren't afraid to use force to get what they wanted carried such things.

Detective Kathleen Reiss interviewed Skylar back at the police station. She read him his Miranda rights and then asked the simple question—why had he robbed his co-worker?

"Money," Skylar said. "I was trying to find money."

Skylar and his friends were charged with burglary in the first degree of an inhabited dwelling, plus an enhancement to the charge that would add an additional year in prison for carrying a gun at the time of the burglary.

A typical new bride would have been furious to learn her husband was sitting in jail on a burglary charge. But if Jennifer was ever cross with her husband for landing behind bars, she kept it to herself. Instead, she turned to her parents for help. Jennifer swore it was all a misunderstanding that snowballed out of control. It was just a practical joke on a co-worker, but the police wouldn't believe that, she said. And now, she begged her father to go down to the county jail and bail her husband out—although some might balk at the image of her "begging" her father to do anything.

"Knowing Jennifer, she probably just ordered them to march down and pay that bail," said a family friend close to Jennifer and Skylar. "She always wore the pants in that family. Especially with her dad. She just told him what to do and he did it for her."

So her father put up the bail money, and Skylar came home.

On May 1, 2003, Skylar opted to skip a trial and plead guilty to the burglary. The charge carried an enchancement for using a firearm, making him eligible for 7 years in prison. The deputy district attorney urged Orange County Superior Court Judge Roger Robbins to hit Skylar with at least one year. Instead, Judge Robbins gave the first-time offender a sentence so light, it would garner harsh criticism from the media in years to come. He granted defense attorney Ernest Eady's request to send his client to the Seal Beach City Jail, a privately run, low-security facility housing non-violent offenders.

The city of Seal Beach participated in a work-furlough program, allowing inmates to work at a job outside the jail all day, then return by sundown to spend the night.

"That was a judge fuck-up," Matt Murphy would say in reviewing Skylar's criminal background two years later. "He gave away the store on that one."

Skylar's attorney, however, defended the judge's decision, telling a local newspaper, "This was not a case that jumped out at you either in its planning or its sophistication. It was a run-of-the-mill burglary between friends. Nobody was hurt. It was not a crime of violence. I'm not minimizing going into people's homes and taking their stuff, but there was nothing abnormal about this case."

Still, the Seal Beach Police Department, which oversees the predominantly civilian-staffed jail and reviews each new inmate's history before acceptance into their facility, say they never knew Skylar's burglary included a firearm enhancement—typically enough to boost the crime to the "violent felony" category. The semi-automatic recovered from his truck was not mentioned in his work-furlough application, nor was there any mention of it in California's criminal database system. Appearing in the same news article as the defense attorney, Seal Beach Sergeant Jim Johnson lamented, "had I known that there was a weapon involved in the burglary, I probably would not have accepted him. I would have said no."

Correctional Systems, Inc., which runs the private jails, offers its services to cities looking to slash the cost of housing inmates. It uses private jailers and managers, who are considerably cheaper than trained law enforcement officers. The theory goes that if a city's police force isn't tied up running the jail, then those sworn peace officers are free to respond to more breaking crime, according to the company's pitch. "Police departments can concentrate all of their efforts on community safety rather than expending energy and resources on jail operations," boasts the company's website.

But on the downside, it could be said that what a municipality saves in revenue, it loses in quality. A city has no control over the background and training of the civilian employees handling its offenders. A high school diploma and clean criminal record are the only requirements for an entry-level applicant.

As part of the work-furlough program, inmates must agree to pay a participation fee, averaging about $70 a day. For a guy like Skylar, who would spend 214 days at Seal Beach jail, his tab hit $14,980. And once again, Jennifer's father covered the bill. Not because he was a wealthy man who could afford it. His blue-collar job as an instrument technician for British Petroleum did pay well, but not that well. He was a middle-class man working his way toward retirement. A nearly $15,000 bill would have crippled him.

The blow could have been eased if Skylar had actually used his time in the work-furlough program at a job, actually bringing in a paycheck. In the beginning, Steve Henderson even managed to get his son-in-law a trainee position as an electrician's assistant for Total-Western, Inc., a company offering maintenance and construction services to refinery, power, and industrial businesses. Mostly, he was a gofer, earning $13 an hour by running errands at various job sites. But it was only a temporary job, and as the work ran out, Skylar was laid off. And he made no effort to find anything else.

Instead, on July 11, 2003, Skylar submitted a written request to Judge Robbins asking that he be allowed to work from home. In the letter, he never specified what kind of work he'd be doing, or if he was running his own business or had a job that required him to check in with a supervisor. "I'm requesting to work from my house to keep supporting my family," was Skylar's simple written request. Judge Robbins approved.

So Skylar went home Monday through Saturday, returning each evening to the jail. But in the entire time he was "working from home," he never reported a single dollar's worth of income, according to court records. And jail officials never caught the oversight.

But job or no job, Skylar made the most of those scattered hours each evening when he was forced back behind bars. It was then that he would befriend two people who would play life-altering roles in his future. And it was then that he'd begin his deadliest con job yet.

CHAPTER FIFTEEN

No one ever said Alonso Machain was a smart man. Not even Alonso Machain. In high school, he was only a C student. And he struggled to earn that. But he liked to think that whatever he lacked in intellect, he made up for in other ways. He tried to be a good person, to do the right thing in life.

At 20 years old, he still behaved like the insecure kid he was growing up in the rough-and-tumble streets of Pico Rivera, a lower-income industrial area of California. It is an area heavily populated by Mexican immigrants, drawn to the city because of its sprawling Hispanic community and cheap housing.

Alonso was, in fact, born in Mexico, to devout Catholic parents. Sunday mornings meant attending Mass. And as an adult, he still went to church services. His family was the kind that would always be very involved in their place of worship. His father even assisted whenever communions and baptisms were held at their neighborhood church in Pico.

His family immigrated to the United States when Alonso was just 7 years old. They were poor, but they never wanted for anything. Alonso always had a clean place to live. He never went hungry. And his parents loved him very much. In his neighborhood, there was plenty of trouble to get into, if he wanted it. But he never fell in with a bad crowd or caused his parents any grief.

He was a good boy, if a reserved one. But as he grew older, he never developed the kind of self-esteem he would need to become a success in life, to stand up on his own. He would always be someone's assistant. A follower. And that would be his downfall.

As a civilian jailer at Seal Beach, Alonso Machain shouldn't have formed a friendship with any inmate. But he was charmed by the fast-talking, wise-cracking Skylar Deleon.

Like all predators, Skylar, no doubt, sensed Alonso was easy pickings. He was young and gullible enough to believe the creative spins Skylar put on the truth and casually dropped into conversation. He wasn't just a former Ditech employee. His grandparents actually owned the company, Skylar said. He didn't just serve in the Marines a few months before being tossed out on his ear. He was a trained sniper who served in the Middle East, racking up twenty-eight confirmed kills.

"Hey, you dropped this," said Alonso, picking up a picture Skylar let slip through his fingers and onto the floor, hitting Alonso's feet. It was a shot of Skylar in uniform, probably from boot camp.

"Oh, yeah, I did," Skylar said, snagging the picture back. "That was me when I was serving in Afghanistan."

And after Skylar had to transfer cells one night, he called on his friend to retrieve some paperwork he left behind.

"I think I left a check stub back there," Skylar told him. "Can you see if you can find it?"

Sure enough, tucked partially beneath the cell's mattress, with just a sliver hanging out for Alonso to find, was a check stub for $30,000.

Investigators believe the check stub was probably from an actual deposit Skylar had made. But not from any job he ever held—or from his grandparents at Ditech. In 2002, Skylar was in a moderately severe motorcycle accident. As he was leaving his grandparents' home in Westminster one evening, a car made an illegal left turn and smashed into the bike he was driving. Of course, it wasn't his motorcycle. At the time, he couldn't afford such a frivolous toy. It was borrowed. From his friend, Ditech co-worker, and future burglary victim, Ted Wangsanutr. Skylar was rushed to Huntington Beach Hospital where, he later said in an interview, he was admitted to the intensive care unit and treated for internal injuries. He would recover, mostly—though he'd claim that the accident left him permanently suffering from incontinence so severe, he had to wear adult diapers. As compensation, he got a $30,000 settlement from the other driver's insurance company.

But he never mentioned any of that to Alonso, who found the check stub for thirty grand exactly where Skylar had left it for him. Alonso assumed it was a cash payout from one of Skylar's much-mentioned "investment deals."

As for why he was in jail, Skylar explained it was all a mix-up, of course. It was just a joke of a friend with a bad sense of humor. But it didn't matter now. He was just going to serve his time and move on. He had bigger things planned. Business plans. Investment deals. Things that would more than make up for his lost time.

Alonso believed it all. And he wasn't the only one listening to Skylar's tales of grandeur. So was a nearby cellmate, Jon P. Jarvi.

There was a time when JP Jarvi had so many things going for him. That's what his mom remembers most about JP as he grew up in their upper-middle-class home in Fullerton, California.

JP, as he'd been known since the day he was born, was bright, with a sharp memory and a reading comprehension level that was off the charts at his elementary school. He graduated high school in three years. And not too many years after earning his license to drive, he started taking flying lessons. In the sky, a rush of adrenaline and freedom flooded his soul. He flew smaller Cessnas, mostly. If he ever wanted to fly the larger commercial jets, he never talked about it. He was content behind the controls in his small, independent flyers.

He was still in his twenties when a job opened up for Team America, the prestigious air show that traveled across the country showcasing the in-flight acrobatics of fighter jets and other small aircraft. JP would never be a show flyer, but he did help ferry the planes to and from show sites and act as Team America's official announcer. And that made him happy.

He also made ends meet earning extra cash as a contract pilot for private companies and individuals. He made enough money to be content.

He was still a very young man when searing back pain began gripping him during flights. Long hours at the cockpit became impossible to endure. JP put off seeing a doctor, at first. But as the pain began creeping into his neck and upper back, even when he wasn't flying, he made an appointment. Only then did JP allow an X-ray, and doctors discovered a hairline fracture in his back and neck.

"He didn't even know when it might have happened," said his mother, Betty Jarvi. "It could have been in high school, and he had been walking around like that for some while. He had been in a lot of pain for a long time."

Doctors recommended a series of operations to repair the break and relieve the constant ache in his upper back, including procedures that inserted a steel plate in his back and another in his neck.

Said his mother, "That took away the pain, except he couldn't bend anymore. Then he felt like he was starting to heal up, so he went in for another surgery to get all that taken out again. And then he broke his back again, in the same place, so he went in another time to have the plates put in one more time."

Along the way, with every surgery, JP went home with a stack of pain prescriptions. And when the prescriptions ran out, it was anything he could get his hands on to ease the suffering.

"That's when he really started to go downhill," Betty said of her son. "I think it was all of the painkillers. That's when he started in on drugs."

Those close to JP say the addiction changed the normally outgoing, happy-go-lucky guy they knew into a moody man whose temper could become so unpredictable, it was hard to say if he was going to greet a friend with a handshake or a cold shoulder.

"He either loved you or hated you," a friend said. "There was rarely an in-between with JP. He still had a lot of friends from

back in high school. That's the kind of guy he could be. Loyal
to a fault. But once he was done with you, if he thought you had
done him wrong, that was it."

"There were periods where he seemed to have it under control and he would be okay for a long time," Betty recalled. "And
then periods where he would get pretty bad again."

Things went from bad to worse during a flight out of Florida,
when the alternator cut out on his plane. He desperately needed
to make an emergency landing, but the plane's landing gear
would not come down. From the air, he spotted an open, grassy
field and targeted it for touch-down. As gently as he could, he
brought the small plane down onto its belly. He was a talented
pilot, and managed to walk away without a scratch.

"Now, this is his story," Betty Jarvi says, "but he told me he
never did file a report on that accident. He was in Oklahoma
City at the time, and the outfit that watches over pilots was right
nearby. But he never filed a written report and it caused him to
lose his license."

JP was devastated. But even during the darkest days, he was
a good son, Betty said. His condo in Orange wasn't far from her
Anaheim home, which he visited three to four days a week.
When his father's health began to slide, JP was there whenever
possible, running errands or showing up if something needed
fixing around the house.

"Which was a good share of the time," Betty said. "And
we'd go out to eat a lot. JP and I, we liked to do that."

But without his pilot's license, JP seemed lost. He was forced
to find a new profession, but nothing interested him as much as
flying. He floundered. Eventually, it was his mother who suggested her profession—jewelry making. It sounded like a crazy
idea, but if you were good, there was a living in it. And he could
be as independent as he wanted to be. So he studied techniques
for refining gold, eventually mastering the art so well, several
area jewelry stores began contracting with him. His interest in
the precious metal thrived. So much, in fact, that he researched
Northern California gold mines in his spare time, looking for
ones to lease. Gold mining became a dream of JP's, who had
romantic notions of sifting through the waters like an old-time

Western settler, looking for chunks to refine into high-end jewels and sell on the market. But the harsh realities of his life would always interrupt JP's California gold rush fantasies.

As his battle with drug addiction raged on, he found a new client, recommended by a friend of a friend, who had a lot of money to spend on custom-made jewelry. She wanted to know if he'd start by making a ring for her mother. JP took the job and made her a ring she loved so much, she struck up a friendship with the fledgling jewelry maker. In the end, she was hanging around his condo all the time, sometimes bringing a group of friends with her.

Life was going okay, looking up again. Then his ailing father passed away. JP flew to Wisconsin with his newly widowed mother to inter his dad's ashes in his home state. When JP returned to California, he discovered that his condo had been wiped out by thieves.

"While we were up there," Betty said, "his condo was literally gutted. They took his furniture, all of his jewelry-making tools, all of his equipment, everything."

JP would later learn that his new high-end customer and her friends had stolen a set of spare keys during a visit. The moment he left town, they robbed him of anything valuable he owned.

Recalls Betty, "After that, he kept saying, 'I've got to be a better judge of people.'"

The robbery sunk JP into a new low. And in the months that followed, federal investigators landed on his door with an arrest warrant. Turned out, his vow to better scrutinize friends didn't last long. JP's girlfriend of the moment had ties to a ruthless white supremacist gang known as Public Enemy Number One, or PEN1. Her friends convinced JP they had a sure-fire way to make a little money. And, sure enough, in court papers, authorities accused JP and friends of literally making their own cash—using his condo as a counterfeiting station. Chemicals found in his home had been used to bleach out five-dollar bills, which were then run through a high-end printer and turned into fifties.

"I guess they did a lousy job," Betty said. "But I know he had no training on a computer. So I don't think it was him doing it.

But, of course, it was done at his condo, so I'm sure he knew what was going on."

Again, Betty remarked on her son's poor ability to distance himself from people who would land him in trouble. He was a good guy, with a big heart. But for most of his adult life, JP Jarvi struggled to get ahead. He battled recurrent back pain, addiction to painkillers, and couldn't hold a job. But his biggest weakness might have been the people he chose to trust.

Looking back, Betty repeated the words her son used every time he relied on the wrong person and landed in trouble: "He just wasn't good about judging people."

After time in federal prison for the counterfeiting scheme, JP was overjoyed to finish out his sentence at a local jail. The inmates of Seal Beach City Jail were sissies compared to the killers and gang members he slept next to in prison. And could there be any greater cellmate than Skylar Deleon? He was a highly trained sniper for the Marines who'd taken out twenty-eight terrorists while serving in Afghanistan. And he didn't even have to serve, if he hadn't wanted to, because his relatives were super rich. His grandparents owned Ditech, and his parents were high-ranking executives in the company.

At least, that's what Skylar told him.

"My parents, you know, they can be very uppity," Skylar said. "Pretty damn snobby, if you ask me. They have more money than they know what to do with. And so do I, I guess. But I liked the Marines. Everyone there is so down-to-earth. We all had a job to do and we just took care of business."

JP never doubted it was all true—he saw the picture of Skylar in uniform, and once, in Skylar's cell, found a $30,000 check made out to Skylar Deleon.

So when Skylar started talking about all of his investments in businesses and property throughout Mexico, JP listened. Finally, here was a guy who really had money and knew exactly what to do with it, JP thought.

"Just wait and see," Skylar said. "I have this one deal that

I'm sitting on right now. Once I invest in that, it's going to make so much money. It's guaranteed, believe me."

JP did believe Skylar. And was overjoyed when his buddy asked if he was interested in going in on the deal with him.

"You just give me the money and I'll handle the details," Skylar said. "How much you think you can come up with?"

"I don't know," said a worried JP, who didn't want to miss out, but also didn't have a penny in the bank and no real prospects for employment once he got out. He couldn't ask his mom for the money. He'd already put her through enough heartache with his arrest. But he had his condo. And his van, maybe.

"Well, the more money you can come up with, the more you'll get back," Skylar promised.

"Don't worry," JP said. "I'll find the money for you."

In the weeks before Christmas 2003, JP Jarvi left Seal Beach City Jail and immediately set about getting his hands on every dollar he could find.

CHAPTER SIXTEEN

It probably wasn't the smartest idea, to take money out against the one thing of value he still owned—his condo. But this was the opportunity of a lifetime. If what Skylar promised turned out to be true, he'd make more than enough to catch up. So he refinanced his condo and took out $50,000 in cash. Then he drove his red Chevrolet Astro van to a local pawn shop to see what he could get for it. He didn't really want to sell his only means of transportation, but the pawn dealer would let JP keep the van, as long as he made payments on the $2,600 they loaned him, with interest, every month. In short, the van was collateral against the loan. Just to be sure JP didn't drive off into the sunset with his money and never return, the dealer put a LoJack device on the van. If JP missed payments, the shop got the van.

JP spent Christmas at home with his mom, his brother, and his brother's wife. They exchanged gifts and just caught up with each other. That night, he took Betty out to dinner. He was in such a good mood—all smiles. Betty hadn't seen him that way in a long time, and it felt good to watch him enjoy himself. Her son had caused her a lot of grief in his lifetime, that was true enough. But she loved him, and he did the best he could to love her back. She was happy to have him home again.

He never mentioned his plans with Skylar. But he did say

that for his birthday, which fell on the day after Christmas, he couldn't think of any present he needed. Maybe just some cash.

The next morning, JP stopped by his mom's house once more, so he could pick up his birthday present.

"He was very upbeat that morning," Betty said. "That's when I gave him his money. I walked him outside to his van. He didn't stay long. We talked for a few minutes and then he left."

From Betty's house, JP made his way to the Wells Fargo Bank in Newport Beach to cash his $50,000 check.

It was JP's 45th birthday, as good a time as any to make a fresh start. Who needed a mining claim to strike gold when he had Skylar? What luck that he'd land a cellmate who turned out to be some rich kid with connections—the kind that made people with money even more money. No doubt, his luck was already changing for the better.

At the bank, the Newport Beach branch didn't have enough cash on hand to lay out $50,000 all at once. Bank vice president Shirley Cantu counted out $25,000 in hundred-dollar bills for JP, then sent him off to their branch in neighboring Laguna Beach to pick up the other $25,000. There, bank manager Ninette Sati greeted an anxious, perhaps even nervous-looking JP. Beads of sweat dotted his upper lip as she counted out his money, all in hundreds, as he'd asked.

Technically, Skylar was still an inmate at Seal Beach jail. But he was out for the day, thanks to work furlough, and was home to pick up the payout. JP left the second bank around 11:30 that morning and drove straight to Skylar. JP gave his former cellmate everything—except for the few dollars from his mom. That rested still in his wallet.

"You won't be sorry," Skylar told him.

"I'll see you tomorrow," JP said.

Michael Lewis looked forward to spending the holidays with his family in California. He even looked forward to seeing his trouble-making cousin, Skylar. As kids, Michael and Jon Jon weren't just cousins. They were close friends. They were the same age. Had the same interests. Same friends. And hanging with him was always an adventure. Whenever Michael thought of Skylar, he thought of their high school days, when his thrill-seeking cousin talked him into being the lookout while he busted into neighbors' homes, stealing money, electronic gadgets, clothes—whatever caught his eye. Even though Michael knew it was wrong, he never tried to stop it. And he never told on him, either. Frankly, he got a vicarious thrill out of Skylar's antics. And anyway, he could excuse the behavior. What else could be expected from a kid raised by a guy like John Jacobson Sr.? The whole family knew about John's criminal connections and penchant for drug dealing. Michael had even been there when Skylar got in on the family business, selling drugs to high school buddies.

"Skylar was exactly like his father," Michael would say later. "But you just got used to that environment. You protect the family. You don't call the police."

As adults, Michael and Skylar were still close, even working together as clerks at Ditech. But that started to change when Michael's life took a radical turn. He became a dedicated Christian, attending church regularly, and telling Skylar he should do the same.

"You should come to church with me," Michael told him. "Just come check it out."

But Skylar blew off his cousin's invitations. He already had enough church talk from his in-laws. So, the cousins drifted apart. And by the time Michael moved to Arizona, the two barely spoke. There was no animosity. They were just different people, leading different lives.

Still, he cared about his cousin and genuinely looked forward to hanging out again. Skylar talked about the two of them going fishing or scuba diving, maybe even driving into Mexico to catch the waves in Ensenada. It might have been winter, but along the Gulf of Mexico, the waters were still warm and inviting.

Despite the distance that had grown between them in recent years, Michael still probably knew Skylar better than most. They'd built a bond over the back of all that troublemaking the two of them caused. Kid stuff, mostly. Some of it more serious, when the drug stuff came into play. But as Christmas Day drew

to a close, Michael couldn't have imagined the kind of trouble
Skylar was about to bring his way.

On the afternoon of December 26, minutes after Skylar
picked up the cash from JP, Michael agreed to run errands with
his cousin. He knew Skylar was supposed to be working during
the hours he was out of jail. But Skylar was so obviously un-
concerned about getting any work done, Michael didn't give it a
second thought. And if he wanted some company while taking
care of a few things, Michael was happy to provide it.

In the car, Skylar mentioned looking into some repairs he
needed on his boat. Indeed, Skylar did own a boat back then.
It was an old, out-of-shape 26-foot Sea Ray, dubbed *Doctor
Crunch*, that used to belong to his Grandpa Jacobson. He told
his grandparents he could use the boat to start up his own chartering business, renting it out to small businesses offering
scuba-diving classes and other pleasure excursions on the sea.
The boat was really too small to hold large groups, including a
class of diving students. And too tiny to be taken out to sea at
much of a distance. But Skylar wasn't going to let that stop him
from slapping $25,000 in upgrades on the undersized, battered
vessel, worth nothing more than a few grand in total. To begin
with, the Sea Ray had a problem with the outdrive, the boat's
power unit. He'd have to have some serious repairs done just to
get the thing moving. At least, that's what Mo Beck, the owner
of Mo Beck Stern Drive Company, told Skylar when he first
dragged the boat down to the boat repair shop three months
ago. It would take over a grand to fix it. Skylar didn't have the
money just then. But he was confident he'd have it soon.

So on that December morning, with a fresh $50,000 in cash
in his pockets, Skylar drove Michael back to Mo Beck's for an
updated cost estimate.

"You know what?" Skylar told Mo, "let's not bother with fixing the outdrive unit. Go ahead and replace it all—a new engine,
the transom, and a new drive unit. How much would that run?"

"A pretty good amount," Mo Beck told him. "I'd estimate
somewhere around seventeen thousand dollars."

"Not a problem," said Skylar, digging into an envelope and

counting out seventeen stacks of ten hundred-dollar bills. It was JP's investment money. But he laid that seventeen grand on the counter with such élan, such confidence, no onlooker would have guessed it wasn't Skylar Deleon's own hard-earned cash.

"Okay," Mo Beck told him. "I'll order the parts and give you a call when they arrive so you can haul your boat over."

With that, the men shook hands and the cousins left.

"Where the hell did you get all that money?" Michael asked, knowing that until now, Skylar didn't even have enough cash to move out of his in-laws' garage.

"I've been working a lot, man," Skylar lied. "I've been putting in twelve-hour days, six days a week with Total-Western. It adds up."

It was already turning into late afternoon and Skylar said he had one more important stop before he had to check himself back into Seal Beach jail for the night.

Skylar made his way to Robbins Bros. jewelry store in the neighboring city of Fullerton. He needed to make a payment on something for his best girl, he said.

Inside, store manager Ronald Jackson remembered Skylar. He'd been there before, to buy Jennifer's engagement ring. At the time, he couldn't afford to buy her the matching wedding band—95 percent pure platinum, dotted with five small diamonds totaling .55 carats. He didn't even have enough credit to make it happen. In fact, back in July 2002, Skylar only got the $10,000 princess-cut engagement ring by submitting a credit application under Jennifer's name alone. He was making up for that now, sort of a combined belated wedding and Christmas gift.

"The band comes to two thousand one hundred and forty-nine dollars and sixty-one cents, with tax," the sales clerk said.

Again, Skylar reached into his stash of hundreds and counted out twenty-two of them.

It was just before 3 p.m. when they left the store. Skylar had just enough time to drive home, give his wife her gift, and make it back for check-in time at the jail.

At home, Jennifer was overjoyed with her ring, even if it was the wrong size. The new band hung loosely on her small finger. But she didn't care too much about that. Nor did she seem to care where the money had come from for such an extravagant purchase. She may have owed her father thousands of dollars for Skylar's legal bills. The tiny paychecks she earned cutting hair may have made her the sole breadwinner for her family. And her husband may have been without a paycheck of any kind for months. But for the moment, this was her ring and she was happy to have it.

The next morning, she returned to Robbins Bros. with the ring resting safely in its box. She held on to the receipt, showing that her husband had paid over two grand in cash for her present.

There was a lot she could do with that money, including put a security deposit and first month's rent down on an apartment of her own. Only weeks before, she'd given birth to baby Hailey. Now, all three of them lived in the cramped one-room garage at her parents' place. It didn't even have a bathroom of its own. She was a grown woman, a wife, a new mommy—but for now, she and Skylar had to tromp through her mom and dad's home to shower and use the toilet. There was little room for privacy in such a setup. And it was embarrassing. She could get pretty angry when she thought about it too long.

But she was married to Skylar now. And just had his baby. It didn't matter that he was a felon serving time in jail for an armed burglary. She loved her husband, in spite of his failings, and wouldn't leave him. She just realized that she'd have to be the one in charge of this relationship. He was too much of a dreamer to ever make real decisions. She'd have to do that for him. He had grand illusions about so many things he wanted in life. But it was up to her to tell him how to actually get those things. Still, that was fine. She was used to telling the men in her life what to do. Didn't her father always do exactly what she told him to, after all?

She looked down at her ring. If she was going to return it and do something practical with the cash, now was the time. She placed the diamond band on the counter and looked up at the salesclerk.

"This was a gift from my husband," she said. "You think you could size it down to a five for me?"

Perhaps Jennifer had reason not to worry about money just then. By the end of the day, she'd write out a $3,800 check to her credit card company. And a $21,000 deposit went into the checking account she shared with her husband.

It was just 8 a.m. on the morning of December 27 when Skylar was released from Seal Beach for the day. He had a big day ahead of him, so he had to get moving early. He'd have to move fast if he was going to get everything done before checking back into jail by nightfall.

He drove straight home, where he met his cousin and threw surfing equipment into the back of his white Expedition. He told Michael to climb into his brother-in-law's black Ford pickup.

"It's a new truck," Skylar said. "But I'd appreciate it if you could drive behind me in it, because I think it's been acting up. It kind of misfires every once in a while, so I want to drive it some distance to check it out."

Michael didn't think twice about it. It was a nice truck, new, would be fun to drive. A nice treat after hauling around in the old, beat-up truck he drove every day.

"Cool," Michael said, grabbing the keys. "Sounds good to me."

At an AM/PM mini-mart, the cousins downed a couple of breakfast burritos while looking into the bright California morning. It didn't matter that it was nearly January. The holiday season in the Golden State meant beach weather no matter what the calendar said.

"Pretty good day for surfing," Michael told Skylar, who nodded in agreement. He promised that Michael would love the beach in San Miguel, Mexico, where they would be going right after breakfast.

As they headed out, Skylar said he needed to stop off at a nearby storage yard to pick up a friend.

JP sat waiting in his red Chevy van. He jumped into the Expedition with Skylar, and Michael drove behind in the truck, heading south down the 405 Freeway until it turned into the 5, the roadway leading into Mexico. In case they got separated, Skylar gave Michael Jennifer's cell phone to use for the day.

The two would talk many times during the two hours it took to reach the border.

As they crossed over, they continued driving until they reached their surf spot in San Miguel. But Michael was confused when Skylar drove on, passing their destination point entirely. Finally, Skylar called Michael to explain.

"Hey, there's a change in plans," he said. "We might be stopping off somewhere for JP."

"Okay," said Michael, though something about Skylar's voice unsettled him. His mood had been so light all day, upbeat. Now, he sounded serious, almost businesslike.

"Just keep following me," Skylar added.

It would be another ten miles, inside the city of Ensenada, before Skylar's Expedition finally slowed to a stop at a bank, Banamex. Michael stepped out of the car and watched his cousin walk toward the bank. It was then, chatting casually with Skylar's friend, that he learned another peculiar detail about the day's trip.

"I can't wait to see Skylar's house," JP said.

"His house down here?" said Michael, sounding a bit confused.

"Yeah, his second house," JP said. "Skylar said it's on the beach and there's fantastic surfing out there. Of course, I don't know how to surf, but Skylar is going to teach me."

"Uh-huh, that sounds great," said Michael, not sure what to say. Clearly, his cousin was giving this guy a snow job for some reason.

As Skylar returned, he walked up to Michael and pulled him aside, making sure JP couldn't hear his next words.

"I need you to watch my back," Skylar told him.

"Why?" asked a startled Michael. "What's going on? What's this about your house 'down here'? And why do I need to 'watch your back'?"

"Don't worry about that house stuff," he said, motioning to JP. "Just listen. That guy? He's the reason I had to go to jail. Everything's his fault. He's just a really bad guy, believe me. So, do me this favor and do what I say, okay? Just watch my back."

"Okay," said Michael, still not sure what Skylar was talking about. But he promised anyway. "I'll watch."

"Thanks, man," said Skylar.

In that moment, Michael could never have known that Skylar met JP for the first time after he was already in jail, when they became cellmates. For now, he just followed along, assuming it was another hare-brained scheme his cousin had cooked up.

"Now," Skylar added, "just get back in the truck and follow me."

Skylar's car backed out and made a U-turn, now heading back in the direction they came from. Once again, Michael stayed close behind. They drove north along Mexico's Highway 1, turning off just outside Ensenada, onto Highway 3, a two-lane country road that leads inland, away from Mexico's coast. If surfing had ever been the plan for the day, this road was not the one that would take them there. He drove in silence for several minutes, eventually losing sight of his cousin as Skylar rounded a bend in the road. Michael paused a moment, then drove on, slowly coming around and spotting Skylar's Expedition stopped off at a dirt turnout, the driver's-side door standing open. He could see Skylar, now holding open the passenger door and helping JP out of the car. As JP stepped down, coming more clearly into view, Michael was startled at the scene. A blindfold of some sort, maybe a rolled-up shirt, tied tightly over JP's eyes. Skylar gently placed one hand on JP's arm, the other around his waist, and carefully guided him along a side road that sloped downhill from the dirt turnout.

"Almost like a father escorting a kid into a room to surprise him with something at Christmas," Michael would say later of the scene.

They crept slowly, walking carefully so the blinded JP wouldn't trip, until they walked beyond Michael's sight.

Michael gently pressed the truck's gas pedal, inching toward JP and Skylar, hoping to catch another glimpse of them. When he didn't, he made a U-turn and paused for just a moment, trying to figure out what he'd just witnessed. Was Skylar planning to beat the crap out of this guy while he was blindfolded? But if there was any hostility between them, why would this guy ever let Skylar blindfold him? JP didn't seem forced out of the car. Skylar wasn't holding him at gunpoint. In fact, Michael was pretty sure he was cooperating fully with whatever Skylar was telling him to do.

Of course, Michael was unaware of the no-lose, get-rich-quick investment deal JP thought he was buying into. It's possible Skylar promised JP his prized investment was just ahead. Perhaps it was land, or a home, maybe a new business opportunity. The only people who will ever know for sure what surprise JP thought was waiting in the distance, beyond his blindfold, are JP and Skylar.

But JP would never tell that story. As he reached the foot of that hill, far out of sight of any passing motorists, Skylar released JP's arm and stepped behind him. With his eyes covered, JP never caught a glimpse of the knife Skylar lifted into the air, just above his friend's collarbone, and plunged downward. The blade sliced JP's carotid artery, causing blood to gush from the wound with each pump of the heart. He fell to his knees and, before he even understood what happened, he was all alone on this rural road. Skylar was gone, leaving JP to bleed to death.

From his seat in the truck, Michael couldn't see the horror unfolding below. But he sensed it. Michael was a big man, weighing in at over 200 pounds. And though that life was behind him now, he used to be a pretty tough guy. He'd been in some rough spots before and could take care of himself. But at that moment, parked down that secluded Mexican dirt road from his cousin and a blindfolded stranger, Michael was frightened. He might have promised to watch Skylar's back, but this was more than he bargained for. Whatever was happening at the bottom of that hill, Michael didn't want to know about it. So he hit the gas pedal and took off, speeding back toward the main road, back to home.

But shortly after he took off, as Michael approached the main highway, Skylar's white Expedition came into view.

"Hey!" Skylar shouted out to him through the window of his car. "Meet me in Puerto Nuevo. We'll grab a lobster dinner."

Michael nodded numbly, agreeing to meet up with his cousin in the Mexican city located a few miles from the U.S. border. But he couldn't stop thinking about JP, who no longer sat next to Skylar, or anywhere in the Expedition at all. He also noticed

Skylar had changed clothes, abandoning the long-sleeved shirt
he was wearing for a short-sleeved tee. Michael shuddered,
piecing together in his mind what it all meant.

In Puerto Nuevo, the restaurants were packed with customers. Skylar didn't have that kind of time. "I've got to hurry,"
he said. "I have to get back to report to jail." He opted to wait
until he was back over the border for dinner.

That was good news, as far as Michael was concerned. Maybe
he'd calm down, Michael thought, once he was back in his own
country. As they walked back to their cars, Skylar asked,
"Would you mind switching cars with me for the rest of the
drive?" He gave no explanation for the request.

But Michael understood.

Michael was never known among his circle of friends and
family for being an intellectual giant. He wasn't the brightest
kid in school and, as an adult, he worked the kind of low-level,
blue-collar jobs that would hardly bring him wealth or success.
But in that moment, he realized his cousin must consider him
an idiot. If Skylar did do something terrible to JP, who was last
seen sitting in the passenger seat of that car, then how could
Michael ever claim he wasn't a part of the plan if border agents
recorded him as the Expedition's driver when it crossed back
into the United States? Every car leaving Mexico and entering
the U.S. must pass by the watchful eye of a border agent, who
stops the car and asks for the driver's name and citizenship. If
the agent is suspicious, he can pull the car over and do a full
search. Suddenly, the real reason Skylar wanted Michael to
drive a second car that day became crystal clear.

"No way," Michael told him. "I'm not getting into that car."

Skylar didn't argue. He just hopped into the Expedition and
headed to the border. As he drove into Long Beach, he picked up
his cell to make a few calls. One to Jennifer. The other to jail. He
knew he'd be late checking back in. But he doubted that would
be a problem, since his buddy Alonso Machain was on duty.

In Long Beach, Skylar and Michael pulled into a California
Pizza Kitchen for dinner. As they ate, Michael was wary of asking too many questions about JP's fate. The more Michael knew,

the more he was involved. But he wouldn't rest easy until he had an explanation. So he asked.

"Skylar," he said, "what happened back there? Where's JP?"

Skylar swallowed his bite of pizza before looking hard at his cousin. Dropping his voice ominously, Skylar gave a cryptic, if terrifying, answer: "You're working with the devil now. Welcome to our side."

Skylar said it to mock his cousin and his Christianity. He was betting on the fact that, no matter how much of a Bible-thumper Michael had become, he'd never turn on family. And Skylar reveled in rubbing his goody-goody cousin's nose in that simple reality.

If Michael had been frightened before, he was petrified now as he looked at this man he'd known all his life. Skylar was never the most moral of men. Michael knew his cousin cut corners in life, a survival tactic Skylar had learned from his father. Even now, as they spoke, Skylar was just wasting minutes before checking himself back into jail for an armed burglary conviction. His cousin was lazy. Maybe even a little mentally unstable. But sitting in the restaurant with him that evening, looking into his eyes, Michael saw pure evil. And he was scared. He didn't need to ask anything more. He knew JP Jarvi lay dead along a lonely dirt road in Mexico. And Michael felt helpless to do anything about it.

As Michael drove back to Skylar's house alone that evening to return the borrowed truck, Skylar made his way back to the Seal Beach jail. Jennifer ran outside to greet him and he reached out to hand over her cell phone and car keys.

"Hey there," she said cheerfully. "Did you boys have a nice time?"

Michael simply stared at her a moment, incredulous. He didn't know what she knew, if she knew. But her overly bright greeting made him sick to his stomach. Wordlessly, he turned his back and walked away.

CHAPTER SEVENTEEN

Ryan Hawks was enraged.

It was bad enough his parents had been gone for fifteen days. But now, investigators were asking questions that were just a waste of time. And an insult, really. At times, their questions made Ryan and his relatives feel like suspects. Then, on top of it all, detectives were questioning his parents' integrity—as if they may have done something underhanded and played a part in their own disappearance. It was hard to take.

"Four hundred thousand dollars, that's nothing to me," Ryan told police. "I could care less about that money or that boat. So you go ahead, look at me. Look at everything about me. I have nothing to hide."

Once again, it was Jim who helped his nephew calm down and deal with the tough realities of a police investigation.

"Ryan," he said, "I would be disappointed if they weren't looking at us, at me. I was one of the last people to see them. They have to investigate us before they can rule us all out as suspects. If my department was investigating this, they'd have to do the same. They're doing the right thing. And you've got to let them do it."

He knew his uncle was right. Ryan had come to rely on him so much in the past weeks—just as he used to rely on his dad.

Anyway, so far, he'd been nothing but impressed with how hard the Newport Beach Police Department seemed to be working the case.

"I don't know what I'd do if it wasn't for Dave Byington, Evan Sailor, Matt Murphy, and those guys," Ryan would say over and over as the pieces to his parents' horrific story slowly fell into place.

But in the beginning, it was tough, since even his parents, the victims, had to be looked at with a dubious eye. Investigators had to ask—could they be involved in anything illegal? Could they have been tangled up in drug-running?

"No," Ryan said emphatically. "Go ahead, audit every bank account, every transaction, every dollar they ever earned. They are by the book. And I'm telling you, there is no way they took four hundred thousand dollars in the street, over the trunk of a car, and then ran across the border."

Sergeant Byington could find, so far, not a single reason to doubt Ryan. He seemed so close to his father and stepmom. And he could tell it pained Ryan and Matt every day that the Hawkses were gone.

"Ryan," Sergeant Byington finally asked, "you knew your parents so well. I want to hear what you think happened."

Without hesitation, Ryan answered, "You know what I think? I think their boat made it back into the harbor without them. I think they are dead and this kid, Skylar, has something to do with it."

The detective nodded. It was exactly what he and Detective Sailor thought, too—even though they still weren't convinced the meager, effeminate Skylar Deleon was tough enough to kill anyone, let alone two people. And parts of his story were checking out. Detectives interviewed Alonso Machain on December 1 and he'd confirmed that, yes, he was there that sunny November afternoon when Skylar and Jennifer had given the Hawkses the cash for the *Well Deserved*. And he was there when the Hawkses hopped in their Honda, intent on heading to Mexico in search of property to buy. But unlike Skylar and Jennifer, who coolly told their stories and went out of their way to be accommodating, Alonso always seemed nervous when he spoke. His eyes darted around the room and he was fidgety, like he couldn't wait to get away.

"He looks all hinked up," Sergeant Byington told his fellow investigators.

Viewing a tape of the interview, Matt Murphy agreed.

"He's a human study of what to do wrong when you're telling a story," Matt said. "Still, he's telling the same story."

So did Kathleen Harris, the notary, when Detective Sailor called her on November 30 to talk about the sale. The investigator told her she was among the last people to have seen the missing couple—if she was really there.

"Yes, I was there," said Kathleen. "I met the Hawkses and witnessed the sale. They were really excited about it."

"Well, they've been missing since that day," Detective Sailor said. "In fact, we believe strongly now that they may have been murdered."

Kathleen reacted with genuine shock. "I wish I could tell you what happened after the sale," she said. "But I just don't know."

Detectives had no reason to doubt her. But Kathleen would later say she shook with fear as Detective Sailor grilled her that day. Outwardly, she'd hidden her nerves well—so well, in fact, that Detective Sailor thought it was hard to get a read on her. But a background check showed she had no criminal convictions, and she had been a licensed notary for several years, with no record of problems. For now, there was nothing he could do but accept her word.

But so much time had passed, few people ever expected to find Tom or Jackie alive, though there was still a chance that their bodies could be recovered. Maybe they were in that missing 1998 silver Honda. And even if they weren't, the car would still be a key piece of evidence, if investigators could find it. Who'd driven that car to its last destination—the Hawkses or their killers?

Though they dreaded it, investigators knew it was time to bring in the media. It was always a double-edged sword. Alerting the hordes of aggressive reporters who covered Southern California meant the Newport Beach Police Department and the Orange County District Attorney's office would be pelted with a steady barrage of questions, some inane, most redundant, and some unanswerable because the information couldn't be released to the public. The latter was the answer reporters working a competitive story wanted to hear the least. And some would go to great lengths to get their answers, even dragging in their newspapers' or broadcast outlets' attorneys, demanding information be released by right of something called the Public Information Act.

But most often, the reporters enjoyed getting the word out for police. And a news story in the public eye almost always generated new tips to investigators. True, a lot of those tips were from crackpots looking for attention. And many were dead-ends. But sometimes, the right person watching that evening news story called in, and suddenly, a dying case gets new life.

On December 1, investigators put out a news release, alerting the media to the story of the much-beloved Newport Beach couple who'd inexplicably disappeared one November afternoon. It was a compelling tale that would certainly draw some attention. But to really grab headlines, they'd need a family member to talk. A lot of families balked at the idea of crying to the cameras. But as cold as it sounds, nothing pulls at the heartstrings of the public like a grieving loved one begging for the public's help. And suddenly, a story that would have run buried in the middle of a newspaper's local section jumps to the front page, a picture of the tearful relative blazing in the center.

Jim Hawks understood this process. It was a ploy his investigators used often, especially in missing persons cases. So when the request came for a member of the Hawks family to speak at a press conference, Jim turned to Ryan.

"I think you should do it," Jim told his nephew.

It was the last thing Ryan felt like doing—putting himself in the spotlight to answer a bunch of questions for a bunch of strangers. But an interview with the missing couple's son would go a long way. He was articulate, and a man so easily likeable, it was hard not to think of the love and laughter this father-and-son team must have shared when they were last together. And it certainly didn't hurt that Ryan was the spitting image of his father—a ruggedly handsome young man with dark hair and a strong square jaw that settled into a sharp line when he clenched his teeth in moments of despair or frustration.

Ryan agreed, remembering the vow he made to push aside grief and do whatever it took to help investigators. "I did it," Ryan said. "But it took all of that self-discipline my father taught me over the years to get through it. I just kept telling myself there would be time to grieve later."

And so it began. On December 8, 2004, Ryan sat in the offices of the Newport Beach Police Department from 10 a.m. until 1 p.m., accepting interviews from any reporter who wanted one. But the media circus wouldn't stop there. For days to come, Ryan found himself standing in front of an endless stream of cameras, microphones, and tape recorders, patiently answering questions, pleading for help from anyone who knew what happened, who may have seen the Hawkses' car. He spoke to the *Los Angeles Times*, *The Orange County Register*, *The San Diego Union-Tribune*, the Long Beach *Press-Telegram*. He appeared on every local news station, and agreed to interviews on the *Today* show and CNN.

"For them to not be in contact for over two weeks," Ryan said in a December 9 interview with a San Diego TV station, "to be completely missing without all their personal items and various other stuff—it doesn't make any sense, and we're not swallowing it, really."

One television set in particular would beam out Ryan's image as he recounted his family's story once again, this time for *Good Morning America*. From his living room, the TV viewer blinked in disbelief as the program flashed a picture of the Hawkses' missing car. Because sitting in a driveway not too far away was that very silver Honda CR-V, bearing the very same license plate number.

"I'm looking at it right now," the tipster said when he got a Newport Beach detective on the line. "I can take a picture of the thing and email it to you, if you need it."

Detectives wasted no time driving to the Ensenada neighborhood. By that afternoon, they were staring at the car—sitting outside a house, in plain view. The homeowner told investigators he'd had the car since November 26, when an American friend and his wife dropped it off, asking to keep it parked at his place for a while.

"Your friend and his wife," the detective asked. "Was that Thomas and Jackie Hawks?"

"No," he answered. "Skylar and Jennifer Deleon."

CHAPTER EIGHTEEN

It was supposed to be a carefree day touring the back roads of Ensenada. The American tourists were hoping to make the most of the lull that comes with the days between Christmas and New Year's Day. But that December 27 afternoon would be marred by the horrific find along a dirt road off Highway 3. JP Jarvi's body lay in a heap near a clump of bushes, a bloody puddle still pooling beneath him.

Ensenada police would later theorize that as he bled out, JP found the strength to crawl up the foot of the hill where he'd been stabbed, to the turnout alongside the main roadway. It would only be a matter of minutes before the Americans found JP. But it was already too late. With his artery cut, the one charged with delivering blood from the heart to the brain, it only took moments before JP lost consciousness, then died.

JP could easily have been added to the list of unknown bodies murdered and then dumped along a remote dirt road in the backlands of Mexico. But authorities would get lucky this time—their murder victim still had his wallet. Inside, they found a driver's license and a little cash. Clearly, they thought, this victim had not been murdered for his money.

Betty Jarvi wept inconsolably when investigators called, informing her of the body found bearing her son's ID. They'd need her to travel into their country to view the body and confirm the corpse was indeed Jon Peter Jarvi. In the way mothers often know when something bad has happened to their children, Betty was certain that her long-troubled son was indeed dead. Yes, she'd come make a positive ID. But she wasn't holding on to any false hope.

When she finally made the trip to Ensenada, her younger son at her side, she gasped in horror at the gruesome stab wound visible at the base of JP's neck. She nodded then.

"Yes, that's my JP."

Coroner's officials handed Betty the personal items from JP's pockets, including the wallet, which still held every dollar she'd given him for his birthday. The discovery brought her to tears again, knowing her son never had the chance to spend the money she'd given him in celebration of his very last birthday.

But it would be the message she discovered on her answering machine when she got home that would hit her the hardest. It must have been on her machine several days, but she only now noticed. As she hit the PLAY button, JP's chipper voice boomed from the tape: "Hi, Mom, it's your number-two son! Give me a call when you can."

"Would you mind if my friend kept his van here a few days?" Skylar sweetly asked his friend, Greg Logan.

Greg was the owner of Jet Automotive, a car repair shop about four miles from the converted studio Skylar and Jennifer called home.

"Is there anything wrong with it?"

"No," Skylar answered. "It's just that it belongs to a friend of mine and he's going to be out of the country for a while. He's got some business to do in Mexico."

Greg said he had no problem babysitting the van—and a wave of relief swept over Skylar. He knew he couldn't leave Jon Jarvi's cherry-colored Chevy Astro van sitting in front of his house for long. It would be nothing short of a gigantic red flag for investigators if they ever came knocking on his door, looking for his friend JP.

But what Skylar couldn't know was that investigators had a tool that would help them track down that van no matter where he stashed it. The LoJack system JP's pawn shop installed when he put the thing up for hock was still working. Police simply had to run the van to learn it was currently registered to a pawn shop. A call to LoJack prompted them to set off the tracking device, leading police to Greg Logan's door.

Los Angeles Police Department's Interpol Liaison Unit helped Ensenada PD impound the van—but not before learning that it was Skylar, not JP, who dropped the van off at Jet.

And so, less than a week after her cash windfall, law enforcement was at Jennifer's front door. Los Angeles Police Detective Joe Bahena and detectives from the Ensenada Police Department wondered if they could have a word with her and her husband.

"Of course," said Jennifer. "But he's not here. You'll have to call him on his cell. What's this about?"

"Jon Jarvi. His body was discovered in Ensenada a few days ago and they're looking into his death," Bahena said, translating for the foreign officers beside him. "We understand Mr. Deleon was in possession of his van before dropping it off at Jet Automotive."

They talked to Jennifer a few more minutes, then handed her their business cards, in case she remembered anything more after they left.

Then put a call into her husband.

Skylar feigned shock upon hearing the news. JP was a friend, Skylar said. They served a little time together at the Seal Beach jail, he told them. And he was just watching the car for a while because JP had to go to Mexico for some reason. And now, he was genuinely upset to hear about his friend's death.

After more than an hour of talking, with Detective Bahena translating every question for the Mexican authorities, they decided to let Skylar go for the moment. They just had one more request, Detective Bahena said. They'd like to see his cell phone records from December 27, 2004. Any calls he'd made that day would be recorded on the nearest cell phone tower, revealing where Skylar had been all day long.

"Sure," Skylar said. "No problem, I can dig those up for you."

"Thanks for being so cooperative," Detective Bahena added. "And give us a call if you think of anything that might help us figure out what happened."

Investigators came away from the conversation with little to connect Skylar to JP's slaying. But he was still the best suspect they had.

Michael Lewis saw the name SKYLAR flash across his phone as it rang. Several days had passed since the fateful trip to Mexico, and Michael wasn't anxious to talk to his cousin yet. He let the call roll into voicemail.

"Hey, if the police call you," Skylar said, "can you just tell them you were in Mexico with my wife? Tell them you took her to Tijuana because she had a craving for Mexican ice cream. Thanks, man. Thanks for having my back."

Michael didn't return the call. He wasn't going to turn his cousin in to police. But he was falling further into this mess, now helping with a cover-up.

A day later, his phone rang again.

"Ha, ha!" Jennifer joked into the phone. "That ice cream we had in Mexico sure was good, wasn't it? Thanks again for letting me come along. Call me."

Jennifer's next call was more urgent.

"Look," she said, "I really need to talk to you. The police are all over your cousin about someone that got killed in Mexico. Call me back."

Not "someone," Michael thought. JP Jarvi. Reluctantly, he dialed her number. He'd better find out what was going on before investigators ended up at his door. Jennifer answered, alarm filling her voice. She said police had been over asking about JP's van and wanting to know where Skylar had been on December 27.

"They can't know he was in Mexico that day because of his probation terms," she said. "If they find out he left the country, he'll lose his work furlough and have to stay in jail for his entire term."

"How will they find out he was in Mexico?" Michael asked.

"They're looking at his cell phone records," she said. "But I want you to tell them I had his phone that day and you had mine. Tell them I was the one in Mexico with you because I had a craving for this ice cream I once had in Mexico. A banana-flavored ice cream. So, you went with me to get it, okay? Tell them the ice cream was a yellowish color and it was really good."

Michael wasn't sure what to do. He was in way over his head. He should have hung up and called the police. But he'd waited so long now, he feared he'd be in trouble himself. And he still felt some sense of loyalty to his cousin, despite all the trouble Skylar was bringing his way. But mostly, Skylar just scared him. If his cousin already killed one man he thought betrayed him, what was to stop him from coming after Michael if he talked?

"Okay," Michael finally said. "If that's what you want, that's what I'll tell them."

Skylar appears in a Santa Ana courtroom to face conspiracy to commit murder charges after he tried to hire fellow inmates to kill witnesses in his pending murder trials. *Photo credit: Tina Dirmann*

The converted garage Jennifer, Skylar and their two children called home. *Photo credit: Newport Beach Police Department (Eastside)*

LEFT: Tom and Jackie at play at a port of call in Mexico 11 months before their death. *Photo credit: Courtesy of Eleanor Hawks*

RIGHT: Jon Jacobson stands proud in his Marine uniform shortly after joining the service. Next to him is his stepsister. *Photo credit: Courtesy of Newport Beach Police Department*

Shot of the *Well Deserved* where her two anchors are stored. The anchor on the left is missing. That detail was one of the first clues investigators had in determining what happened to Tom and Jackie Hawks. *Photo credit: Newport Beach Police Department*

Mug shots of defendants
in the Hawks and Jarvi
murder cases:

RIGHT: Skylar Deleon

LEFT: Jennifer Deleon

RIGHT: John F. Kennedy

LEFT: Alonso Machain

RIGHT: Myron Gardner

LEFT: Michael Lewis

Photo credits: Newport Beach Police Department

Tom and Jackie Hawks pause a moment to pose on their pride and joy—*Well Deserved*. The photo appeared in an article written about the couple in the nautical magazine *Latitudes and Attitudes*, which ran several months before their death. *Photo credit: Chuck Silvers*

The ever physically fit Tom Hawks demonstrates his workout routine on board his beloved boat, *Well Deserved*. The photos appeared alongside an article Tom wrote for a nautical magazine on how to stay fit while living at sea. *Photo credit: Chuck Silvers*

Orange County Senior Deputy District Attorney Matt Murphy.
Photo credit: Tina Dirmann

Newport Beach Police Detective Evan Sailor and Sergeant Dave Byington. *Photo credit: Tina Dirmann*

Dixie Hawks, Tom's first wife and mother of Ryan and Matt, taken in the San Diego home she once shared with her former husband. *Photo credit: Tina Dirmann*

The Newport Beach police detectives who worked tirelessly to deliver justice to the Hawks family. Pictured (left to right): Det. Joe Cartwright, Det. Joe Wingert, Det. Evan Sailor, Sgt. Dave Byington, Det. Jay Short and Det. Keith Krallman. Not pictured: Det. David White, Det. Don Prouty, Det. Kristen O'Donnell and Officer Mario Montero. *Photo credit: Tina Dirmann*

Tom and Jackie tying the knot at their Arizona home, surrounded by friends and family. Acting as Tom's best man is his son, Ryan. Little Matt, Tom's youngest, is on Jackie's left. *Photo credit: Charles and Eleanor Hawks*

Ryan Hawks at home in San Diego, California. *Photo credit: Dixie Hawks*

CHAPTER NINETEEN

Skylar had big plans once he fixed up that old boat, the *Doctor Crunch*. It would be a crucial part of his new business, giving dive lessons to people in the United States and Mexico. Technically, he wasn't certified to give lessons. He wasn't even certified to dive, though he'd done so countless times in Mexico, where regulations are less strict. But he'd fix that by taking formal classes. He'd become a certified diver, then move on and get a dive master's license, qualifying him to become an instructor.

Until then, he could always start his chartering business, earning a few hundred bucks here and there by taking dive students out on the water with their instructor. Of course, there was another problem. His boat was too small to hold many people, or take deep into ocean waters. The Long Beach pier to Catalina Island was about as far as he dared. But that was enough.

By early spring of 2004, Skylar returned his boat to Mo Beck's shop, eager to finish the work he had begun the previous December.

"Mo, I've got a few more things I want you to do for me while you're finishing up this other stuff," Skylar said. "I want a new water heater pump put on. And an instrument package."

"Well that's going to run you more, of course," Mo said. "An instrument package alone is about a thousand dollars."

As he'd done weeks before, Skylar counted out $1,000 for Mo in hundred-dollar bills.

"That's a good start," Mo said. "But in total, with all the upgrades you want, and figuring in my labor costs, it will still run you higher than this."

"Fine," Skylar said. "I also need a washdown system and a bait wash, anyway. So add that on to my tab. Just let me know when you figure out the total and I'll settle up with you then."

Mo Beck didn't really know what to say. Skylar was asking for upgrades that just didn't belong on a 26-foot vessel meant mostly for leisure afternoon boating trips. The boat itself probably wasn't worth more than $10,000—but he was asking for better than $20,000 in equipment upgrades. Then there was that odd coating Skylar had put on the boat before bringing it back to Mo Beck's shop. The entire back portion of the Sea Ray was now lined with the sort of material usually sprayed into the bed of a pickup truck to protect it from getting scratched. In the more than twenty years he'd been working around boats, he'd seen a lot—outlandish and expensive upgrades of all kinds. Men, mostly, who had too much money and couldn't wait to spend it on toys for their prized vessel. But this lining—he couldn't explain it. He'd never seen anything so crazy.

But it was Skylar's boat and Skylar's money. So, if Skylar wanted the upgrades, Mo would give them to him.

"I'll call you when it's ready," he said.

By April 16, 2004, Mo had everything done—a new engine, all new wiring, new transom, instrument package, washdown system, bait wash, and water heater pump. He called Skylar.

"She's ready to pick up," Mo told him. "But as I suspected, the cost ran over that eighteen thousand dollars you gave me."

"What's the new total?" Skylar asked.

"We're at twenty-five thousand two hundred and sixty-one dollars and four cents," he said. "So, that leaves you with a balance of seven thousand two hundred and sixty-one dollars and four cents."

"I'll be there later today," Skylar said, without hesitation.

But in truth, Skylar had no plans to pay off his bill. He couldn't. He was out of money.

Only four months before, he murdered a man for roughly $55,000 in cash. By April, he and Jennifer had spent every penny. It's not clear where all the money went. Jennifer never gave any to her father to reduce the better than $30,000 they owed him. And they never moved out of the converted garage connected to her mom and dad's place. They spent $18,000 at Mo Beck's, $2,200 at Robbins Bros., $3,800 on a credit card bill, and some cash went toward car payments. But the rest was simply frittered away. Jennifer took a break from cutting hair just before her delivery date, and they needed some of that left-over money just to pay living expenses. And so, the JP money spent, Skylar was left with not a single penny to pay off his debt to Mo.

But he needed that boat.

Skylar called Mo back hours later. "Look, I can't really come by today after all," he said. "Some things came up at home, so, would it be okay if I came by tomorrow instead?"

"Yeah, that's fine," Mo said. "I'll keep it locked up here another night for you."

But on April 17, as late afternoon approached, the *Doctor Crunch* still sat idle in Mo Beck's garage. He called Skylar, repeatedly, anxious to find out what time he'd be by. Skylar never answered his phone. At 6 p.m., Mo closed up for the night. He hauled the boat and its trailer just outside the fence aligning his shop's back yard and attached a thick metal lock on the tongue of the trailer, meant to prevent anyone from towing it away.

Still, that morning, when Mo Beck arrived at work, *Doctor Crunch* and its trailer were gone. Left behind was the snapped-off trailer tongue and a snippet of the broken lock, tossed carelessly beneath a Dumpster.

Mo had no doubt who had the Sea Ray. He jumped in his car and drove to Skylar's home. But he wasn't there. He wouldn't be home all day—and, of course, he never answered his cell phone.

In the end, Mo would have to settle for filing a civil suit

against Skylar. But in reality, he doubted he would see his money, or the Sea Ray, ever again.

It felt good to spend nights at home again, curled up next to Jennifer. By spring of 2004, Skylar walked away from the Seal Beach jail for the last time. He still had three years of probation to fulfill, but at least he didn't have to check in with a jailer at the end of each day.

Once more, it could have been a time of fresh starts for Skylar. He could have chartered out *Doctor Crunch*, after successfully stealing it away from Mo Beck. He could have earned that license and taught diving. He knew he'd never make a lot of money in such a business. But he lived along the sun-kissed sands of Southern California, where the demand for water sports, like diving, would always be high. He'd always have work.

But that wasn't enough. Life's pressures were building on Skylar, once again.

In May 2004, Jennifer announced she was expecting another baby. Another person to live in their 19×19 room, another round of medical bills, another absence Jennifer would need from work. Already, they were struggling to make ends meet. The year before, Jennifer's tax return showed she netted a mere $18,000. By the time she took out the money she spent for renting her chair at the shop and other business expenses, her take-home salary for the year was $7,000. Skylar brought home less than $15,000, before taxes.

Meanwhile, their expenses were looming: $199 monthly payment for Jennifer's car, $687 for Skylar's truck, $4,000 a year in car insurance, $14,000 in credit card debt, a $12,000 loan from Bank of America. Then there was the more than $30,000 they owed Jennifer's father.

And Skylar hadn't earned a paycheck in six months.

The pressure was on to find some cash somehow, somewhere.

At least investigators weren't asking him questions about JP anymore. Skylar tried to believe they had nothing on him. It had been five months since he'd left JP alone and bleeding to death along the road in Mexico. If police were going to hold Skylar accountable for it, they surely would have done so by now.

He should have felt overcome with relief. Instead, he was emboldened. With that money gone, he'd have to come up with another plan. Jennifer would expect another cash windfall soon. And he'd make sure she'd get it.

But for now, Skylar decided to spend his days at a little shop just three miles from his home. The Pacific Sporting Goods Scuba Center offered dive classes, and Skylar wanted to be part of them. He needed to be part of them, actually. In August, he posted an ad online, boasting of credentials he did not yet have and offering to teach students in the Puerto Vallarta area:

> I'm a certified Dive Master with all my own equipment. I have all equipment necessary for rentals. I will have my instructor certification in 2 weeks. I have 650+ logged dives. Contact BajaSkylar@yahoo.com.

Skylar was short on the cash he needed to enroll in classes at Pacific Sporting Goods. So he cut a deal, volunteering to take classes out on his boat and act as a gofer for instructors on the water and in the classroom. In exchange, he earned hours toward his diving certificate.

Adam Rohrig was young, just in his mid-twenties, but a highly trained diver. He grew up near the ocean and had been diving since he was 19 years old, when he first signed up for classes at the same dive shop. After high school, he enrolled in the elite Navy SEALs program. He never worked so hard in all of his life. But no matter how much he gave, how much he tried, it was never enough. He still found himself struggling to keep up with the training considered by most military experts to be among the toughest and most competitive in the world. Ultimately, the Navy told him he'd have to wait another two years before he could be promoted. So he dropped out and decided to enroll in California State University, Long Beach.

Meanwhile, he earned a living through a bartending gig in Long Beach and teaching dive lessons at Pacific Sporting Goods.

That's how he met Skylar in March 2004.

Adam pegged Skylar as some know-it-all rich kid with too much time on his hands. He never talked about a job, or mentioned responsibilities of any kind, really. But he did let it slip once that his family owned some sort of very successful insurance company. But he was trying to make his own way in life, refusing to let them support him. That's why he joined the Marines, he said.

"That's where I learned to dive," Skylar told Adam, knowing how it would impress the former Navy SEAL trainee. "It was a big part of my training in the Marines."

Skylar talked a lot about his training among the elite Special Forces unit. To look authentic, Skylar even had a Special Forces Recon tattoo stamped on his arm. He casually flashed it to Adam more than once.

Maybe his determination to "make it" on his own explained why he never seemed to have a lot of money around, despite his claims that he sometimes earned up to $2 million a month through his family's business. After all, he wasn't even paying for all of his diving lessons. Instead, he offered to act as Adam's assistant in class, helping him set up before students arrived and clean up after. That's what he was willing to do to become officially certified, then move on to earn his dive master's license.

At first, Adam was grateful for the help. And he kind of liked the guy. Skylar was certainly entertaining. He was the kind of person who always had a story, even if a lot of his tales were more fiction than fact. Adam was certainly savvy enough to see that. Still, they became friends, hanging out after classes to share a few beers, or taking off to Catalina for the afternoon to get in a quickie dive. Then there was the afternoon that Skylar pulled up for lessons driving an $86,000 Dodge Viper Roadster. It was thrilling to ride in that thing, zooming from 0 to 60 in 4 seconds. It was rented, of course. But Adam never knew that. According to Skylar, his parents had bought it for him.

"I just don't like to drive it that much because, you know, it's so flashy," he told Adam.

Adam liked his student enough that he introduced Skylar to Thomas Maggiore, a dive master who independently contracted with Pacific Sporting Goods to teach. Thomas needed a boat to take out his latest group of students so they could get some dive time under their belts.

"I've got a Sea Ray," Skylar said. "I just had it totally made over, all new equipment. Why don't you let me take your students out?"

Thomas agreed, paying Skylar $200 for the afternoon, and letting him use the trip as a dive credit toward certification. Thomas, however, was unimpressed with the outing. The boat was way too small for his students and all their equipment. Mostly, everyone felt cramped all afternoon.

And Skylar realized it, too. If he was really going to make this business work, he simply needed to get his hands on a much bigger boat.

CHAPTER TWENTY

"You want to make a lot of money?" Skylar asked Adam as they cleaned up after class one evening in the fall of 2004. Skylar lingered behind until every student was long gone before posing the question. He was pretty sure his friend, who'd been juggling two jobs since leaving the Navy, just might be interested.

"Of course," he said. "Why are you asking?"

"I know how you can," he said cryptically. When he offered no more details, Adam pushed.

"Well, tell me," he said. "How can I supposedly make all this money?"

"Can you drive a boat for me?"

"Yes," he said. "You know I could. But what for? Why do you need me to drive a boat for you?"

"I might need some help getting rid of some bodies."

It sounded so absurd, Adam laughed.

"Right," he said. "Sure you do."

"I'm serious," Skylar said. "You know I used to be a sniper in the Marines. Now, this is what I do. I get paid to take care of bad people. And I have a new job to get rid of some very bad people."

"You're shitting me," Adam said. "You can't possibly be telling me you're some sort of paid assassin."

"Trust me," Skylar said, lowering his voice. "Maybe the less you know here, the better. But these are people who are into some bad stuff. They've done terrible things. And they need to be disposed of. They have a huge boat. A yacht, actually. So it'll probably happen there, once we're out to sea. I just need someone to drive the boat while I'm working."

Adam looked at Skylar in disbelief. He couldn't figure it out. This had to be yet another one of Skylar's wild stories. Or maybe he was playing some sort of sick joke? But Skylar's deadpan face told him otherwise.

"And how do you expect to get away with something like that?" Adam asked.

"No bodies, no crime," Skylar said simply.

"No fucking way," Adam told him. "You're out of your fucking mind."

"Okay, okay," said Skylar, trying to calm Adam down. "Forget I ever said anything."

But Adam couldn't forget it. He'd never forget a conversation like that. In fact, it was all he could think about months later, when headlines told the story of a couple who turned up missing after selling their yacht to a Long Beach resident and his wife. And when Adam would finally recount his story for Detective Sailor, he was sick with regret for not taking the conversation seriously, for not calling police. If he had, maybe Jackie and Thomas Hawks would be alive today, he told the detective.

"I don't know why he didn't go to [the] police," Detective Sailor said later. "But I know it's something he's living with every day."

As Jennifer prepared to deliver her second baby, she was still the main earner for her family. She showed up to her station at Little John's Family Hair Styling in Long Beach every morning, pulled out her combs, scissors, and hair dryer, and put in a full day's work.

She wasn't just an employee of the shop. She actually rented her chair space, making her an independent contractor. She set her own schedule, so she could come and go as she pleased. It came in handy now that she had a baby. And she talked of taking as much time as she needed to recover when the second arrived. Who knows?—maybe she wouldn't even come back at all, she told her fellow stylists. The news saddened co-workers, who genuinely enjoyed having her in the shop. That's because at Little John's, she presented quite a different side of herself—she was outgoing, helpful, considerate. Happy.

"An angel, just like the girl next door," was how stylist Gary McHenry, who worked at the station next to Jennifer, described her. "If you took sweet and then went to sweeter, Jennifer was even sweeter than that."

Gary met her husband, because Skylar often popped by to take his wife to lunch, usually with little Hailey at his side.

"Whenever he came in to see her, he'd say 'Hi, hon!' " Gary remembered. "We all thought he was such a nice guy, always coming in to take her out to eat. They were a cute, young, loving couple, and you thought that they'd be married for a long time and have lots of kids. Her parents would even come in occasionally and we all just thought, 'What a nice family.' "

But at home, life wasn't so idyllic. In fact, by 2004, as fall drifted into winter, life grew more complicated with every passing day.

Skylar did find temporary work, once again as an assistant with Total-Western. He even convinced his old pal Alonso Machain to ditch his job at Seal Beach and come work with him as an apprentice electrician.

"Don't worry," Skylar told Alonso. "I have connections there through my father-in-law. I'm just here helping out some of his friends for a while. But I can totally hook you up. You'll make good money."

In truth, it was just a gofer position. Another low-paying, temporary job that would probably lead nowhere for both of them. But Alonso was happy to follow Skylar's lead.

Skylar never gave Alonso a chance to wonder why the heir to an enormous mortgage company needed to work some petty blue-collar job.

"I have money, of course," he told Alonso. "A lot of it, in fact. But it's all tied up right now. It's just not a good time for me to access, if you know what I mean."

Actually, Alonso didn't know what Skylar meant, but he trusted his friend, so he nodded his head in agreement anyway.

The job would be a fateful one for the duo, for it was there that they met site supervisor Myron Sandora Gardner.

Myron Gardner was a man with whom few people would trifle. He stood just 5'9" tall, but weighed in at 205 pounds and grew up in the very toughest neighborhoods of Long Beach. In fact, as a kid, he ran with the roughest members of the Insane Crips, one of the most notorious street gangs the city has ever known. The ICG, as they were known, short for Insane Crips Gang, were responsible for everything from petty robberies to homicide, according to Long Beach police gang detectives. As a teenager, Myron earned the moniker "Fly," detectives said, and before his 18th birthday, he was serving time in the California Youth Authority in Chino for voluntary manslaughter. He was paroled in 1982, but would spend the next two decades in and out of jail. He earned convictions for domestic violence against his wife in 1992, possession of a controlled substance in 1995, and driving under the influence in 2002 and 2004. His longest sentence came in 1995, when a judge handed him 3 years in prison for a robbery, plus another 5 years for carrying prior felonies. He actually served just five of those years before he was paroled.

By 2004, at age 41, Myron had considerably tamed his wild side. He held a steady job at Total-Western, rising to a supervisory role over the temps and gofers the company employed. Younger gang detectives didn't even consider him a player with Insane Crips anymore. Still, he lived among them. Old members considered him a friend. New ones considered him an ally—in their eyes, he was OG, an Original Gangster, and that meant he was a man who had earned their respect.

Skylar and Myron had little in common. But Skylar developed a knack for knowing when to cultivate a friendship. Myron, with his extensive gang connections, could certainly come in handy some day, Skylar thought. Myron, no doubt, thought the same thing of the tough-talking white kid, who once again boasted about his connections and, once he accessed it, his cash. The two developed a fast friendship that would continue even after Myron's bosses decided Skylar wasn't working out. He was fired in October 2004.

At the time, he had a total of $500 in the bank. His wife was five months pregnant. But those realities would mean nothing to Skylar, a man who thrived on his dreams of grandeur, even as his checking account dwindled. The money would come, Skylar thought.

So, on October 22, he bought a brand-new Toyota Highlander. The price tag on the sporty SUV was $30,000, and saddled the Deleons with a $687-a-month car note.

And when Skylar spotted the item in a nautical magazine advertising a yacht for sale by a man in the Seattle area, he couldn't resist. He called the seller, asking for more details. The nearly half-million-dollar vessel sounded amazing. But there was only one way a man like Skylar would ever lay his hands on a ship like that. He wasn't afraid to do what needed to be done. He'd already gotten his hands dirty once in the pursuit of a payout. But this would be a bigger scheme. He'd need help.

Obviously, Adam was out. He needed somebody closer to him. Somebody who wasn't afraid to bend a few laws. Somebody who might even be impressed with his plan. He needed his father.

Skylar's relationship with John Jacobson was as complicated as ever. Even after he married Jennifer, Skylar couldn't cut ties with the father he grew to hate, but needed to love. In fact, the older he got, the more Skylar's behavior began to mimic the darkest parts of his dad's personality. Skylar would never be outwardly violent, like his dad could be. But it took a sadistic soul to callously slice a friend's throat for cash. Or murder strangers for a boat.

Yet as Skylar's malicious side evolved, John's mellowed. He was still a mean-tempered man, prone to putting down his children and ex-wives. But by now, most of his battles were fought with verbal blows, nothing more. Age, bringing ebbing levels of testosterone, and a reluctance to return to prison, forced John to earn a legitimate living. For a time, he moved to Kingman, Arizona, earning a few dollars as a DJ for Big Rig Doll House, a strip club that catered to truckers breaking for the nearby diesel fueling station. But in recent years, his main source of income came from his bumper sticker business. Main Line Stickers, as it was called, operated from the back of the converted U-Haul truck he bought at an auction. John drove between surfing and skating competitions from Arizona to California to hawk his goods, or sometimes set up shop at a local swap meet. He lived a transient life, sleeping in his U-Haul truck and refusing to use anything but a cell phone, reasoning that it was harder to trace. Those close to John said he'd grown paranoid, convinced someone was always out to get him. Relatives said it was because he worried his former drug-dealing partners were searching for him. Apparently, he'd skimmed $80,000 off his last successful deal. At least, that's what he told his son and his ex-wife, Lisa.

But he was also in terrible health.

"He's HIV positive," Skylar said in an interview. "He's really sick."

Others close to John believe he has the disease that leads to AIDS. And he struggled, particularly, because he carried no health insurance.

Maybe that's why Skylar was convinced his dad would want in on his plan. What could a man carrying a fatal disease have to lose? And so, he went to his father, spinning a wild tale about a group of Israeli gangsters hiring him as a hit man to take out a couple involved in some drug deal gone bad.

In a May 28, 2007, interview with the *Los Angeles Times*, John explained that his son told him the gangsters offered two options for payment: collect $50,000 for taking the couple out to sea and handing them over to assassins on another boat; or slay the couple himself, pick up a $100,000 payment, and retain their yacht and everything else on it.

"He told me it was going to be the simplest money he ever made," Jacobson would later tell the newspaper.

But Skylar was wrong about his dad's desperation level.

"I can't," John told his son. "It's a bad idea and you're going to get yourself caught. And when you do, trust me, you won't make it in prison. They won't put you in no Seal Beach country club jail for sissies this time."

Unlike Adam, John had no doubt his son was serious. And if Skylar went ahead with the plan, John figured there wasn't much he could do about it. He just wouldn't help.

With Adam, and now his father, turning down his offer, Skylar turned again to his old childhood ally. After all, his cousin never told the police about JP Jarvi. So just maybe, he'd want in on another scheme, especially if this time, Michael got a little money out of the deal. He made the call.

"What if," he told Michael, "I needed your help transferring some people off a boat? There could be some big money in it for you."

"You know what?" Michael said. "I'm not hanging out with you anymore. At least, not one on one. The only way I'll ever see you again is when we're surrounded by the rest of the family. I'm done with you and your schemes."

Still, Skylar was determined. He even tried Adam one more time.

"Are you sure you don't want to help?" he asked casually after class one night in October.

"You are fucking crazy," Adam told him. "No is no."

So he had no accomplices. Yet. But he wouldn't give up. There was always someone willing to do dirty work if it meant scoring a big enough payout. And he became even more determined after picking up the November issue of *Yachting World* magazine.

That's where he learned, for the first time, of the 55-foot cabin cruiser for sale some twenty-five miles away, in Newport Beach harbor. And Skylar's plan went into overdrive.

"Get ready," he told Jennifer. "In fact, why don't you go ahead and call that client of yours, the one who's a realtor? We're going to need our own place very soon."

In late October, Jennifer did call a realtor, one who specialized in showing homes in the most posh sections of Orange County. Terry Rogers worked for Coldwell Banker real estate and was a long-time client of Jennifer's at the hair salon. She promised to take good care of the couple and was already searching for multimillion-dollar homes to show them when the Deleons paid her a visit. It was November 2, 2004, the day after the *Well Deserved* ad ran. Jennifer, in unusually high spirits that afternoon, did most of the talking.

"Believe me when I tell you that we'll have a lot of money to spend on our place," Jennifer said. "We can offer a two-hundred-thousand-dollar down payment. And we'd like to be in it before the baby is born."

"Of course, of course," Terry said. "When is the baby due?"

"February second," she said, rubbing her swollen tummy.

The realtor nodded, but was dying with curiosity. Jennifer couldn't be making that much money cutting hair. And she never talked of her husband's work. So Terry had to ask. She had to be sure Jennifer wasn't just wasting her time.

"Do you mind if I ask . . . Where's all the money coming from? Did a rich relative pass away?"

"Something like that, yeah," Jennifer said. "My husband has family in Mexico, and they have a lot of money. So we're coming into a large amount through them. And they're giving us a boat."

The realtor nodded and smiled at the story. She saw no reason to question it. Some people just got lucky like that, she thought.

"Anyway, I just wanted to mention that whatever you show us," said Jennifer, "make sure it's on the water. And make sure it has a boat slip. Something big enough to accommodate a fifty-five-foot yacht."

CHAPTER TWENTY-ONE

The first time Jackie laid eyes on the Lien Hwa trawler, she knew it was the one. It had everything she wanted: three stories with a spacious living room that spilled into a fully equipped kitchen, a small stairway leading to a master bedroom complete with queen-sized bed, plus a large cockpit, and a beautiful hand-carved teak interior throughout. Walking through, it didn't feel like someone's boat. If felt like someone's home. She reveled in the thought of living there with Tom. The boat had room for two refrigerators, a freezer, an icemaker, a washer and dryer, a fully operating stove, and a microwave—even room for a bar to keep their preferred wines and, of course, Tom's favorite, Pacifico beer.

Tom, meanwhile, was impressed with the 10,360-amp-hour battery system, the large cockpit, the solar and wind generator, dive compressor, bait tank, and the paravane stabilizer. And it boasted a 1,600-gallon fuel tank, meaning if they were smart about fuel efficiency, driving no faster than maybe 10 mph, they could be at sea for many days without refueling.

"Tom, are we really going to do it?" Jackie asked.

"Yeah, we really are."

Technically, they weren't quite prepared for the $300,000 purchase. They hadn't sold their home yet. And Tom had obligations to tie up at the probation department. But in their minds, they had planned this for years. And for months now, they attended countless boat shows, toured marinas, talked to brokers, all with an eye toward finding their perfect home on the ocean.

Now that they found it, they wouldn't let it get away just because of a few loose ends.

"We'll take it," Tom told the seller. Jackie was thrilled. And terrified.

"She was just nervous about buying the boat and not having the house sold yet," Tricia Schutz said. "And they had been doing their homework, researching and researching, trying to figure out if it was feasible for Tom to retire."

Of course, Tom's department fought not to let him go so early, offering him a $500-a-month raise on his retirement pay if he would put in just one more year. Tom, always a financially prudent man, agreed. He'd just keep the yacht where he bought it, in Mexico, so he could put off luxury taxes on his new toy a little longer—until he was ready to go.

He continued working. Until Judge Kuebler died. A tragic car accident took the life of his long-time friend while the respected jurist vacationed with his family. He'd only retired from the bench a few weeks earlier. Tom got the message.

"Money isn't everything," he told friends and family, and resubmitted his retirement notice. "More money won't buy us more time."

After their friend's funeral, things moved quickly, remembered Tricia. "They just sold the house and it all just sort of fell into place."

Fellow probation officer John Ryder hated to see his longtime friend and co-worker go. He'd known Tom and Jackie since 1989, meeting them in the months just before they got married, and just before John transferred into Tom's office in Prescott. Back then, Tom hadn't been with the department too long himself. He'd just sold his bar, Matt's Saloon, even though it became something of a local legend in the area—a must-see stop along the town's historic Whiskey Row. Tom still spoke of the July 4 evening when the fire marshal threatened to fine him if he didn't thin out his crowd.

"How much is the fine?" Tom asked the marshal.

"Five hundred dollars," he answered.

"Really?" said Tom, quickly figuring that a round or two of drinks with this crowd would earn him far more than that. "No problem. Fine me!"

Still, after a few years running Matt's, he was done.

"It's just not a business to be in when you're trying to raise a family," he told friends.

And so, he sold the place and became a dedicated probation officer. Tom already had a few years in the Prescott office by the time his pal John came in from another branch in the county. And Tom didn't make his friend's transition easy.

"I'm a very tall guy, about 6'7". But Tom, he was very muscular," John remembered. "And so, he'd pick on me a bit. I mean, he would piss me off a lot. But it was all in good humor."

Later, as John's confidence grew with his new co-workers, he got even with his pal for all that early teasing.

"He couldn't read out loud very well, and we loved to pick on him about that stuff," John said. "I mean, half the time, he didn't pronounce our own county correctly! We do have a weird name, Yavapai. But he'd call it 'Yappai.' Or he'd be working on budget stuff and instead of saying 'fiscal year' he'd say 'physical year.' So we'd pick on him and we'd all laugh about it. That's the thing, Tom could always laugh. He had the best sense of humor."

Over time, the duo rose through the department together, both earning supervisor titles. Outside of work, their friendship flourished, too. Tom loved inviting John and co-workers Bill Paiano and Len Ezell out for weekend getaways on the lake.

"Just bring your swimming suit and whatever you want to drink," Tom would say. "We'll have everything else."

John had such wonderful times with the Hawks family on those trips that he made it a priority to go with them anytime he could.

"After seeing how much fun that was, for me, any time I could be a part of that, I wanted to," John said. "After Tom taught us about boating, Bill Paiano and I went in together and got a boat of our own so we could enjoy those outings even more. And we'd always hook up with Tom and Jackie and the boys. We'd try to get out there at least once a month."

Often, Jackie was the only woman on these weekend get-aways. She was even the lone female during one two-week excursion with the men to the Sea of Cortez.

"Poor Jackie," said John, remembering the hundreds of beers the boys put away that trip.

Now, such excursions together would come to a halt with Tom and Jackie selling their home and living far away, on a yacht along the Mexican Gulf. But John couldn't have been happier for his friends.

John and a friend flew to La Paz, Mexico, to meet Tom and help them bring their new purchase into California. Jackie opted to fly ahead, leaving the maiden voyage home to just the boys.

"She's beautiful," John told them when he first laid eyes on their new home. "What are you going to call her?"

"We've been kicking around a few names," Tom said.

They considered *Sea Hawks*, *Knot-So-Sex-Sea*, *Well Sea-soned*, *Wish Granted*, *SunSeeker*, *Timeless Wonder*, *Sea Roamer*, *Well All Over*, *Sea Foam*, *Hooked*, *Heavenly*, *Paradise* . . .

"But you know, we've worked so damn hard to get to this point, I'm thinking I ought to just name her something like '*Well Deserved.*' "

" '*Well Deserved,*' " John repeated. "I like it."

As they approached the California coastline, the *Well Deserved* was forced to ride against the waves. Each oncoming swell slammed into the cabin cruiser, rocking it wildly, leaving her new passengers more than a little nervous.

"There was this constant banging from the waves," John remembered. "And we weren't sure with this new boat how rough our ride would be. So we went real slow. You have to understand, going from their twenty-eight-foot Skipjack to that boat, it was like going from a sports car to a semi-truck."

Concerned that there could be a few hiccups on the trip home, Tom hired a boater with a captain's license to help him steer his new pride and joy home safely. All the men took turns steering *Well Deserved*, changing shifts every three to four hours.

Mostly, it was smooth sailing—until a rough patch of weather caught everyone off guard. Swells reached twenty feet high.

The *Well Deserved* rocked with terrific force, diving hard into the trough of each wave. When Tom, exhausted from fighting the boat's wheel to keep it on course, finally lay down, a fierce wave knocked the boat so hard, he tumbled out of bed and onto the floor.

"We had autopilot, which kind of steers the boat for you," John said. "But that went out, so we're really having to drive it. And I remember just being up there, you're out at night, looking at radar, which might show the shore is fifty miles off to the side, but you can't see it. You can't see anything in front of you and you don't run lights because that just makes it worse. It's spooky. You're just constantly fighting the waves, trying to make the boat go where it's supposed to go. If you get sideways to waves like that, you could roll the boat."

It was a terrifying experience. But even then, Tom found a way to make jokes and keep his tiny crew laughing.

"Tom's laughing the whole time, but I just kept thinking, 'Here we are, driving his three-hundred-thousand-dollar invest-ment, and if we screw up, we can sink the whole thing!' I think I was a lot more nervous than he was."

It was nearly dawn before the men were able to steer the boat into calmer weather, still enough to drop anchor and rest awhile.

When they finally arrived into Newport Beach harbor, the men cheered.

"It took us two weeks," John said. "But it was all so exciting. It was the trip of a lifetime."

It would take a few months before Jackie and Tom could ship out on their own adventures. First, they did everything they could to prepare for a life at sea, spending countless hours read-ing, studying. They learned everything about operating their vessel, repair work, emergencies at sea. Tom pored over the ship's autopilot and global positioning unit, learning how to op-erate them, and how to operate without them, if necessary.

In the days before they set sail, Jackie's best friend came to stay onboard for a visit. That week, Jackie's nose was often in a book, reading about the ocean and all the creatures they would likely see on their travels.

"She loved all outdoor water creatures," Tricia said. "So she read a lot of books and watched a lot of movies about them. She was prepared for anything."

Only one minor complication remained—how to get mail, check their rental properties, and pay bills while in the middle of the Pacific Ocean for months at a time. Tricia, who had always been there for her dear friend Jackie, offered the solution.

"I just took care of their mail, their affairs, paying their bills, collecting their rent, watching their property," said Tricia, who would then forward Tom and Jackie stacks of mail as they landed at a port of call long enough to get to a post office.

With that settled, Tom and Jackie set off, starting with test trips to and from Newport Beach harbor and Catalina Island. Tricia tagged along.

"I remember, they worked as a team running that boat, like no other couple I've ever seen," Tricia said. "And I'll always remember them like that. They were a team. A true team."

Finally, on October 17, 2002, Tricia hugged her friends goodbye and watched as they pulled up anchor. *Well Deserved* moved slowly, gracefully, to the south, with a course set for Mexico. Tom and Jackie stood side by side, eager to embrace the adventures lying on the horizon before them.

"We are in Ensenada, Mexico," Jackie emailed friends and family on November 11, 2002. "Tom loves the street taco stands, I think the margaritas are killer!"

It became the main way to communicate with friends and family as they moved slowly along the anchorages dotting the Pacific coastline. For a long time, they tried to get a satellite phone on board to help ease time away. For a couple with so many close friends and relatives, no word for weeks at a time was a difficult adjustment. But there was no choice. In the beginning, sporadic emails from their exotic ports of call had to do. And Jackie wrote of their travels every chance she could get.

December 2002, Cabo San Lucas:
   Just a small note to say we are leaving Cabo San Lucas and heading on down to an island above Puerta Vallarta, called Isla Isabela. It will be

*a 30hour passage. That means no stopping along the way. But we really
enjoy the night crossings. They have their solitude. And when the
dolphins play along they make for a beautiful sight in the phosphores-
cence. They look as if they are covered in tiny lime green lights, and when
they come out of the water and splash back in, it's even more beautiful.
The skies are full of stars and we almost have a full moon. This will be
our longest passage so far. The last was 22 hours from Magdalena Bay
to here, in Cabo. Once we reach the island, we will play for several days
before crossing to Nayarit on the mainland. Then we'll hit several nice
anchorages along the way. It may take us two weeks to reach Puerto
Vallarta, where we will email with all our news. We would like to wish
you all a very Merry Christmas and hope to wish you a Happy New year
in our next email, from Puerto Vallarta. We love and miss you all. Tom
and Jackie, Well Deserved.*

It wasn't all easy living, of course. Jackie wrote of expensive
repairs. The boat's propeller needed replacing, then the autopilot system went out. Such repairs could take weeks, leaving
them stranded at one tiny harbor or another and giving them a
case of what Jackie called the "boatyard blues." Plus, such repairs were always an unneeded expense for a couple trying to
live out a life on retirement pay.

"It is a great financial setback," Jackie wrote when the boat's
propeller shaft bearings had to be replaced and the vessel's bottom had to be re-varnished. "But it has to be done."

But most of Jackie's emails were full of sights they'd seen,
people they'd met.

December 9, 2002, Cabo San Lucas:
    *We have been eating a lot of lobster, the weather is hot and sunny, the
water temperature is 77 degrees, the color of the water is turquoise. We've
seen many humpback whales. I even got to see one breech out of the
water. It was fantastic!*

Jan. 10, 2003, Banderas Bay:
    *We are now in the Banderas Bay, just 8 miles outside of Puerta
Vallarta, in a small town called La Cruz. We have to stay here for
awhile because we've ordered some parts for the boat. And we are*

trying to order an email unit for the boat. It is a priority and we hope to have it before we move on. Tom is keeping himself occupied with the dingy, kayaks and surfing. He is off surfing now as I write this note to you.

Jan. 15, 2003, Banderas Bay:

Now for the good news—we have ordered an email unit for the boat. This is making me very happy, now we can hear from all our loved ones! Yeah!

There are 32 boats anchored here and we often share meals together, along with stories. We have enjoyed taking the bus into Puerto Vallarta and seeing the sights. We even saw an animal keeper from one of the nearby resorts walking a baby tiger on a leash! The sea life here is amazing, with all the humpback whales, dolphins, and a few four-foot Rooster fish. We have Brown Boobie birds perching on the stabilizers, watching for their meals below. Tom found a Boobie bird's beak on the beach and has made a necklace out of it. So now he is called Boobie Head by all. He even ate raw oysters from a Mexican diver's catch on the same afternoon, and from these shores, it may be questionable. What a Boobie Head! Hugs and kisses, Jackie and Tom.

Feb. 5, 2003, Mexican Riviera:

Right now, we are surrounded by plush resorts and homes all painted in bright colors of blues, yellows, oranges and reds, with Palm Trees everywhere. It's like seeing something on the program, The Rich & Famous. We spend our day kayaking and snorkeling around the island, and the time just whizzes by. We are heading south another 40 miles in the morning to Bahia Tenacatita. We may spend a whole month there, a big cruisers handout with lots to do. Will update you later. Love and miss you lots, Tom and Jackie.

Feb. 14, 2003, Tenacatita:

Happy Valentine's Day! Tom says he is going to catch me a fish for my Valentine gift. It is our last day with the cruisers in Tenacatita. Several couples came by to use our windsurfer, then we went to the beach for a beer. Our neighbors were over for a movie after. Will tell you more about our new spot once we check it out. Heading up to the Sea of Cortez and into the Baja. Love you.

March 3, 2003, Chacala. From Tom:

We just left Chacala this a.m. Sandy beaches, palm trees, plapas and a fantastic reef for surfing. The ocean is alive today. Lots of whales, dolphins, feeding fish and sea turtles. We call them the speed bumps of the ocean. Headed for Mazitlan, approximately 100 miles away. Jackie is really learning to handle the seas. She is a real trouper. It is a fantastic way of life. Fresh air, new adventures daily. Heard you got some snow. We sure need it, but prefer the 80 degree air and water temps. Wish you were here. Luv, Capt. Tom.

March 8, 2003, Mazatilan:

We have been at sea four months now and it is time to take a break from the rocking boat. Plus, I need a chance to clean and cook with all the fresh water and power I need! There is a Wal-Mart here, too. Maybe I can even get a Big Mac from McDonald's. What a treat! I really miss pizza, too! Hugs & Kisses, Jackie and Tom.

There was much the couple missed about being home—Jackie missed her mom's birthday, and had to check in with her by email and satellite phone when Gayle O'Neill had a brief battle with cancer. Jackie wrote of those regrets, as well as her longing to hang out with her old pal, Tricia. "She is such a wonderful friend," Jackie wrote to her mother. "I really miss having her around to talk to."

But in general, they were in love with their life on the ocean, and only had plans for more in the year to come. They signed up for classes to become certified ham radio operators, and to understand Morse code.

April 15, 2003:

We are sooooo busy! This going to school every morning for three hours is killing us! Then we study of and on all the rest of the day. Yuk! We have stress again! Sure hope we pass this HAM radio exam. We are too old for this! Take care. .-. .--- . . . -. (Love, in code) Jackie & Tom..

April 26, 2003:

We had our class this morning and everyone had to listen and write the song Happy Birthday, Jackie in MORSE code. The teacher gave me a

muffin. Tom got me two pairs of beaded parrot earrings that I wanted
and a little shorts outfit. Our new boating friends got me a boating
cookbook and are having me over for dinner. It's been pretty nice so far.

There's a big boaters festival out here on the 2ⁿᵈ. Tom will probably
get in on the dingy races. I will probably attend a cooking seminar,
besides all the dinners, dances and parties!

Thanks for thinking of me today. Wish I was there, too. Hugs and
kisses! You're old kid, me.

Time drifted by for Tom and Jackie as easily as a sea breeze rip-
pling over the ocean.

Their life was so idyllic, the nautical magazine *Latitudes &*
Attitudes featured them in their December 2003 issue, noting
that the couple had logged 2,500 miles during just nine months
at sea.

"Cruising has become their life and they love it," the article
read.

They have met many new friends and visited over 50 anchorages. They
enjoy fishing, diving, kayaking and living off the sea. Tom has found some
surf spots that were fantastic, and when the wind blows, he gets out his
windsurfer. He thought he might get bored, but at the end of the day, he
and Jackie still ask each other where the day went.

Tom repeated his favorite line to the magazine writer.

We have been told that God doesn't count time on the water towards your
lifespan, so I'm sure that Jackie and I will have many more cruising years
ahead of us.

"Amen to that," the article ends.

The following year, Tom penned his own article for the magazine, headlined "Staying in shape while underway." Tom, ever
the avid bodybuilder, didn't abandon that lifestyle just because
the *Well Deserved* wasn't equipped with a gym. Instead, he
turned the boat into his personal workout arena. Pictures show
the 58-year-old, muscles bulging, sitting on the deck of his

boat, lifting gargantuan dumbbells and pulling chin-ups from his boat's hand railings.

Tom wrote:

> When my wife Jackie and I first began cruising, we believed that walking, kayaking, swimming, snorkeling and scuba diving would keep us relatively fit. Wrong! . . . When you consider all the cocktail parties with other cruisers, with hors d'oeuvres, chips, salsa, and my so dearly loved Pacifico Beer, I was doomed. My definition was fading as my root beer belly began growing larger by the week. . . . I developed a workout that takes less time than most people take having their morning coffee . . . Cruisers can be creative when developing a work out plan, as they can do dips on the bow pulpit or between two chairs, chin-ups on a hand railing, or put your wife in a harness and pull her up the mast. I think I like that one the best.

Nearly two years had passed, and Tom and Jackie never seemed happier, Ryan Hawks recalled. He mostly kept in touch through an endless stream of emails. Eventually, they did get that satellite phone working on the boat. But each call was so expensive, the very frugal couple used it sparingly. So if Ryan's cell phone rang and the *Well Deserved* was on the other end, it was a special occasion.

"Hey, what's happening, man?" Ryan would say excitedly into the phone.

"Oh, not much, son," Tom would answer. "Mom's making me go catch dinner."

"Gee, life's rough," Ryan teased.

Ryan missed just hanging out with his dad and stepmom. So did Matt. But they were so proud of their parents for pursuing their dream, they'd never ask them to change their life of travel. And as luck would have it, they didn't have to. In the fall of 2004, Matt's fiancée delivered their first grandson, baby Jace.

"After that," Matt said, "they were ready to come back and be grandparents."

Tom and Jackie traveled to Arizona to visit the new baby. They bought furniture for the nursery and Matt spent an entire afternoon alongside his dad, putting everything together. In the early evening, they relaxed playing a game of catch in Matt's front yard. That's when Matt learned of their latest plan.

"Looks like we're going to sell the boat, Matt," he said. "We've had our fun. But we're thinking now a little house, maybe here in Arizona. Or maybe something in Mexico would be the thing for us. Then just buy a smaller boat and we can travel back and forth to visit with the little guy. What do you think?"

He talked about Jackie's idea to maybe live half the year in Arizona, near Jace, and the other half, probably the winter months, in a house in Mexico, wandering up and down the coast in their smaller vessel.

Matt was taken aback, knowing his father and stepmom would give up the *Well Deserved* for more stability, more time with Jace.

"They wanted that because family was that important to them," Matt would later recall. "We always were."

Tom wanted to see his grandson go through all the stages of babyhood. From the deck of his trawler he could never see Jace stumbling through first steps, likely with all the grace of a little drunken sailor. He'd miss him struggling to leave baby talk behind and wrestle new words. But just maybe, as important as it all was to Tom, it meant even more to Jackie. Tom still remembered watching his own boys as toddlers. But Jackie never had that chance. Because of that devastating motorcycle accident years before, she never raised a baby. Until now, with her grandson. She wanted to be there for as many precious moments as possible.

And so, by October 2004, Jackie and Tom parked inside their home port of Newport Beach and penned the ad, set to run on November 1.

As October drew to a close, Ryan took time off from his competitive job as a medical supply salesman to lounge on the *Well Deserved* with Tom and Jackie. Ryan reveled in the time, soaking up their attention. Jackie prepared munchies and meals for her stepson, while Tom mixed up rounds of Black Velvet whiskey and Coke. One evening, sipping cocktails during a viewing of Tom's favorite movie, *The Last of the Mohicans*, Ryan found himself rip-roaring drunk. Clearly, Tom ribbed, Ryan wasn't used to holding his liquor.

"Let's go out," Ryan exclaimed.

The trio cut the movie and climbed into the *Well Deserved*'s dinghy, headed for land. Just a few feet away stood Blue Beat, a bar frequented by Newport Beach locals. Immediately, Ryan went to work, chatting up a group of pretty female employees sharing cocktails after a long shift.

"Hey, ladies," Tom chimed in, doing his best to embarrass his son. "Have you met my little brother? He's not as handsome as I am, but give him a chance anyway."

Ryan could only laugh at his dad's efforts. Thankfully, he was so tipsy, nothing his dad said bothered him anymore. Still, he was grateful when Tom tired of embarrassing him and made his way back to Jackie, laughing at the father and son duo from a nearby table. A good hour passed before Ryan realized his parents had, in fact, left the bar entirely. Not only did they sneak away, they'd taken the dinghy and were already back home. "Damn," he thought, knowing he'd have to make his own way back to the *Well Deserved*. It's just the kind of practical joke his dad loved to play.

At the dock, Ryan had no choice—he stripped down nude and rolled his cell phone and wallet deep inside a ball of his clothing. Lifting the bundle high overhead, he jumped into the chilly water. It was only about a five-minute swim back to the yacht, but he'd have to make it paddling with one arm, careful so not a drop of water touched his cargo overhead.

Onboard, his parents were already fast asleep. But Jackie left out warm towels and blankets on Ryan's bed.

The next morning, Tom boomed when he saw Ryan curled up in bed. "Hey, stinkpot!"

Ryan groaned at the sound of triumph in Tom's voice. It didn't help that a slight hangover had settled in.

"I knew it!" Tom shouted. "I told her! I knew you'd do it! I knew you'd swim back! Didn't I tell you, Jackie?"

"Yeah, well, thanks for leaving me," said Ryan, chuckling in spite of his headache.

"Don't worry, son," he said. "If it makes you feel any better, Mom pushed me in the drink last night, too!"

"Right," Jackie chimed in. "I did no such thing. He was so drunk, when he tried to push off the dinghy last night, he completely missed the dock and fell in the water!"

"And the worst part, I lost your present," said Tom, referring to a pair of rainbow flip-flops Ryan had given his father as a gag gift the night before—a belated Father's Day present since Tom had been at sea that June. Tom had laughed uproariously when he unwrapped the brightly colored shoes and eagerly slipped them on. "Now they're floating somewhere under the dock! You've got to be a good son and swim under there and get my present back!"

"Dad," Ryan laughed, "I'm not swimming under that dock looking for your rainbow shoes! Hell, I'll just buy you a new pair and give them to you the next time I see you, okay?"

Ryan spent ten days on board the *Well Deserved* that late October. After so many months passing with Tom and Jackie at sea, he was grateful to have them back home. When he finally left, Ryan was in high spirits. If only he could have known as he drove away, back to his job in San Diego, that he had just spent the last vacation of his life with his beloved parents. In a few days, the "for sale" ad would run.

Tom could have hired a broker to handle the sale, the same way people do when buying and selling any home. But, always money-conscious, he couldn't see why some agent should get a cut, typically 9 percent of the sale price, when Tom was perfectly capable of handling the advertising and paperwork himself—just as he had for nearly every piece of property he'd ever bought and sold in his adult life. If the sale was going nowhere, he could always turn to a broker later on. But that never was necessary. Within days of the ad running, Tom's phone rang.

"I'm calling about the boat for sale," Skylar said. "When can I come by and see *Well Deserved*?"

CHAPTER TWENTY-TWO

"How much money would I make?" Alonso asked when Skylar first brought up the idea.

"Two million, at least," he said. "Now, understand, I normally don't get paid when I do a job like this. I just take care of the people and then, basically, I get whatever possessions they had."

Skylar had just days to get his plan into place. He had plans to meet Thomas Hawks on his boat November 6. And by the end of that meeting, Skylar planned to be the owner of that yacht. He'd do most of the dirty work. He just needed someone to act as backup. Alonso wasn't an ideal candidate. He was young, just 21, and had never delivered so much as a good punch to anyone in his life. He wasn't even quite 5'9" tall, and was so petite, he looked more like a child than a man. He weighed, soaking wet, maybe 145 pounds. But he was easily duped. Whatever Skylar told him, Alonso would believe it. And that made him the perfect guy for the job, in Skylar's eyes.

"But you've done this before?" Alonso asked.

"Oh yeah, of course," Skylar said.

"And it doesn't bother you?"

"Listen," Skylar said, "I keep telling you, you can't think about it like that. These are some really bad people. They've been dirty all of their lives. You think they bought that boat with their own money? Hell, no. I've already talked to the guy on the phone. Said he was some retired probation officer. Do you know any probation officer who can buy a yacht like that? No way. They're bad and now they've done something to piss off the wrong people. And I've been asked to make them disappear."

"The way you put it, sounds like the world would be a better place if we take them out," said Alonso, trying to justify what he was about to do.

"Exactly," Skylar said. "An eye for an eye, tooth for a tooth. That's what it's all about."

Alonso took in everything his friend had to say. He didn't like the idea of helping two people die. But if they were really bad guys anyway . . . Plus, Skylar promised he wouldn't actually have to do it. Skylar would take care of that part. But in the end, it was the idea of earning a couple million that drew Alonso in.

"Okay," he said. "Okay. But just tell me, how do you do this without going to prison?"

"Don't get caught," said Skylar. "Just don't get caught."

The next few days flew by as the duo scurried to prepare for their big meeting. They drove to Lakewood Mall, where Skylar used a credit card to buy two Taser guns from a store called Sword and Stone. Skylar then sent Alonso off to another store to buy a pair of handcuffs.

"We'll stun them and then cuff them up," Skylar explained.

Skylar downloaded pictures of the *Well Deserved*'s ad onto his laptop. The ad showcased several rooms of the ship, and Skylar wanted Alonso to study the layout.

"We'll take them down to the boat's lower level, in the engine room," Skylar said. "That way, no one will hear them if they scream."

Alonso was getting nervous. With each detail, each new level of planning, it was becoming all too real. But he felt like he couldn't back out now. Skylar was counting on his help. So he said nothing, and continued soaking in each instruction.

"Before I get started," Skylar added, "I usually try to look around for any weapons the people might have. So, be sure to keep an eye out for that. And look for any radio equipment, too. Anything they could use to call for help."

On the morning of November 6, Skylar picked up Alonso in his Highlander SUV and drove into Newport Beach, parking several blocks from the Balboa Peninsula. From the car, the men watched the *Well Deserved*, anchored in place, gently rocking in the distance.

"Can you see anyone else onboard?" Skylar asked. "We can't have anyone else onboard aside from the couple."

"No," Alonso answered. "I don't think so."

They sat, just watching, for a long time before Skylar felt convinced the couple was alone. He called Tom.

"Hey, we're here," he told Tom. "You want to come out and meet us?"

Within minutes, Tom stood on the dock shaking Skylar's hand. Skylar was nothing less than shocked at Tom's appearance. The guy may have been pushing 60, but he was in better shape than 25-year-old Skylar had ever been. He was maybe 5'8" tall, so that put Skylar about an inch over his victim. But the guy carried a 185-pound solid physique. His muscles bulged beneath the T-shirt he wore and his shorts revealed strong, well-defined legs. Immediately, Skylar was worried. Stun guns and all, he didn't know if he and his scrawny partner could carry off the job.

But Skylar wasn't the only one having his doubts that afternoon. Tom was surprised that his potential buyer turned out to be so young. And there was something else. Maybe it was all those years as a probation officer, an entire career spent dealing with liars and thieves, that made his inner alarm bells go off. Tom, normally gregarious and outgoing, was standoffish with the men. So when Skylar asked to take the *Well Deserved* out to sea for a bit of a test drive, Tom said no.

"I can't do that right now," he said vaguely. "It's not a good time. I can take you out to see the boat, but we can't go anywhere."

"Sure, that would be great," Skylar said. "And if I like the boat, maybe we can set up another time to take her out."

"Yeah, maybe," Tom said skeptically.

From the deck of the boat, Skylar caught Alonso's glance and quickly shook his head. Alonso understood. Skylar didn't want to go through with it. His sidekick breathed a sigh of relief.

But back on deck, away from the Hawkses, Skylar explained his next step. "We need another guy," he said. "We need someone else who can help me handle Tom. That guy's a lot bigger than I expected. It's going to take two of us to take him down, and then you can handle Jackie."

Then he flipped open his cell phone to call Jennifer. He read Tom's reactions perfectly and understood he wasn't buying the story of Skylar being some child actor with a bunch of cash stashed away. He needed something else to convince the Hawkses. Something else to make him seem for real. He called his pregnant wife.

"Hey," he told her. "You need to come down here yourself and look at this boat. I need you to put their minds at ease and, you know, help me make the transaction look more legitimate. And bring Hailey."

"Okay," she said simply. "Come pick us up."

So Jennifer returned to the yacht that afternoon with her husband and their 9-month-old toddler. And the mood changed instantly. Jackie's heart melted when she saw the little girl and chatted animatedly with Jennifer, whom she couldn't help but notice had another little one on the way. She had a baby in her life too, Jackie boasted to Jennifer. A new little grandson, Jace. The couples chatted for more than an hour. By then, Tom dropped his defensive demeanor and even agreed to let Skylar come back three days later to learn how to operate the boat's autopilot and Global Positioning System.

"And after that," Skylar suggested, "maybe we can take her out for a run? I'd sure hate to buy a boat without taking it out first, you know."

"Sure," Tom said. "I understand. I'm sure we can make that happen."

There was no doubt in Skylar's mind who he'd turn to for the extra muscle he needed. Not long after wrapping up with the Hawkses, he called his old supervisor, Myron Gardner.

"I just need someone who can act as a little extra muscle while I get the job done," Skylar said. "Someone who can just stand there and be intimidating. Maybe step in if it looks like I'm losing control of the guy. There's a lot of money involved for whoever wants the job."

Maybe in his younger years, Myron would have never missed a chance at easy money. But now, he'd have to pass. Still, he figured he knew a guy or two who might be interested. He promised to look into it for Skylar.

He immediately turned to his old pal from the neighborhood, CJ. After a lifetime of running with the Crips gang, CJ was big, mean, and fearless. He fit the bill perfectly. He stood 6 feet tall and was full of muscle. He'd been born and raised in Long Beach's gang neighborhoods and now, at 39, carried an impressive record, with twenty-one arrests for crimes including possession of narcotics, grand theft, battery, and attempted murder. He was a respected member of ICG, and just cold enough to offer his muscle while two people he never met were tossed into the ocean to their deaths.

Still, when CJ heard the plan, he paused. Despite the money involved, he wasn't sure this was a deal he wanted in on. He'd done a lot of horrific things during his service as a Long Beach gangbanger. But this would bring him a hell of a lot more than just a few years behind bars. Still, the money, up to a few million, sounded pretty good.

In the end, CJ told Myron to check elsewhere. "If you still can't find someone to handle it, I will."

But on the morning of November 15, Myron was still scrambling to find his muscleman. He had someone all lined up just the night before. But by morning, that someone called to say forget it, he changed his mind. That left Myron with no choice. He reluctantly went back to CJ. And this time, he agreed to help out.

Within minutes, Skylar was on the phone to him.

Skylar picked up CJ at a liquor store on Martin Luther King Boulevard and Pacific Coast Highway in Long Beach. But Skylar took one look at his accomplice, standing there in his oversized jeans and baggy T-shirt, and knew Tom would be suspicious. He had to make a change.

"You're going to be introduced as my accountant," Skylar told him. "So we've got to have you dress like an accountant."

"Let's go to my place," CJ said. "I've got some clothes I use for church."

At home, he threw on a pair of slacks and a dark green sweater. Skylar looked him over. CJ looked less menacing, but even a conservative sweater couldn't hide the fact that he was a very big guy—just what he needed.

It was already early afternoon and Skylar had a lot to go over with CJ before they met the Hawkses. Skylar popped open his laptop and went over pictures of the yacht.

"Bascially, the plan is to overpower them with stun guns," Skylar said. "You and I will handle the guy, Tom. After I stun him, we'll take him to the ground and handcuff him. He's a big guy, looks like he works out a lot, so it'll take both of us. Alonso here will handle the wife, Jackie."

Skylar added that he'd be introducing CJ as his accountant, so it was best if he just kept quiet. Skylar realized the minute he opened his mouth, Tom and Jackie would see through that lie.

"I'll do all the talking," Skylar said.

With that, the trio drove the short distance from that scruffy Long Beach neighborhood into the well-heeled streets of Newport Beach. Skylar flipped open his cell phone and called Tom.

"We're here," he said, "at the dock on Fifteenth Street. You want to come pick us up in the dinghy?"

"I'm on my way," Tom said.

From the shore, people who watched the *Well Deserved* pull out to sea under that late afternoon sun must have looked on in envy. She was an impressive ship, no doubt carrying a lucky crew of passengers. What would onlookers give to be part of a trip like that?

But before sundown, a terrible tragedy would occur on the decks of that gorgeous boat. And by midnight, the *Well Deserved* would return home, without her captain, and without the captain's charming wife.

CHAPTER TWENTY-THREE

It was very early in the morning on November 16 by the time Skylar dropped CJ off at home. CJ was disappointed there wasn't much cash onboard—about $1,000 for each man. Before the attack, Skylar also promised Alonso an extra $15,000 for putting his signature on the power of attorney papers, asserting he'd created the document. So far, he'd only collected $1,300.

But Skylar told his partners not to worry. More was coming.

CJ climbed out of Skylar's Highlander, pausing to drop his head into the driver's-side window.

"Get with Myron about the rest of my payment," he said.

"Sure thing," said Skylar. "Don't worry."

It's not clear where Skylar thought he would find the "millions of dollars" to pay off Alonso, CJ, and still carry enough profit to buy Jennifer's dream home. He could have been bluffing his partners. But likely, he also overestimated how much money he'd find in Tom and Jackie's private bank accounts. Likely, he considered his power of attorney papers to be keys to bank accounts holding untold wealth. People who owned a yacht like that, he thought, surely were loaded. He didn't know that nothing was further from the truth. Jackie had been a stay-at-home mom, Tom, a career probation officer who made enough from a few property investments to retire early. They had enough to live on.

Certainly, they wanted for little. But no one would ever consider the Hawkses rich. No one except a guy who never earned anything of significance, accomplished anything real, in his life. The only way he knew to get what he wanted was to murder those who had it. Ironic that a boat named *Well Deserved* ultimately landed in the hands of a man who couldn't have deserved her less.

Skylar called his dad with the news.

"It's a done deal," Skylar said.

"I don't believe you," answered John. But even as he spoke, he feared the worst. "Tell me you're lying."

"I'm not," Skylar said. "I did it."

Jennifer couldn't wait to step aboard her new boat, and Skylar was delighted to show off the big score to his wife and family. The Hawkses had only been dead a handful of hours when Jennifer climbed on deck, inspecting all the luxuries onboard the ship she'd now call home—a queen-sized bed, a washer and dryer, a fully loaded kitchen. She was giddy with excitement, and anxious to make the place her own. First up, cleaning out the closets. She decided to make two stacks—a keep pile and a throw away pile. She ravaged Jackie's closets, tossing items per her discretion. Of course, Jackie was a much tinier lady than Jennifer, so there wasn't much of her clothing she could use. But there were other things—cameras, jewelry, dishes, linens.

As her piles began building, Jennifer called her dad, ordering him to run to the store and buy a large bottle of bleach, trash bags, and a pack of gum. The boat and other possessions, Jennifer had breezily explained to her family, were part of an inheritance Skylar just came into from his Mexican relatives. Later, she changed her story to say he actually inherited cash and they bought the boat from an old, retired couple. The deal even came with their car, she said, referring to the Honda Civic now parked in front of her parents' home.

Either way, no one questioned the story.

"It was part of my 'Don't ask, don't tell' policy when it came to Skylar," Steve Henderson, Jennifer's father, later would tell others. "It didn't sound right to me, but I didn't say anything about it."

And so, he not only bought the items his daughter wanted, he helped them swab down the boat, and brought his son and nephew back the next day for a fishing trip out at sea with Skylar. Lana Henderson, meanwhile, drove her daughter's new Honda to run errands.

But what Skylar really wanted to do next was get a look at the Hawkses' bank accounts. He had the power of attorney papers, complete with the couple's signatures. But they were worthless unless he could get them notarized.

Despite Adam's violent reaction several weeks ago to Skylar's request for help dumping a few bodies, the men were still on friendly terms. So, again, Skylar turned to him. And as fate would have it, Adam's close friend, Kathleen Harris, was a notary.

"If she would be willing just to backdate a few papers for me," said Skylar, purposely vague on the details, "there would be a lot of money in it for her."

Adam knew Skylar's family was in the mortgage-lending business. Probably, that's all it was, a bunch of real estate papers. He didn't see much harm in that, and agreed to convince Kathleen to help Skylar out.

On November 22, three days before the Thanksgiving holiday, Jennifer called Kathleen and invited her to their hotel room at Extended Stay America. When Kathleen arrived, she found $2,000 in hundred-dollar bills fanned out on a small table in the room. The power of attorney papers she was to notarize lay beside the cash.

"All I need you to do," Skylar said, "is backdate everything."

"Make the date November 15," Jennifer added.

Kathleen had never committed a crime in her life. And she knew putting her signature on that paper was a fraud that could cost her her license to practice if anyone ever found out. But she considered those chances remote. She wasn't a rich woman, and so, a little extra cash for a little white lie didn't seem so bad—until she realized she wasn't being asked to sign mortgage papers.

There was a title transfer document regarding some boat. That wasn't so bad. But the other papers, giving the Deleons power of attorney over someone else's finances, looked suspicious. She was beginning to worry. Suddenly, Kathleen just wanted out of that room. And so, without asking anything more, she signed the papers. And with her signature, Skylar and Jennifer now had access to every financial asset the Hawkses owned.

"If this deal goes through," Jennifer told Kathleen as she headed for the door, "you can expect more money to come later."

It was meant to bolster Kathleen's confidence, and ensure her silence over what she'd just done. But it had the opposite effect. She was scared now. And couldn't wait to call Adam.

That evening, she met her friend for a drink.

"What the hell was that about?" she asked. "And who are the Hawkses?"

"I don't know," Adam said. But now, he was worried for Kathleen, too. As she told him about the boat transfer papers, and the power of attorney documents, it started to come together for him. He remembered now the conversation with Skylar, who begged for help getting rid of two people on a boat. Apparently, he wasn't joking. "The crazy bastard actually did it," Adam thought. But he didn't say that much to Kathleen. He didn't want her any more scared than she was already. Suddenly, he felt sick that he'd gotten his dear friend involved in Skylar's mess. He wanted to put the whole thing behind them. But that was impossible.

Skylar called back, saying he forgot to have another document notarized—a bill of sale this time. Skylar and Jennifer needed to show one to a detective to prove they bought the yacht, Skylar said in a message. Adam didn't respond to Skylar's call at first. But he didn't stop calling. He rang repeatedly, sometimes every five minutes.

Finally, Adam encouraged Kathleen to seal the papers once more. As Adam saw it, it was better to get all the paperwork done to avoid suspicion.

"The last thing you need is to have the police start poking around because you notarized some documents, but not all of them," Adam said. "So as much as I hate this, I think you need to sign off on the rest, then forget the whole thing. Forget all this ever happened. I don't know what this is all about, but something tells me it's bad. You don't want to fuck with these people."

Kathleen signed off on the crucial bill of sale document, even though, unlike the last set of papers, this one didn't have Tom and Jackie's signatures. Instead, Skylar signed in their place and noted that, as power of attorney, he had the authority to act on their behalf. Kathleen knew that would never fly if anyone really started to look into the deal. But she did what they wanted, applying her notary seal. Then, terrified, she got the hell out of town. But she wasn't running from police. She almost couldn't care anymore if they found her. She was hiding from Skylar and his wife.

The day before Thanksgiving, Skylar and Jennifer caravanned to Arizona with Jennifer's dad, intent on accessing the Hawkses' accounts. They drove Skylar's Highlander, taking turns behind the wheel. Steve kept an eye on his granddaughter, taking her for a drive with him while her mom and dad went into the Stockmen's Bank in Kingman, Arizona. Operations manager Sheri Murphy couldn't shake the feeling that the young couple before her seemed nervous as they asked how to use their power of attorney to access a bank account.

"Specifically, I'm wondering how I would write a check from this account," Jennifer said.

Sheri explained she'd have to sign Tom and Jackie Hawkses' names, then put her own signature underneath, along with the initials P.O.A., indicating power of attorney.

"Well, is it okay if I just print their names?" Jennifer asked, pulling out a stack of blank checks with the Hawkses' names and account number on them. "I don't feel right signing their names."

A lot of things didn't feel right about this couple, Sheri thought.

"How long have you known the Hawkses?" Sheri asked, her suspicions on high alert.

"About a month," Skylar said. "They went to Mexico and we're helping them out handling their bills and financial stuff."

Excusing herself, Sheri made a call to the Hawkses' home branch in Prescott, Arizona, where operations manager Luann Kenney advised Sheri to interoffice the power of attorney papers. She wanted a better look at them. And she wanted to talk to the Deleons herself. As Sheri broke the news to the Deleons that they'd have to work with the Prescott office, Luann Kenney reviewed the Hawkses' account further. She noticed that a third name already appeared on it—Patricia Schutz.

Fear took hold of Trish when Luann called, explaining that a Jennifer and Skylar Deleon claimed to have power of attorney over the Hawkses' account.

"I pay their bills," Trish said. "These people are strangers. There's no way [Tom and Jackie] would give them access to their money. Not without talking to me first."

Trish hung up and called Jim Hawks. He had been scrambling for any word from his brother and sister-in-law. They'd been missing for nine days. And now this—it wasn't good news. As Jim listened to Trish, his worst fears took hold. He knew filing a missing persons report was the next step. But he knew what kind of signal that would send to his nephews. It was an acknowledgment that something bad had happened to their parents. He'd have to call and brace them. But first, he called the police.

CHAPTER TWENTY-FOUR

There were nine days left before Christmas of 2004. It was a time when most people were putting in fewer hours at the office, scrambling to get home to holiday parties or squeeze in Christmas list shopping. But Detective Sailor sat at his desk that afternoon determined to make some headway on the Hawks case. He called Skylar.

"Hey, man," he said casually when Skylar picked up the phone, "how'd you like to come pick up your boat?"

Well Deserved had been in police custody since the day Skylar gave them permission to search her. Though they found little evidence of it onboard, they couldn't escape the feeling that the ship had become a floating crime scene. They held the boat as long as they could, but knew Skylar was anxious to get her back. So the call from Detective Sailor was a welcome one.

"That's good news," he said. "Where can I pick it up?"

"Just come down to the station, I'll have to give you some papers to sign," Detective Sailor said. "After that, I'll give you directions to where you can go get it."

"I'm on my way," he said.

Detective Sailor hung up the phone and turned to his sergeant. "He's on his way," he said.

"Perfect," Sergeant Byington said. "This should be good."

Skylar arrived cradling Hailey in his arms. Detective Sailor led him into a conference room, where Sergeant Byington was seated and waiting.

"Have a seat," Detective Sailor said. "Turns out, we've got a few things we have to talk to you about before we can let you have the boat."

Gone was the friendly demeanor of two investigators looking for help on a missing persons case. Only hours ago, the detectives learned the Hawkses' car was sitting in Mexico, where it had been hand-delivered by Skylar, Jennifer, and Jennifer's dad.

Skylar sensed the change. He was agitated, almost nervous, for the first time. He talked of not having that much time, of having to get Hailey back home.

"Well, here's the problem," Detective Sailor said. "We believe you know a lot more than you've been telling us. We believe Tom and Jackie Hawks were murdered. And we believe you know how. So we're here basically to tell you, the jig is up. It's time to start talking."

Skylar shook his head furiously. "I don't know what you're talking about. How could you say that?"

"Skylar," Detective Sailor said, "we found that car. It was in Mexico, sitting in front of a house that belongs to a man claiming to be a friend of yours. And you know what he says? He says you and Jennifer dropped that car off."

As he delivered the news, Detective Sailor watched Skylar carefully. He couldn't help but notice as the color drained from Skylar's face. He said nothing, but his face was white with fear. Just then, baby Hailey, maybe sensing the tension in the room, began to cry. Skylar gave himself time to think as he tended to her. But she cried louder and then spit up. Skylar stood abruptly.

"I've got to go," he said. "I've got to clean this up."

He walked quickly toward the door and out of the station, Detective Sailor in step behind him, continuing the chatter.

"You don't understand," Skylar said as they reached his car. "It's my dad. It's all my dad."

"What about your dad?" Sailor asked.

"He's a really horrible person," Skylar said.

"Why?" the detective encouraged. "What do you mean?"

"I can't," Skylar said. "He's threatened my family. I want to tell you everything, but I can't. The life of my family is at stake."

"Why would he threaten you?" Detective Sailor asked.

"Because he knows I've been talking to you," Skylar said. "He knows and he's not happy about it. He warned me not to talk to you. Look, I can prove it."

Skylar pulled out a cell phone and shoved it toward the detective. Sure enough, a message played from John Jacobson Sr. In truth, Skylar had confided in his father, in part bragging about the boat he scored, and in part looking for advice as police became more and more aggressive.

"Don't say anything else to the police," the message said. "I have an attorney for you. Just don't talk to the police."

Once again, Detective Sailor found it impossible to tell if Skylar was telling the truth or spinning a lie. He knew by now he was an adept liar. But he still didn't think he murdered the Hawkses alone. Maybe he was covering for his dad?

"He forced me into this," Skylar said. "He's the one who wanted that damn boat. But I can't say anything more. You know, my dad, he just runs with some really bad people. You can't understand how much my life is at stake just by standing here."

"So you didn't really buy that boat, did you?" Detective Sailor said.

"No, that's the crazy thing, I did," Skylar said. "I did give them money for the boat. That part is legitimate, I swear. And I don't know where the hell they went after that. But you know, I'm really angry with the Hawkses."

"You're angry with the Hawkses? For what?" said an incredulous detective.

"For putting me through this," said Skylar, clearly regaining his momentum. "When you find them, I want you to let me know, because I'm thinking about filing a lawsuit for putting me through this with the police. They're sitting in Mexico somewhere, refusing to contact anyone, and I'm being put through hell because of it!"

Skylar turned then and lowered Hailey into her car seat. He was itching to get out of there. He didn't like this conversation.

Anyway, he didn't plan on being around much longer. He and Jennifer were already planning their escape to Mexico. Just days before, Jennifer paid a visit to her obstetrician, asking for advice on where she could get good medical care across the border.

"Nowhere," the doctor told her. "I suggest you wait and have that baby here, in the United States."

But they couldn't wait, clearly. Time was running out. The police obviously considered them suspects now. Running would mean Skylar would also violate his probation, which he was still on for the robbery at Ted's house. Technically, he could not even leave the county without permission. But his probation officer liked him well enough. He'd just call in and ask for permission to go, explaining he'd found a job opportunity down there. Since his probation was in a different county, in neighboring Los Angeles, he could be long gone before Newport Beach detectives knew a thing. But even if the probation department denied his request, it might not matter anymore. If the detective let him drive out of the station that day, he and Jennifer had to put their plan into action.

For now, Detective Sailor did let Skylar drive away.

"I'll let you get her home," he said, gesturing to the baby. There wasn't much else he could do. A found car still wasn't enough to prove they killed the Hawkses, no matter how strongly the detective thought it was true.

But the need to arrest Skylar would jump from desirable to critical within just a few hours.

That same day, an officer with the Los Angeles County Probation Department called Sailor and Byington. What Skylar didn't know was that detectives had long ago contacted his probation officer. So he was well aware his probationer was being looked at in the Hawks case. That's why he wanted to let them know—Skylar just called claiming to have found a job teaching diving lessons to students in Puerto Vallarta. He wanted permission to leave the country.

There was no job, obviously, Sergeant Byington thought. Deleon was running. He couldn't let that happen. But what could they charge him with? They still had no evidence of murder. And once he was behind bars, Matt Murphy would only have sixty days before he'd have to present evidence to a judge demonstrating why Skylar should go to trial in the killing of Tom and Jackie. So far, they had no bodies, no DNA, no eyewitnesses.

He needed to talk it over with Matt. Knowing that the Hawkses' car had been found in Mexico, where the Deleons had dropped it off, was fantastic evidence. But he agreed, it wasn't enough to make an arrest for murder. They'd have to come up with another way to take Skylar off the streets.

"You know, he's already confessed to a money laundering," Matt said. "For now, arrest him on that."

Detective Sailor wrote up the arrest warrant. As he worked, he was stunned to learn Jennifer was on the phone, screaming to Sergeant Byington about the boat.

"You keep telling us you are going to release the boat, and then you don't," she yelled into the phone. "You guys are just bullsh . . . You aren't being straight with us!"

Quietly, the detective chuckled at the near slip. His mind flashed back to the first time he saw her, demurely pushing her cleaning cart around church. "You almost had us fooled," he thought. But when he spoke, his words were soothing. He wanted to keep her cooperating for as long as possible—even if that might only be a few more hours.

"No, you have it all wrong, Jennifer," Sergeant Byington said. "We want you to have the boat back. We've just got to make sure everything's wrapped up so once it's returned to you, that's it, it's yours, and we won't ever have to pull it back for anything. You understand, right?"

"This has been very hard on me," she said. "I'm so stressed out over it all that it's putting my pregnancy at risk!"

"Well, we can't have that," Sergeant Byington said. "That baby is your priority, so you need to try to calm down and make your health your first concern right now. Everything else will work out, so just relax."

"Okay," she said, her temper subsiding. "I'll try."

On the morning of November 17, a judge signed the arrest warrant. Sergeant Byington contacted the surveillance car that had been sitting outside of the Deleon house, there just in case

Skylar started packing up his car before they were ready for him. But now, they were ready.

"Detective Sailor's on his way," the sergeant told Detective Joe Wingert, who sat just a few feet away from the Deleons' front door. "We're taking him in."

As Detective Sailor arrived, Jennifer, Hailey, and Skylar walked out of their house and started toward their car.

"Hey, man," Detective Sailor said, "we've got a warrant for your arrest."

It shouldn't have been a surprise when the Newport Beach police detectives greeted them on the driveway, announcing Skylar was under arrest. But Jennifer and her husband looked stunned.

"What's the charge?" Jennifer demanded. "Why are you arresting him?"

"Right now, it's money laundering," Detective Sailor said, placing the cuffs around Skylar's wrists and escorting him to the back of his police car. "And you probably won't make bail because, you know, you're already on probation for the burglary."

"This is ridiculous," Skylar snapped. "I sit and try and help you guys and I get in trouble? What's going on with my wife?"

"You're the only one under arrest now," Detective Sailor said.

"What grounds do you have for you arresting me?" he asked.

"I can't discuss that with you right now," the detective replied, settling him into the police car before returning to the house.

Jennifer looked on as a team of investigators crawled through her home. She was still holding the search warrant notice when Detective Sailor found her.

"This is going to affect his probation, isn't it?" Jennifer said to the detective as he approached. "And he's got joint suspension over his probation."

The detective paused to look quizzically at Jennifer.

" 'Joint suspension,' " he echoed. "I'm not familiar with that term."

In fact, nobody talked like that. Nobody but prosecutors. It was a slang term the deputy district attorneys used to describe a defendant whose remaining jail time has been suspended in exchange for probation. His time in "the joint" is literally suspended. But if he screws up again, he goes back to jail. "Joint suspension" over. Only a woman aggressively involved in her husband's case would know a term like that. Clearly, this was no shrinking violet. From the sound of it, she knew more about Skylar's case than he did.

"Joint suspension, that's what it's called," she said, educating the detective. "You do less time unless you get in trouble again. Then you have to go back and do the maximum. So he'll have to serve the rest of his sentence for the burglary. That's seven years."

"I don't know," he said, deciding not to get into it with her any further. "I don't know his probation specifics."

"Okay," she said. "Can he kiss his daughter good-bye before he goes?"

"No, ma'am," the detective said, glancing at Skylar sitting quietly in the back of the patrol car, and at the growing number of curious neighbors coming out to take in the commotion. "I'm afraid he can't. I'm not trying to be an ass, but you've got a lot of people out here. I think we've drawn enough attention. I'm just going to get him out of here now."

While he drove Skylar to his new room at the Orange County jail, investigators spent the afternoon at the Deleon/Henderson home, pulling out pictures, computers, paperwork and clothing—all appearing to belong to the Hawkses. But perhaps the item that told the story of the Hawkses best was the camcorder investigators boxed away that day. Much later, when Matt Murphy reviewed the evidence from the Deleons' makeshift home, he lingered longest over that camcorder. He sat in his office, riveted to the frames of Tom and Jackie laughing on the decks of their boat, shots of Tom swimming with humpback whales, footage of Tom dressed down in a thick raincoat as he braved winds and pelting rain to help fellow boaters prepare for an approaching hurricane. The camera even caught Tom wrapping up a rare boys' weekend at play, without his adoring wife. Stubble clung to his normally clean-shaven face as he looked wistfully into the camera. "Jackie," he said, suddenly grinning from ear to ear. "I can't wait to see her."

"It's heartbreaking," Matt thought as he watched Tom's face. "He loved her so very much."

The last frames show Jackie and Tom aboard the *Well Deserved* on November 13, hosting their good-bye dinner from the waters off Catalina Island. Jim Hawks was there, along with a handful of their boating friends. "This is our last voyage onboard *Well Deserved*," Jackie said. "I'm really going to miss living here."

As she talked, the camera panned over her friends, over the living room she shared with Tom for the past two years, then back to Jackie. "Oh, well," she said. "I just wonder what's coming down the road next."

Her last words hit Matt with all the force of a punch in the stomach, knowing that just a few hours later, the Hawkses would completely disappear. He kept watching as the footage flickered into blackness. Then came to life again. But this time, scenes of Jennifer Henderson's parents at a dinner party flashed onto the screen. It's Thanksgiving Day. Steve Henderson is laughing in the background, other relatives are milling about, a chunky little boy lingers on the couch, Hailey crawls across the floor. Instinctively, Matt knows it must be Skylar holding the camera swiped from the *Well Deserved*. His guess is confirmed as the camera sweeps across the room, then pauses, focusing for a moment on Jennifer. Wordlessly, she turns to the camera and offers an enormous smile.

Looking at Jennifer's beaming face, an incredible need to find justice for the Hawks family swept over Matt. These had been good people who led honest lives, who loved each other, loved their friends. And watching the two people who likely had a hand in their demise laugh and play with the Hawkses' personal belongings left Matt feeling emotionally spent. It was never a smart idea to get too personally involved in a case he was prosecuting. But there was no shutting off how he felt now. As with every case, he wanted a conviction. But this time, it was more than that. It's a sad but true fact that in most homicide cases, often the victims aren't such innocent figures. Often, they are involved in gangs, drugs, an abusive relationship, something . . . Many times, it was the activities and lifestyle of the victims that helped put them in the place that ultimately cost them their lives. But not this time. The Hawks? Just good folks. Had been all of their lives. And they didn't deserve this. Perhaps more than any other time in his career, he couldn't wait to send Skylar and his wife to prison. And if possible, death row.

CHAPTER TWENTY-FIVE

It was a hard call for Ryan to take. Maybe some part of him should have been relieved when his uncle called to say investigators had found his parents' Honda. Isn't that why he'd been giving countless interviews to TV and newspaper reporters, begging for help finding the car? He'd told his story so many times, his stomach was in knots. He couldn't eat. He couldn't sleep. And now, the work had paid off—some guy watching him plead his heart out on TV had turned in the car. At least it was progress, a new development in the still-unsolved puzzle. And more importantly, it led to Skylar's arrest.

But it was not comforting news.

Ryan called his mother. As he told her of the discovery, he broke down.

"You know," he said, "for some reason, I just kept thinking that maybe there's some two percent chance that they'd still be alive. I kept thinking that maybe this guy just kidnapped them and was holding them for money. But Uncle Jim kept telling me, 'If they were kidnapped, there'd be a ransom note by now.' But now that they've found the car, there goes all hope. They're dead."

"Honey," Dixie answered her son gently, "you knew that. You've known all along they were gone."

"I know, I know," Ryan said. "But it still hurts. It hurts to think that this one asshole has just wrecked my entire family. It hurts because things are never going to be right again."

By late December 2004, Skylar appeared in court to enter a plea on the money-laundering charges. Sitting in the courtroom to support her husband was Jennifer, flanked by her mom and dad. Ryan was there, with his mother and uncle. His face was an emotionless stone cast as he looked at the Henderson family.

"I'll never so much as break a sweat in front of them," he said. "They'll never see me show any emotion. That's the way my dad would expect me to act."

In the moments before Skylar stepped into court, Matt Murphy took a seat next to Dixie. She was the ex-wife of Tom. Typically, any ex-wife had a pretty sharp ax to grind against a former spouse. Though his heart told him Tom had been a clean man, Matt felt it was his obligation to ask Dixie once more. If anyone had a reason not to keep secrets, it would be Dixie.

"I just want you to know," Matt began, "what the defense will try to do. They will say Tom was a drug dealer and that someone else killed him in a drug deal gone bad. I'm only telling you this because I really need to know . . . If there's any truth to . . ."

"My ex-husband has never done an illegal thing in his entire life," Dixie Hawks said, not even giving Matt a chance to finish the thought. Her words were measured, passionate.

"Without a doubt, she's telling the truth," Matt thought.

He looked up then to see Skylar, dressed in his orange jail jumpsuit, led into court. He was looking down at the floor, appearing so docile, so timid, like he'd never hurt a fly. And in that instant, Matt realized—he was looking at a complete sociopath. Matt prosecuted very few of them in his career. That kind of pure evil was rare. But the minute Matt locked eyes with Skylar, he knew what this defendant was all about.

"I could see it in his eyes," Matt would say later, after Skylar entered his "not guilty" plea and was on his way back to jail to await his next court date. "He was a sociopath and he drowned that retired couple for no other reason than he wanted their boat."

In the days following Skylar's arrest, the U.S. Navy would assist investigators in a scan of the ocean floor, in search of Tom and Jackie's remains. Authorities based their search on coordinates stored on the *Well Deserved*'s Global Positioning unit on the afternoon of November 15. It was just a hunch that the Hawks were probably dumped somewhere along that route. And a lot of time had passed. Considering the ocean's currents, finding two bodies attached to an anchor would be nothing short of a miracle. Still, the naval operators dipped a radar/sonar into the ocean, looking for those remains. Finding them would be significant evidence for the prosecution if found—and would mean the Hawks family could give the beloved couple a proper burial.

But after hours of scouring, they turned up empty. In truth, the Hawkses' remains had probably been swept deep into the sea by now. It would be a setback, to try someone for murder without the bodies to prove a murder had been committed.

"It certainly helps to recover the bodies, but I don't need them to get a conviction," Matt said after the unsuccessful search. In fact, in another case, years ago, he'd won a first-degree murder conviction against a defendant, even though the body, believed buried in the California desert, was never found. "Skylar murdered them, and we'll get enough evidence to convince any jury in the world of that."

John Jacobson was mad as hell when Newport Beach officers arrested him outside the U-Haul truck he called home.

"You've got no right to do this," he yelled as he was booked into custody.

"Yes, we do," Sergeant Byington corrected him. "You've got an outstanding warrant for unpaid traffic tickets."

"That's not why I'm here, and you know it!" John shouted. "This isn't over any traffic ticket. I'm here because of my son. This is about Skylar's thing."

In fact, the detectives tried talking to John on his cell phone many times. But he was always uncooperative.

If the investigators thought they'd have better luck by forcing an in-person chat, they were wrong. John was furious. And verbally combative.

"As a matter of fact, I do want to talk to you about Skylar," the sergeant said honestly. "You know, since you're here anyway."

John didn't appreciate the sarcasm.

"Hell, no," he said. "I'm not telling you a thing. Just because you arrested me doesn't mean I have to say a damn thing."

"Look, I'm just looking for some help to find some missing people," Byington said.

"No you're not," John said. "You're looking for information against my son! Now you've arrested me because of Skylar and you're out there illegally searching my van!"

"You're in here belly-aching because we arrested you on some traffic warrant? We have dead people out there we're trying to find! What's wrong with you? And if your son had nothing to do with it, then why don't you talk to me? Help him out? What kind of a father are you?"

"I'm not telling you shit," he said. "Get me a lawyer."

With that, the interview was over. Twenty minutes later, John Jacobson had bailed out of jail. And the detectives were no closer to knowing if he was involved, or if that was yet another of Skylar's lies.

Seven months pregnant, her husband in jail, Jennifer was in crisis mode. She was scared. And not just about what might happen to Skylar—but what might happen to her.

Christmas was just six days away when Jennifer called her family together for an evening talk. She sat with her children, her parents, even Skylar's aunt, Colleen Francisco.

"I'm going to prison," Jennifer told them. "I know it now. It's just a matter of time."

"Why?" Colleen answered in shock. "How could you think that?"

"Because of the Hawkses," she said. "We were the last ones to see them. And now, Skylar and I are going to prison."

Skylar's aunt was unnerved by Jennifer's erratic behavior. This wasn't like her. Normally, Jennifer was the strong one. Cold, actually. She never showed emotion. Now, as she spoke, panic gripped her face. She looked terrified. Watching her nephew's wife, Colleen realized that Jennifer knew exactly what became of that missing couple.

"And the last time you saw them, Jennifer," Colleen asked, "were they alive or dead?"

In response, Jennifer looked away and began to cry. Tears spilled down her cheeks. Suddenly, she looked so lonely. Vulnerable.

When she finally spoke, her voice was hushed and broken. "We needed the money," was all she would say. "We needed the money."

Although notary Kathleen Harris confirmed she witnessed the sale of the boat, the detectives had doubts about her story.

She had no criminal history. And no other known ties to Skylar, as far as they could tell. So why would she lie for him?

Still, they couldn't yet explain one major problem with her story—she gave the wrong description of Jackie Hawks.

According to Kathleen, Jackie was overjoyed with the sale of the boat, and spoke of her excitement when she signed the bill of sale papers and the power of attorney documents.

"I remember what a pretty lady she is," Kathleen said. "She was petite. And she had dark hair, cut really short. And it was very curly."

Jackie was petite. And quite attractive. But it was the hair that the detectives couldn't figure out. Jackie had, in fact, dyed her hair very blond, and wore it straight, even a bit spiky. Poring over the latest photos of Jackie, they were at a loss to come up with a reason for the "dark, curly hair" description.

Still, in every follow-up interview, Kathleen stuck to her story. And to that description.

But as she spoke, Kathleen must have sensed the detectives' skepticism. And once she learned she may have unwittingly assisted in ripping off two missing people, she grew scared. She could lose her license to practice. Worse, she could end up in jail.

Christmas Eve, Matt Murphy was home to answer his ringing phone.

"Matt, it's Paul Meyers," said the voice on the line. Paul, a friend of Matt's for many years, was a talented defense attorney well-known to Orange County prosecutors.

"Paul," Matt said. "Mighty thoughtful of you to call and wish me a Merry Christmas."

Paul chuckled before breaking the news to Matt.

"We've got to talk," he said. Paul was representing Kathleen Harris. And she wanted to set up a meeting.

"Okay," said Matt. "After Christmas. Let's do it."

Days later, Matt and Sergeant Byington met with Paul and Kathleen. Paul wanted a deal known affectionately among attorneys as a "Queen for a Day" arrangement. In short, Matt couldn't prosecute Kathleen based on anything she said in the interview. In exchange, she'd tell him everything she knew about the sale of the *Well Deserved*. Matt agreed.

"As long as she tells me the truth," Matt said. "No holding back on anything."

Kathleen nodded and began her story.

"I know I told you that I was there when Tom and Jackie sold their yacht to Skylar and Jennifer," she began. "I wasn't."

She recounted everything—how her friend Adam asked her to backdate some documents for friends of his, about her meeting with Jennifer and Skylar at the hotel, about the money.

"She told me if this all worked out, there would be more," Kathleen said. "But I just thought it was some kind of insurance fraud scheme. Nothing more."

"You don't know what happened to Tom or Jackie?" Matt asked.

"No," Kathleen said. "I never asked about them. And I was never on that boat."

"What about Adam?" he asked. "What does he know?"

"Nothing," Kathleen assured them. He was a good guy who only knew Skylar because he signed up for dive lessons.

"Did Adam get a cut of the money you were paid?" Matt asked.

"No, he didn't," Kathleen said. "I kept all the money."

"What did you do with it?"

"I spent it on bills, went shopping, nothing exciting," she said.

"And how are you so sure Adam isn't more involved than you think?" Matt asked. "He set this up for you, right? Maybe he was on that boat the night they disappeared?"

"I'm sure because I know Adam," Kathleen said. "He's a good guy."

The investigators weren't willing simply to take her word about that.

Within hours, Detective Sailor called Adam to request a meeting.

"There's a Starbucks not too far from your house," Detective Sailor told him. "Let's meet there."

"Okay," Adam said. "When?"

"How about now?" Detective Sailor said.

"Okay, I'm on my way."

But as Adam stepped out of his house, he realized he'd just been set up. Police surrounded his Long Beach home. Detective Sailor stepped forward to hand him a search warrant. For all they knew, he wasn't just the guy who helped Skylar get a dirty notary. He could be a partner to murder.

But investigators began to drop their suspicions about Adam the minute they spoke with him. He readily talked, saying he knew Kathleen was going to police. He'd even encouraged her to do it after the news began running stories of the Hawkses' disappearance. He implicated himself, too, in the Kathleen Harris deal.

"We split the money," Adam admitted. "She gave me a thousand dollars for hooking her up with Skylar. I really regret that now. I should have never gotten her mixed up with someone like Skylar. He's a bad guy."

The revelation meant Kathleen lied in her interview. She did give money to Adam. It was irritating, but they realized she was probably trying to keep her friend from being dragged into this any further. They'd have to call her later and verbally rough her up a bit over the fib, reminding her that she could easily end up in jail on a murder charge if she hid any more details.

But in general, they believed she hadn't been involved in the disappearance. And a gut feeling told them Adam wasn't either. He had a clean record, seemed eager to talk to police, and wasn't at all nervous when they showed up at his door with a search warrant.

"How do you know he's a bad guy?" Sergeant Byington asked.

Adam recounted for them Skylar's request for help in dumping a couple of bodies at sea.

"I told him he was crazy," Adam said. "I really thought the guy was joking."

Sergeant Byington called Matt Murphy with the news.

"I knew it," said Matt. It still wasn't enough to charge Skylar with murder, but they were so close. "We're going to get him."

"Wait until you hear what else we found," the sergeant said. "Remember how we couldn't figure out why Kathleen kept describing Jackie with dark curly hair?"

"Yeah," Matt said.

"We found a crumpled-up paper near a trash can in Adam's house. You know what it was? Color copies of Tom and Jackie's drivers' licenses," the sergeant said. "Adam says Skylar gave them to him so he could pass them on to Kathleen. They're older photos, but in Jackie's? She's wearing her hair cut short, dark, and very curly."

"So she was telling the truth," Matt said. "She never laid eyes on them. She was just describing them from their outdated DMV photos."

The sergeant nodded from his end of the phone. "Exactly," he said. "They were already dead by the time she was signing those papers. So she never saw them."

With Kathleen's admission on the record, it was time to go back to Alonso, the only other person alleging he witnessed the *Well Deserved*'s sale. If Kathleen was covering for Skylar and Jennifer, likely, Alonso was, too.

Detectives took a ride out to Irvine, where Alonso was working as a clerk for a mortgage company. In his pocket Detective

Sailor carried an arrest warrant for conspiracy to commit forgery.

"Kathleen's already told us what happened," Detective Sailor told him. "She wasn't there when that sale went down. She was paid to sign those papers days later. And so were you."

If Alonso looked nervous talking to police before, he looked like he might pass out now as they put the cuffs on him and drove him back to the Newport Beach Police Department. Sergeant Byington thought he could see the young man physically shaking.

The sergeant did his best to calm the boy down and convince him now was the time to come clean, before he ended up with a murder charge.

"I lied," Alonso said simply. "You're right, that sale never happened, as far as I know. Skylar just asked me to sign those papers later."

"So why'd you do it for him?" the investigator asked.

"Because Skylar paid me," he said. "I only did it because Skylar promised to give me a lot of money if I helped him out."

Sergeant Byington pushed for more, convinced Alonso, who had some history with Skylar dating back to their Seal Beach City Jail days, knew more than he was saying.

"Alonso, where are Tom and Jackie?" he asked.

Alonso knew everything. He knew Tom and Jackie were dead, and that their bodies had been at sea so long now, investigators would never find those remains. Likely, the only way the Hawks family would ever know for sure what happened out there that terrible night was if he talked. He'd go to prison, probably for the rest of his life. But the Hawks family could finally grieve properly and maybe find some peace in knowing the truth.

Alonso knew all of this. Still, when he looked at the investigators, all he said was, "I don't know."

He still couldn't bring himself to admit out loud that he'd participated in the gruesome deaths of two innocent people.

"Skylar never talked to you about them?" Sergeant Byington asked. "He never told you where they went and why he needed you to pretend you witnessed buying the boat?"

"No, we never talked about all that," Alonso lied. "He just said he'd give me a bunch of money if I helped him out, so I told him I would."

The detectives nodded, willing to give him the benefit of the doubt for now. At least he was cooperating—and they wanted to keep it that way. So when his attorney, Roy Peterson, asked that Alonso be released from jail on his own recognizance, they agreed.

But it was a mistake to trust Alonso, as the detectives soon found out. Days later, he was nowhere to be found. Best guess was that he had run to Mexico, where he was born and, therefore, still a citizen. He had relatives there, too, so hiding out would be easy enough.

Matt Murphy refused to let the setback get him down.

"It's not as bad as it used to be," Matt said. "There have been a lot of changes to make it easier to get cooperation from Mexican officials. I'll get him. It's just a matter of time."

Still, the detectives were furious. It wasn't the first time they'd had a bad guy run across the border to hide out. It was a common frustration for law enforcement officers working cases so close to the Mexican border. A lot of their suspects were Mexican citizens who could slip back home with relative ease. And often, would never be seen again. Cooperation with Mexican police officials had always been difficult—corruption and bribery ran rampant. And even working with the most honest cop was problematic. It meant asking an already overworked officer to interrupt his caseload to help out an investigator he'd never met, in another country. They placed a surveillance team outside Alonso's home, just in case he came back for a visit. But they didn't hold out much hope for that. It was possible they'd never see Alonso Machain again.

Perhaps the only person more outraged than the detectives about Alonso's escape was Ryan Hawks. He was devastated by the news. But as he'd done since this nightmare began, he pushed aside his feelings and sprang into action. While forcing himself to do all those interviews for all those days, he got to know quite a few reporters. He used that power now, calling journalists in his phone book.

"You go down to his parents' house," he told them, "and you interview them, put them on the news. Because wherever he is, I want him to see his family crying. I want him to see what it's like to watch your family break down on television."

CHAPTER TWENTY-SIX

"There is no way Skylar is getting out of jail," Matt thought. "The minute he's out on his own, he'll be heading down to Mexico. He's already admitted to having ties down there, through his dad. And it's where he stashed the Hawkses' car."

But with Kathleen's admission that she faked those documents, and Alonso saying he never saw a sale go down, it's doubtful any money had changed hands. Therefore, there was no money that was ever laundered. Matt couldn't go before a judge and argue that he had the evidence to keep Skylar in jail on a money-laundering charge. Because he didn't.

But maybe there was another way out—Jon P. Jarvi.

Newport Beach police detectives were well aware of the case. During the search of the Deleon home in December, they had found a business card belonging to Los Angeles Police Detective Joe Bahena.

On December 18, Newport Beach Police Detective Keith Krallman put the call in to Detective Bahena.

"We found your card at this house we served a search warrant on," Detective Krallman told him. "The guy who lives there, Skylar Deleon, is a suspect in a possible homicide case we're working. I thought I'd call you and see if you had a case on him, too."

In fact, Bahena said, he did.

"Actually, it's Ensenada PD's case," he continued. "I'm with the LAPD's Interpol Liaison Unit. I was just assisting them, but they were looking at Skylar as a suspect in a murder out there. A guy by the name of Jon P. Jarvi. He was found stabbed to death on the side of a dirt road."

"Any idea why Skylar would want to kill Jon?"

"Well, he took out about fifty-five thousand dollars in loans the day before he was murdered," Bahena said. "That probably had something to do with it."

It didn't take long for Newport detectives to catch up on the case. They re-interviewed Greg Logan, who told them about Skylar's request to leave JP's red Chevy Astro van at his Long Beach company, Jet Automotive, for a while. They talked to the Wells Fargo bank manager who'd cashed JP's $50,000 check. And after serving a search warrant on the Deleons' joint account, it was obvious Skylar and Jennifer suddenly came into a large lump of cash the day after Jarvi died. They put $21,000 into their account. Receipts recovered from the Deleon home showed they spent another $2,200 on a ring that same day. And paperwork from Mo Beck Stern Drive Co. in Costa Mesa, showed Skylar ordered over $18,000 in repairs on a boat.

During a visit to Mo Beck, the boat mechanic told detectives how Skylar flamboyantly laid out $18,000 in crisp hundred-dollar bills for the boat upgrades. He'd never forget that, Mo told them.

But it was the boat theft that made Skylar such an unforgettable customer. With seven grand left on the tab, Skylar's boat disappeared, Mo told investigators.

"I even hired an attorney and sued the guy over it," he said.

"Where does that stand?" Detective Krallman asked.

"We haven't gone to trial yet," he said, "but we've had depositions. Can you believe Skylar's attorney submitted some paperwork acknowledging he had the damn boat?"

The theft may have been bad news for the repairman. But for the investigators, it was a sorely needed stroke of luck.

When the sergeant called, Matt was overjoyed to hear the news.

"We can drop the money-laundering charge and hit him up with grand theft," he said.

Obviously, it still wasn't the charge the two wanted to slap on Skylar. But it would buy them more time to make a charge for the Hawkses' murder stick.

"And before we're through, we're going to get him for murdering Jarvi, too," Sergeant Byington said. "The way things are lining up, he's just as guilty on that one."

As the walls closed in on Skylar in early February 2005, Jennifer lay in a hospital bed giving birth to their second baby. A son this time. Jennifer named him Kaleb. Skylar wasn't there to welcome his son into the world. In fact, as the investigation evolved, it seemed unlikely Skylar would ever be out of confinement long enough to hold his new son. He'd have to settle for Jennifer's visits, when she would lift Kaleb's tiny body up to the glass partition that separates inmates from their visitors. Hailey was always there, too, peering into the glass to watch a father who, even in time, as she grew, she'd still likely never understand.

Investigators again raided the home Jennifer shared with her parents on February 22. Jennifer was forced to stand by with her two children and her mother, Lana Henderson, as police rummaged through their house for the second time in nine weeks. This time, they were also after evidence in JP's murder. The warrant included an order for a DNA sample from Jennifer. Jennifer complied. After all, she was nowhere near JP when he was killed. Just like she was nowhere near the Hawkses when they were dumped overboard. Maybe that knowledge was enough to keep her calm, even brazen enough to casually chat with Detective Krallman without calling an attorney.

"How does Skylar support you and the kids?" the detective asked.

"He doesn't," she answered quickly. "I do. I'm the breadwinner in the family."

"So you know about all the money that comes and goes into the household?"

"Yes," she said. "I handle all of our finances and bills."

"Would you describe your relationship with Skylar as a close one?" he pushed. In a way, his questions were giving her every opportunity to distance herself from her husband and the mounting criminal investigation against him. But at every turn, she pushed away the opportunity.

"Oh, we're very close," she said.

"So you know what he's doing on a day-to-day basis, is that right?"

"Of course," she said. "I know my husband. I'm not a naïve wife."

Investigators, still trying to give her every benefit of the doubt, pressed her family, looking for signs that Jennifer may have had reasons to fear Skylar. Was he an abusive husband? they asked.

"Are you kidding?" her father laughed. "No way. Jennifer would never put up with that."

"Who wore the pants in the family?" Detective Krallman asked him.

"Jennifer," he said. "Jennifer's always in control."

Detective Krallman also knew Skylar parked Jon Jarvi's red van in front of the Hendersons' house for several days before dropping it off at Jet Automotive. He wanted to know what she knew about the van. And the van's owner. Later that afternoon, he brought up the subject.

"Do you remember your husband parking a red van in front of your residence towards the end of December?" he asked.

"No," she said, "I don't know anything about a van."

"Are you sure?" he pushed. "You sure your husband didn't park a van here before he moved it to an automotive shop?"

"Oh, right, now I remember," she said. "It was just so long ago, I forgot. I don't even remember what color it was. Yeah, it was here briefly. But it wasn't like we had it. I think it belonged to some guy my husband served some time with over at the Seal Beach jail. And he just left it in front of our house."

"How long was it in front of your house?" the detective asked.

"It was only here for a minute," she said. "A day, not even. We didn't want it in front of our house. Parking on our street is already atrocious. So we dropped it off at some automotive shop. We figured they'd know what to do with it better than we would."

"And you never met the van's owner?"

"No," Jennifer said. "I never met him."

"So he just came over to the house one day and said, 'Here, here's my car'?"

"Pretty much . . . My husband said the guy was kind of off," she said.

"Did he ever come back and ask for it?"

"No," she said.

"Really? Never?"

"Honestly, I don't know what happened to him," Jennifer said.

"But there was some kind of investigation after that, right?" the detective said.

"Um, yeah, some people came and talked to me," she said. "They were some kind of detectives. I don't know who or from where. I'm not really familiar with the different levels of different police, honestly. But, yes, they came to the house."

"Obviously for some reason," he said.

"I honestly don't remember," she said. "I think . . . Well, not like I wouldn't remember this, it would be a big deal, but if I'm not mistaken, they said they found that . . . That he wasn't . . . I don't know if it was that they couldn't find him?"

"Uh-huh," the detective urged.

"Or if it was because he showed up, um, not alive?"

"Uh-huh," he said again.

"I mean, I don't want to say dead, but . . ."

"But you heard that?" Detective Krallman said.

"Honestly, I don't remember a hundred percent," she said. "I think they said he went down to Mexico for some reason and his throat got slit."

"Oh, they told you that, too, huh?" Detective Krallman said.

"Yeah," she said.

Detective Krallman made a note of her statement. It was true, another police agency had come to her house to talk to her about the van and JP. But he couldn't imagine Detective Bahena and the Mexican officers would tell Jennifer how he was killed. As he left Jennifer's house, Krallman called Bahena to ask about the detail.

"No," Detective Bahena said, "I never told her that man had

his throat sliced up. I couldn't tell her that because I didn't even know. The Ensenada cops just told me he'd been found stabbed, on the side of a road. But I didn't know someone cut his throat. No way."

If Jennifer didn't get that detail from the police, then she knew a lot more than she was letting on. A detail like that is something only the investigators—and the killer—should know.

Krallman didn't believe she participated in the actual murder. Murders. But she knew about them. From his desk at the police station, he reached for the phone, anxious to talk to her again. This time, with another approach. He'd throw her a lifeline. Offer her protection. He'd tell her not to be scared, promise he would see to it she was taken care of, if only she'd cooperate. It could be her last chance to survive this thing. If she could be made to see that, maybe she'd talk.

The phone rang.

"Hello," Jennifer answered.

"Jennifer, it's Keith Krallman, from the police department. How are you?"

"I'm okay," she said.

"Everything going okay or what?"

"Yeah," she said.

"Look, I know you feel like you are being pulled in a hundred different directions," he said.

"I do."

"You know, Jennifer, I can tell things aren't okay, just by talking with you earlier today," he said. "I could read your face, your body language. And I could tell you're under a lot of pressure. You've got a brand-new baby boy who needs his mom. You've got a beautiful thirteen-month-old girl. She's just a doll. I'm not just trying to placate you, I'm being honest."

"No, I understand," Jennifer said.

Krallman remembered how the detectives first found her cleaning a church. He remembered her family went to that church often, were active members. He decided to play on that knowledge, hoping there was a sense of faith deep within this woman, if he could just help her find it.

"But I've got to tell you, the only thing, right now," he said,

"I'm having a hard time with you. I know you want to do the right thing. I know you want to be an honorable, Godly woman."

"Yes," she said. "I do."

"Then I think doing that right thing starts right now," he said fervently. "Right now, Jennifer. It just takes a decision on your part not to sit there. Because the man upstairs, God, knows what's going on, Jennifer."

"I know that," she said meekly.

"He knows the truth, the decisions we've made. It's just whether or not we confront those demons, if you will."

"Right," she said.

"And you know, Jennifer, I personally would like to help you out. Whatever way I can. But I simply want to know the truth."

"I know," she said. "Really, I understand."

"And I know you want to tell me everything that's going on, Jennifer. I know you do."

"What I know, yeah," she said. "But it's not everything."

"But you know something," he said. "And I can tell you want to be truthful. Do what's right here, Jennifer. And if you need my help, I will. I'm your ear, I'll listen. But this is a double homicide. It's not just going to go away."

"I'm just—" she paused. "I'm . . . scared."

"She's so close now," he thought. With enough coddling, enough reassurance, she'll talk. He just needed her to believe he could see her as another Skylar victim—even if he wasn't entirely convinced of that. But she needs to feel safe enough to talk. He pushed on.

"I'm just trying to make the right decisions for my children," she added. "It's bad enough that Daddy's not here right now."

"Jennifer, you know what you need to do in order to protect your children," he said. "You need to do the right thing."

"I have a little bit of a control thing," she said. "You know, where I like to know everything and have a little say in everything. But I'm learning that I don't. I think that's my struggle right now. I think I'm being tested right now."

"Well, I can anticipate what the next step is going to be, if things stay the way they are right now," the detective said bluntly, hoping to force her into seeing reality.

"More charges?" she said. "For Skylar?"

"Yes."

"For me?"

"Uh-huh," he said honestly. "And, Jennifer, until then, be honest with yourself. You don't want to worry and look over your back every time you walk out the front door, worried the cops will keep showing up with search warrants, interrupting your life."

"I know, but I'm afraid of other things, too."

"Like what? Who?"

"John," she said, falling back on the lie she and Skylar had fed the detectives since the beginning. "Skylar's dad showing up at my door."

"I can take steps to protect you, if that's true, Jennifer," he said, not altogether buying her excuse. "But I can't do anything if my hands are tied behind my back. If you don't talk to me. You need to take that next step because you are a grown woman, capable of making your own decisions. Just tell me. What do you think happened to the Hawkses?"

There was a long pause. A sigh into the phone. Then, she answered him.

"I don't know," she said.

"Did you kill Tom and Jackie Hawks?"

"No."

"Did Skylar?"

"No."

"Did you have anything to do with their disappearance?"

"No."

"Nothing at all?"

"No," she said. But she began to cry.

"Did you have anything to do with this guy who dropped off his van at your house?"

"No," she said again.

He decided to change tactics. Get harder.

"Jennifer, what if I told you we recovered the Hawkses' Honda Civic in Mexico, and someone told me you helped drive the car down there with Skylar? That someone saw you?" he said. "Does that information scare you?"

"Yeah," she said.

"I know it does," he said. "I'd be scared, too. So, we're at a crossroads. And now is your chance to do the honorable thing. The Godly thing. What are you going to do?"

"I want to do the right thing," she said. "It's just hard. Really hard. I need to think. Talk to my lawyer. And I'll be in touch after that."

No, she wouldn't, he thought. It's over. She wasn't going to talk. Not now. Probably not ever. He'd spent over an hour on the phone with her, begging her to come clean, even offering her protection. But in the end, she wouldn't betray Skylar. Even if it meant saving herself.

Later, as police went through stacks of receipts noting deposits and purchases made in the days surrounding Jon's murder on December 27, they could only chuckle at one particular purchase. As a cop working around homicide for a few years, you tend to develop a black sense of humor. It kicked into gear now as they read a receipt for $936 in sex toys, including a blow job kit, a cock box shaft, and a large contraption with an enormous rubber penis protruding into the air called the VersaCock. The purchase was made online at 1:18 a.m. on December 28, just hours after Jon Jarvi's brutal killing.

Even more odd were pictures downloaded from websites of men in various stages of gender reconstruction surgery. The pictures illustrated how a man's penis could be fashioned, through surgery, into looking like a woman's vagina. No telling how such pictures figured into the increasingly twisted world that Jennifer and Skylar lived in. But no doubt it had something to do with the receipts the detectives found for payments Skylar made to a doctor specializing in sex change operations. As Skylar was booked into jail, a full physical exam showed all his boy parts were properly in place. If he'd ever considered such an operation, he never went through with it. So, for now, the cops simply shook their heads in amusement and carried on.

On February 26, 2005, Matt Murphy faced Skylar's lawyer in court. Edward Welbourn was a competent defense attorney, but clearly had no idea just yet who he had for a defendant. Ed broached Matt about a plea bargain on the theft charge, something that might have Skylar home after a few months in jail.

"No way," Matt told him flatly.

As Judge Susanne S. Shaw took her seat in the Santa Ana courtroom, Matt aggressively argued against Skylar's right to bail. He publicly declared for the first time that Skylar was "the main suspect in a double homicide out of Newport Beach." And just to make sure Judge Shaw fully understood, Matt announced Skylar was also a suspect in a third murder, something related to the theft charge.

"The People's very strong position is that he poses a substantial risk to the community," Matt said. "We also believe he is a flight risk."

Matt's candid announcement in court made newspaper headlines. "Yacht Buyer Is Suspected of Killing O.C. Pair," the *Los Angeles Times* would announce in the next morning's paper. A shocked Ed Welbourn told reporters he had no idea what the third murder was about. But the allegations were enough for Judge Shaw to deny Skylar bail. He'd remain in jail until trial. Already, they were so close.

Detective David White was weary from combing through so many telephone numbers. After a while, the digits have a way of blurring together. Still, it fell to him to get a name behind every number on cell phone bills belonging to Skylar, Jennifer, Alonso, Tom, and Jackie. He narrowed down the time frame to the weeks just before and after the death of Jon P. Jarvi and the disappearance of Thomas and Jackie Hawks.

But to do that, he had to write up the search warrants that forced the cell phone companies to hand over the call logs. Once he got those, he had to write up new search warrants for every number he couldn't readily identify with a simple phone call. And there were a lot of those.

Sergeant Byington could only look on in pity at Detective White, who worked for hours, non-stop, tracking every call.

"It's a logistical nightmare," Sergeant Byington said. "So

many times the phone may be registered to one person, but that doesn't mean Skylar was calling that person. It's a matter of finding out who the registered phone owner might know that has a connection to Skylar."

But a few things immediately stood out from the calls. Skylar dialed one number repeatedly in the weeks leading up to November 15. In fact, Detective White counted 132 calls to that same number in the month before the Hawkses disappeared.

"Who the hell was he calling that much?" Sergeant Byington asked.

"Your runaway," Detective White said. "Alonso Machain."

Clearly, Alonso, the naïve jailer who'd allowed Skylar the inmate to befriend him, was in way over his head. With that level of contact, it was likely he was much more than just some signature for hire.

It wasn't the only thing they noticed about Alonso's calls. Every single time someone makes a cell call, the signal hits a nearby cell phone tower, and that signal is logged by the phone company. Skylar's cell pinged off cell phone towers in and around Catalina Island for several hours the night of November 15. It was good evidence, even if it wasn't all that surprising to detectives. But Alonso's phone pinged off the same towers that night.

"You know what that means," Sergeant Byington told Matt. "He was on that boat, right alongside Skylar."

It's why he was so scared whenever he talked to police. It's why he ran. He knew at the time of his arrest that investigators were only scratching the surface on his involvement. It was only a matter of time before they found out everything.

"Fine," said a determined Matt, "then he'll also go down on a first-degree murder charge, right alongside Skylar."

Even more than that, Matt thought, at this point, he could convince just about any jury in the world to hand them both the death penalty.

Nailing down Jennifer's role in it all, however, worried Matt the most. He knew she was involved somehow. She was the one who called Jim Hawks after she found his card on the *Well Deserved*, and who'd lied about seeing the Hawkses off to Mexico. She was the one who'd escorted her husband to their Arizona bank, and then to Ensenada to drop off the car. And she was the one who'd promised the notary more money to backdate papers.

"And," Detective White pointed out, "all those calls Skylar was making from the deck of the *Well Deserved*? They were to Jennifer's cell. He called her twelve times that night."

"Twelve times!" Matt said, astonished. "There's no woman in my life I've ever had to call twelve times in one night. But you know what I think? You know why he called her twelve times that night? He was checking in with her every step of the way. He was giving her a blow-by-blow of the action."

In fact, that's exactly what happened. He called her when he got on the boat. He called her when they were out to sea. He called when he overpowered the couple, when he punched in the autopilot for Catalina waters. He called just before he dumped their bodies. And again, when the job was done.

"She's into this up to her eyeballs," Matt said. "Every new detail we get supports that. Think about it, she's living in a nineteen-by-nineteen–foot room with Skylar, and she doesn't hear any of those hundred and thirty-two calls he makes to Alonso? No way. She knows exactly what was going on."

"There's just one call that I can't figure out," Detective White said. "Jackie's family gave us her last cell phone bill. It shows her last call going out at six a.m. on the morning of November sixteenth. She dialed Skylar's number. The call only lasts a few seconds. But it's where the call is coming from that's weird. Nowhere near Catalina Island. It's pinging off a tower in San Ysidro out in San Diego County."

The town sat just north of the Mexican border. Had the Hawkses really driven to Mexico before they were killed, the investigators wondered.

"Or maybe," Matt theorized, "maybe they were kidnapped and killed in Mexico. For all we know, she was stashed in the trunk of some car and randomly dialed a number on her phone, trying to get some help."

"If that's true," Sergeant Byington said, "she certainly chose the wrong person to call."

CHAPTER TWENTY-SEVEN

Alonso Machain may have been living in Mexico, but he was carrying so much guilt, he felt like he was living in hell. It was easier for Skylar, who grew up in chaos; Alonso was raised in a loving and deeply religious home. How could he even face his mother? Or his father, the man who still spent so many Sunday mornings as a church volunteer, helping the priest perform communions and baptisms? Alonso thought of his own Sundays in church, when he listened to his Catholic priest speak of morals, of right versus wrong, and consequences for those who participated in sin.

He may have escaped prosecution, but not punishment. In his mind, images from that tragic night played over and over again. He couldn't forget Jackie's sobs as she begged Skylar for mercy.

"How could you do this to us?" she asked Skylar. "You brought your family on our boat. We met your wife, your little girl. Why do this?"

When those moments flashed into his mind, he quickly shut his eyes and prayed for relief. But it didn't come. He was guilty. He helped murder two people. And there was only one way he could make amends with God. He knew what he had to do, but he struggled to find the courage to do it. He talked to his parents and told them how he loved them. He talked to his family priest, who told him to do whatever was necessary to find peace with God. Then he called Roy Peterson, his attorney.

"You have to turn yourself in," Roy told him. "Wherever you are, just come in. It's not too late to make this right. I'll call the prosecutor, I'll set everything up for you. But you can't keep running. You're only making it worse for yourself."

"I know," he said. "I'm ready. I'll come home. Just let me spend one last night with my mom and dad. If they can give me that, then I'll talk to the police the next morning and tell them everything."

As Roy hung up with his client that afternoon, he breathed a sigh of relief. Then picked up the phone again and dialed Matt.

Matt was thrilled to hear he'd get another crack at Alonso. He agreed to give Alonso his last night home with Mom and Dad, but placed a police car outside the Machain residence to keep an eye on him. It was there when Alonso had his homecoming, and sat outside, unmoved, until morning. And so did Alonso.

Matt and the detectives were anxious to get the interview started. With new evidence that unfolded in his absence, including two cell phone calls—one to his girlfriend, one to Jennifer—proving he'd been at sea on November 15, Alonso had no choice but to cooperate. Matt would certainly make him understand that. *Come clean this time—or face the death penalty.*

It was the main thought that raced through Alonso's mind on the morning of March 2 as he entered the Newport Beach Police Department. It was 9 a.m. when he took his seat in the police chief's conference room. Sergeant Byington was already there. Detectives Evan Sailor and Keith Krallman joined in. It was surely an intimidating room for Alonso to walk into. But oddly, as he began to speak, Roy Peterson at his side, Alonso seemed more relaxed than investigators had ever seen him.

"We're all ears," Matt told him. "I can't promise you any kind of special treatment based on what you are about to say. But I can tell you, if you lie to us, even just once, you are worthless to me."

Alonso nodded solemnly.

"So tell us," Matt said, "what happened to Tom and Jackie Hawks."

Ten minutes into the conversation, Matt had no doubts this time that Alonso was telling the truth. For eight hours straight, he answered every question. And volunteered whatever they didn't ask. He told them how Skylar had the murder all planned out, weeks in advance. Skylar said he was a hired hit man for the Mexican Mafia and had been hired to get rid of some bad people. He offered Alonso $2 million to help out. He talked about trips to the mall to buy stun guns and handcuffs.

"He even went up to this group of Mexican day laborers," Alonso said. "You know, the ones who stand around along the street waiting for work? He gave one of them one hundred dollars to take a hit with the stun gun so he could make sure he could cuff him before the shock wore off."

He told them, too, about their aborted attempt that first afternoon when they met Tom and Jackie.

"[Tom] was real stand-offish when we first met him," Alonso said. "Like he didn't believe us or something. He took us on the boat, but he wouldn't take us out to sea. So we didn't do it that day."

After the meeting, Skylar called Jennifer down to meet the Hawkses, make them feel more at ease, Alonso said.

In another room, Detective White scrambled to verify that detail. It was an easy way to check if Alonso was still telling the truth. Detective White pulled Skylar's phone records and scanned for a call from Skylar to Jennifer on the date and time Alonso alleged it happened. And the call was there, just like he said.

Detective White sent the message back into the interview room, to Sergeant Byington. "He's telling the truth," he said. "The call's there."

Alonso told them he didn't stick around for Jennifer's meeting, but he knew it happened because Tom was a lot nicer to them after that. And then there were Jackie's words before she died.

"She kept telling him, you know, just asking how he could do this to them after they met his pregnant wife and little baby," said Alonso, looking anguished at the memory of Jackie begging for their lives. "She was having a really hard time with it. But Skylar didn't care. He just went on, forcing them to sign all those papers. It was horrible. Horrible."

For detectives, it was a riveting meeting. They learned about Myron Gardner, a former boss to Skylar and Alonso, who helped bring in extra muscle after Skylar had seen how physically fit his intended victim was.

"But Myron wasn't on the boat with us that night," he said. "He sent us some other guy. I never met him before. He just went by some initials. Something like TC, I think."

They grilled him about the mysterious "TC." Alonso told them everything he could—that they picked him up in Long Beach, where he was a member of some gang. He gave a description, a huge man, black, maybe around 40. But Machain didn't know where "TC" lived, his phone number, what he did for a living. There was a lot of work ahead.

"Did TC throw that anchor overboard?" asked Sergeant Byington, still believing Skylar didn't have the guts to do it himself.

"No, that was Skylar," said Alonso, recounting how mad Skylar got after Tom, desperate to fight back, kicked him in the groin. He got so mad, he picked up that anchor and hurled it overboard. But it was "TC" who kicked Tom in the back, forcing him off his feet. He winced remembering how Jackie's head slammed against the ship's side rail before going over, tumbling behind her husband.

"Alonso," Matt said, "if Tom and Jackie drowned that night, can you tell us why there's a phone call from her cell the next morning?"

"That was me," he said. "Skylar told me to drive to Mexico and make a call with her phone. That way, when her relatives saw her bill, they'd think she and Tom did drive to Mexico that night. And then, you know, maybe they'd just think something bad happened to them over there."

Sitting there with Alonso, it was hard to picture him on the boat that night. He seemed like a decent enough guy, if not that bright—someone who probably would have led an uneventful but honest life, if not for meeting Skylar Deleon.

Finally, Detective Sailor asked the question on everyone's mind. He'd spent the most time with Alonso, grilling him about the paperwork on seven different occasions. He talked with Alonso's parents and knew he came from good, God-fearing people.

"So why'd you agree to do this, Alonso?" the detective said. "How did Skylar talk you into this?"

"I don't know," said Alonso, looking down as regret overwhelmed him. "He told me they were bad. Really bad. He said no retired probation officer could live like that. That he really made his money running drugs. He made it sound like we would make a lot of money if we just got rid of people who were bad anyway. And I believed him."

It was near 5 p.m. when, his confession complete, Alonso was led back to jail.

"Do you believe him?" Sergeant Byington asked Matt.

"Yeah," Matt said. "This isn't a sophisticated kid. He's not savvy enough to make up a story like that."

"I'll write up an arrest warrant for Myron," Detective Sailor said.

"And let's to work on finding out who 'TC' is," Sergeant Byington told his detectives.

"Yeah, let's get those guys hooked up," Matt said. "Then you know who I want? Jennifer."

Matt had listened in disgust when Alonso talked about Jennifer. He pictured her, six months pregnant, dragging her 1-year-old by the hand onto that ship, parading her toddler around for the people her husband was about to murder. Skylar might have been the one who physically pushed that couple over, but as Matt saw it, Jennifer killed them just the same.

"Tom was a lifelong probation officer," Matt said. "He was used to dealing with dirtbags. I bet he took one look at Skylar and saw another dirtbag. He could sense it. But Jennifer, she threw him off. I'm telling you, if it weren't for Jennifer Deleon, I swear Tom and Jackie would still be alive today."

Brand-new mommy or not, Matt resolved to have her in cuffs as soon as possible. For now, he'd have to be satisfied hitting Skylar with the charge he really deserved—murder. With

Alonso's confession, Matt had plenty to make that charge stick. "And that feels great," he said.

Only two days would slip by before the media circus began anew. Reporters, photographers, and television cameras filled the small Santa Ana courtroom. Journalists representing outlets all over Southern California turned out to catch a glimpse of the three men charged with murdering Tom and Jackie Hawks. The mystery behind what happened to the much-beloved, long-missing Newport Beach yacht owners had apparently been solved, and no one wanted to miss out on the story.

Skylar sat stoically as he waited for the judge. He wore the bright orange jumpsuit assigned to all inmates. Cuffs shackled his wrists and ankles. Myron Gardner was there, too. He didn't resist when police arrived the day before to arrest him at a gas plant in the city of El Segundo, where he was working a job for Total-Western. And Alonso was in court, looking desperately uncomfortable. He didn't look at Skylar. He couldn't.

Matt Murphy stood before the judge discussing the charges. The murder offense carried special allegations, because the crime included multiple deaths and was committed for financial gains. The two special circumstance enhancements meant the district attorney could go after the death penalty, if they're convicted.

Attorneys for all three defendants entered "not guilty" pleas on behalf of the clients. Alonso was terrified. His attorney told him Matt would eventually offer him a reduced sentence, after he testified at trial. At the very least, he expected the DA not to go after the death penalty. Alonso would live. And that was something to be thankful for. For now, he'd await his fate in a separate jailhouse, safe from Skylar's clutches. Matt didn't want anything happening to the prosecution's star witness.

From time to time, Skylar looked out into the courtroom, scanning the crowd for Jennifer. She was there, perched in the fourth row, gently rocking 3-week-old Kaleb. The infant, nestled in a soft lavender blanket, was lulled into sleep, blissfully oblivious to the drama unfolding around his parents. After court, Jennifer smiled for reporters and told them how her husband was a former child actor. In fact, he even had recurring roles in the hit children's show *Power Rangers*, she bragged.

How was she holding up, reporters wanted to know. Surely, it must be horrible to see her husband charged with murder just as she'd given birth to their son, they said. Was she afraid for Skylar, they asked?

"I'm just beside myself," she answered demurely. "As any wife would be."

And to a local newspaper reporter, she added, "These last few months have been horrible. I'm trying, for my kids, to keep their lives as normal as possible."

From his side of the aisle in court, Ryan seethed. It was hard watching Jennifer, sitting there with her baby, knowing she helped her husband cover up what he did. But it wasn't just her. Myron's family was there, too. Ryan looked on with icy coldness. Outwardly, he never flinched. But inside, he struggled to control the wild rage building in him.

"I just hate them all, everything they represent," he said afterward. "These were people who were too lazy to go out and make their own money. They couldn't earn it themselves. So they had to go out and murder a retired couple. So I have no sympathy. I hate them. And when their family members walk into court, I hate them, too."

Alonso's parents were in court that day, as well, sitting side by side. They watched the Hawks family ever so briefly, taking in their emotionless faces. They looked over several more times that morning, as if they wanted to somehow convey to the family, if only in a pleading glance, how sorry they were for it all. But Ryan didn't look back. Still, he felt it, every time their eyes stole a glimpse in his direction. It was their son who finally confessed. If not for his story, nailing Skylar could have been damn near impossible.

"I know his guilt led him to eventually do the right thing," Ryan said outside of court. "But I just can't forget he's the one who took my mom down with a stun gun. I can't stop thinking about that."

On the evening of March 9, Ryan appeared on the CNN show *Nancy Grace*, to talk about his lost parents.

"I know that they are together," he said. "And I know that one doesn't work without the other, so, I guess I'm thankful for that."

"Ryan," Nancy said, "when I think of my mom, I think of her playing the piano, and when I think of my dad, I think of him going to work on the railroad. When you think of your parents, what's your vivid memory?"

"I think of my dad fishing," he said. "Or doing some kind of creative water activity. And I think of my mother just yelling at him, 'Get back on the boat. Do some work, old man!' It's clear as day. And I constantly relive it in my mind every single day. But, God, we sure do miss them. And I only hope that all this will be answered truthfully, which I'm determined it will. And that my family has some answers. No matter what, justice will prevail."

"Ryan, Ryan," Nancy said, "I wish the very same."

CHAPTER TWENTY-EIGHT

Detective Jay Short could only shake his head in frustration thinking of the task Sergeant Byington had just handed him.

"I need you to find the gang member that was on the yacht with Skylar and Alonso."

"Okay," Detective Short said, happy to pitch in on the investigation that had gripped the hearts of so many in the department. A lot of man-hours had gone into it so far. But clearly, Skylar's arrest wasn't the end point. There was more work ahead, more arrests on the horizon.

"What do we know about this guy so far?" Detective Short asked.

"That he's out of Long Beach," Sergeant Byington said. "And he's black."

"That's it?" Detective Short said, hoping the sergeant was joking.

"Oh yeah, he's an older gangbanger, maybe about forty," the sergeant said. "He's a big guy, muscular type. And he goes by initials."

"That's it!" Detective Short said again, this time with a hefty dose of sarcasm in his voice. "So, I'm guessing we don't have which initials, right?"

"No, you're not right," the sergeant shot back jokingly. "It's TC. Or maybe CT."

"Maybe?" Detective Short said.

"Yeah, maybe," the sergeant said. "And maybe neither one. Alonso's not sure. Sorry. You've got your work cut out. But you've got to find him."

With a pat on the shoulder, he walked away, leaving Detective Short to figure it out with his partner, Detective Joe Wingert.

The men started on the computer, scouring their databases in search of all Long Beach gang members on record who went by initials. The computer spit back a list so long, the detectives could only laugh out loud in frustration.

"Okay, let's narrow this thing down, or we're screwed," he said.

They entered more search terms: men in their late thirties to early forties, African-American men, men who weren't in prison on the night of November 14. The list dropped to thirty-nine names. Still too long. But more manageable.

"Let's check out Skylar's cell phone records," Detective Short said. "Maybe we'll get lucky and one of the numbers comes back registered to a TC."

"No such luck," Detective White said when they approached him. "So far, no one with initials comes up in the bunch."

"Okay, then let's look at the calls to other Long Beach numbers," Detective Short suggested.

Poring over the digits, another calling pattern stood out. Skylar made multiple calls to two Long Beach numbers in particular in the days leading up to November 15. One was registered to Myron Gardner. The other to a woman, someone named Antoneisha Farrington.

"Who the hell is Antoneisha Farrington?" Detective Short said.

She was, in fact, the girlfriend of Orlando Clement, according to Detective Sean Hunt. Detective Hunt was a cop for the Long Beach Police Department, working in its gang unit. Newport Beach investigators called him once they began their search for the unidentified Long Beach gangbanger with the unknown initials. They needed somebody who knew these gang members personally—their nicknames, tattoos, who they ran with, and who they didn't. That was Sean Hunt. He knew these guys because he walked their neighborhoods, talked to them, to their families. He treated them fairly when it was warranted, and took them to jail when necessary. And it was often necessary. The gangs in Long Beach were some of the most active, and deadly, in all of California.

As Detective Hunt listened to the scant clues on the gang member they were looking for, he already had a few ideas who the mystery man could be. It had to be somebody ruthless, somebody willing to kill strangers on short notice. And for no other reason than someone asked him to. Maybe promised him some cash for the job. Orlando was a tough son of a bitch. He stood somewhere around 6'4" tall. Beefy guy, too. That much certainly fit the description of the guy they were looking for.

But Hunt doubted Orlando was the guy.

"Yeah, Orlando's one of ours," he said. "He's with Insane Crips. But he's too young. The man you're looking for is about forty. Orlando is only in his twenties."

"How about the initials? Does he go by Orlando or does he have a nickname?" Detective Short asked. "Maybe something with initials?"

"No," Detective Hunt said. "I've never heard anyone call him by any initials. But we can ask him. He's just sitting up in prison now. Been there a few weeks on a drug charge."

"Sounds good to me. Let's go pay him a visit," Detective Short said.

Orlando had no idea an entourage of detectives would be paying him a visit. So he must have been stunned when the Delano prison officials escorted him into a room filled with investigators. Detectives Short, Wingert, and Hunt waited for Orlando to take his seat. Hunt's partner, Detective Jim Kloss, another expert on the intricate workings of Long Beach gangs, joined in. Orlando gave a nod to Hunt and Kloss. He knew them all too well.

"So, what's up?" Orlando finally said. "Why am I here?"

"These are Newport Beach detectives, Orlando," Sean Hunt said. "They think you might be able to help them with a case they're working on."

"Yeah?" he said. "What case is that?"

"Do you know a guy by the name of Skylar Deleon?" Detective Short asked.

Just because Orlando was an inmate, it didn't mean he had to cooperate. He could say nothing. He could ask for an attorney.

But he didn't. Instead, he nodded his head and told them everything.

"Yes, I do," he told them. "I don't know him too much, but I met him."

According to Orlando, he only met Skylar once.

"And that was enough," he said. "That's one crazy white boy."

"How did you come to meet him?" Detective Short asked.

"He worked with my friend Myron," he said. "Myron said this guy he worked with was looking for someone to help him with a job."

"What kind of job?" Detective Short asked.

"Just acting as the heavy, you know, standing around to make sure nobody gave him any trouble while he took care of some business," Orlando said.

But he didn't know all of the details until Skylar drove into his neighborhood one afternoon last November to tell him personally. And that's when Orlando got scared.

"Skylar scared you?" Detective Hunt said incredulously. "How exactly did this kid scare a big tough gangbanger like yourself?"

"Look," Orlando said, "a white guy coming alone into my neighborhood, to meet with gang members, and he's not the least bit worried about his safety? I figure this guy's got to be crazy."

"So what happened?" Detective Short asked.

"I told Myron no way," he said. "I didn't want anything to do with this guy."

"So why do you think Myron asked you in the first place?" Detective Short wanted to know.

"John told him to ask me," he said.

"John?" Detective Short said.

"My dad," Orlando said. "Well, I'm pretty sure he's my dad. That's what my mom says. But I don't call him Dad."

"His real name is John Fitzgerald Kennedy," Detective Hunt said. "And I'm not kidding. That's actually what his mother named him. But he doesn't go by JFK. He goes by another set of initials. His gang name is Crazy John. But everybody calls him CJ."

He was 39, a muscular guy, and mean. He fit the bill exactly. And he was Myron's buddy.

"That's going to be your guy," Detective Hunt said after the interview. "I'm certain of it."

As the investigators made the long drive home from Delano prison, Detective Short called his office. Sergeant Byington was practically giddy to learn they probably just nailed another one of Skylar's partners in crime. Detective Short suggested the sergeant get together a photographic line-up of mug shots to show Alonso and see if he identified John. All Sergeant Byington had to do was run John's name, and a list of prior bookings, complete with mug shots, would come up. He got to work setting up a photo of John alongside five other shots of men with appearance and stature similar to their suspect's. If Alonso positively identified John, it would be enough for an arrest.

"Alonso, do you see the guy that was on the boat with you in any of these pictures?" Sergeant Byington asked as the men stood over the six-pack of pictures.

"That's him," said Alonso, pointing to one shot without hesitation. From jail, he was still working with police in the hope of redeeming himself. In hope of escaping the death penalty. "That guy there. He was on the boat with us. I'm sure."

The detectives were still making their way home from the prison visit when Detective Short's phone rang.

"Jay," Sergeant Byington said, "Alonso just identified John as their third man. Detective Sailor will write up the arrest warrant from here and fax it over to the Long Beach department. It'll be there waiting for you. Let's go pick him up."

Detective Short snapped his cell phone shut and broke the good news to the other officers in his car.

"You're going to make a lot of cops in the Long Beach gang unit awfully happy today," Detective Hunt said. "We've been waiting for a reason to put this guy away for a long time.

In particular, Detective Hunt had been waiting to see John screw up so badly, he'd end up exactly where he belonged—in jail for the rest of his life.

"I hate that guy," Hunt said. "I've hated that guy since the moment I met him. And he hates me."

"Let me through," John screamed at the Long Beach police officers blocking the pathway to his nephew's house. Yellow crime-scene tape framed the yard, making it off limits to anyone but investigators.

It was a homicide scene. And there was no way police would let John through—even if the house did belong to his beloved nephew.

Aviante Hale, 21, lived in the North Long Beach home with his stepfather, Gregory Clover, since his mother, John's sister, passed away in May of 1997. Robin Kennedy's decomposing body had been found in the apartment of a Long Beach man, who stabbed her to death following a heated argument. Afterward, a lost Aviante clung to his uncle for solace. And John, aching over the loss of his sister, was happy to have him around. Aviante looked up to John so much, he followed after him into the gang life, even earning the gang name "Little CJ."

But it was that gang life that police believe led to the drive-by shooting that cut down Little CJ as he stood in the driveway of his home around 1 in the morning on August 1, 2004.

"I've been hit!" neighbors heard him howl before he collapsed onto the pavement. He died there, before an ambulance could even be called.

The shooting that cut down John's beloved nephew took place just three-and-a-half months before John even heard of Tom and Jackie. And he was devastated by the loss. Ironic that he could be so overwhelmed by grief when it touched his own life, and yet, just fifteen weeks later, would prove himself completely incapable of empathy for the Hawks family.

For the moment, he wanted revenge on the gang members responsible for taking Little CJ from him. But to do that, he needed all the details he could get from the cops.

"Let me through," he scowled again when he saw Detective Hunt's face. "I'm a city employee, damn it. I have a right to be here."

In fact, John did work for the city. But Detective Hunt always thought that was the biggest joke of all. Somehow, John was hired to work in an office the city created to promote gang prevention. In the last decade, the city invested $3.5 million into a gang intervention and prevention program. John was one of their gang prevention officers. It was just a civilian position. He didn't carry a gun or a police badge. Still, his appointment was a controversial one. The unit's supervisor, former LA County probation officer Alvin Bernstein, reasoned that only someone who has "been there" could relate to the young men considering a life in the gangs. The problem with that, Detective Hunt frequently told Alvin, was that John never stopped being a gang member himself. He'd been one since he was 13 years old. And a guy like that didn't change just because the city gave him an employee badge.

"He was snowing the city," Detective Hunt said. "He was working both sides of the fence. And he knew I knew it. So we never got along."

In fact, the detective suspected CJ used his position to get information from cops and city officials on pending investigations. It put John in the unique position to hear when his friends were under investigation, and then tip them off to everything, Detective Hunt realized.

"So what do you think of that murder case?" John would often say to detectives Hunt and Kloss.

"Oh, you know, we're still just working it," was all they'd ever answer.

So they certainly didn't want him in on his nephew's crime scene. In response, an enraged John pushed his way across the line anyway. In response, officers hit him with a Taser gun. He dropped to his knees. When he recovered, police arrested him for obstruction.

The clash was the culmination of more than a decade of run-ins Detective Hunt had with John, who grew up along the streets east of the 710 Freeway. More than 1,300 gang members live in the area, police estimate.

"And once you're in, gang members stay gang members. Unless they move far, far away. Or die," Detective Hunt said.

As a kid, John bounced from house to house. Various relatives took turns raising him. But trouble started early for John, who spent time in the California Youth Authority for battery. He launched into a life that cultivated his penchant for violence. And for the rest of his life, he drifted in and out of jail, with more than a dozen arrests on his record, including the four years he spent in prison for attempted murder.

When he wasn't serving time, he trained for an underground version of the extreme sport ultimate fighting. And hung out at Grandma Robinson's house. She wasn't actually John's grandmother. That's just what they called her, all the gang members who hung out at her little home on the corner of 20th Street and Martin Luther King Boulevard. Her sons, grandsons and their friends congregated on her front steps, drinking beers and playing music. It's not clear if Grandma, an elderly woman who lived hooked up to an oxygen tank, was aware her home had become a magnet for ICG members. But it had, in fact, become such a symbol for gang life, the famous rapper Snoop Dogg, himself a former Long Beach Crips gang member, shot one of his videos outside of her house.

Still, not just any gang member could hang at Grandma's. You had to be a veteran. You had to be a shot caller. And that was John. He'd been in the gang long enough, put in enough time behind bars, that he'd earned the respect of his crew.

But running a gang wasn't the only thing he learned from his rough life on the streets. He'd run up against the system so many times, he learned how to work that, too. He sucked up to former probation officer Alvin Bernstein, and was rewarded with his city job.

And so began John's double life.

At times, he went to community meetings, presented reports

to the city council about gang prevention programs, even became active with a local church.

"He was learning the scriptures, spoke a few times in church," said Pastor Leon Wood, with the North Long Beach Community Prayer Center. "Then, under my leadership, he began studying to become a minister. He wanted to be a pastor someday. He was a role model for the members of his former gang, because they trusted him and he had changed. We even had a name burial ceremony one day, where we buried his gang name, Crazy John. He was really moving forward."

In public, John talked about his kids, a 5-year-old daughter, another daughter in high school, and a teenage son who lived with his mom in Las Vegas.

He seemed so dedicated, John convinced many community officials he had become a different man.

But not Detective Hunt—he saw the other times. On patrols with the city, he caught John at Grandma's house, hanging with the old crowd. To Detective Hunt, that meant John was still nothing more than a run-of-the-mill gangbanger. And Hunt treated him accordingly. He even rolled up on John one afternoon as he sat in Grandma's yard, puffing a marijuana joint. Detective Hunt busted him for the offense, of course. And John was stunned.

"Hey, Hunt, why are you always riding me?" he demanded. "I'm just working out here."

"So am I," Detective Hunt told him. "So am I."

"John always thought I was picking on him," Detective Hunt said. "But I was fair. I never made up anything on him, and he knew that. If you're dirty, we'll get you. And John, he was dirty."

His only regret was that he never caught John doing anything big enough to end his game of charades for good. But Hunt knew it would just be a matter of time.

By the time Detective Short and his team arrived back at the Long Beach Police Department, the entire gang unit was already being briefed on the Hawks case. They would assist in the arrest, scouring John's Long Beach neighborhood until they found him.

As Detective Short scanned the room, he was struck by the faces of the cops as they listened to the Hawkses' story. They looked disgusted, heartbroken. Angry. They heard how it was John who kicked Tom in the back that night. Kicked him hard enough to knock him off his feet, forcing Tom, Jackie, and that anchor into a slide down the deck, then over the boat's edge.

"There were a lot of seasoned veterans in that room," Detective Short remembered of the moment. "Guys who had been working gang crimes for years. So you come in with a homicide case to that group, it's not a novel event. But this case, the circumstances here, you could see how they softened up to the story and took such an interest. Before we could finish telling them everything, they just wanted to go get him. But that's been a common theme through this whole thing. Once people get to know what happened to this couple, it pulls at the heartstrings. And you want justice for them."

It was just before 8 p.m. on the night of March 9, 2005, when the officers hit the streets, in search of their man. They cruised all night, but came up empty. Still, Detective Hunt was confident. John rarely wandered too far from his home turf, where he considered himself king of all he surveyed.

Within hours, Hunt was proven right. On the afternoon of March 10, an officer called the detective to let him know he was following a 1988 gold-colored Cadillac—John's car.

"We'll be right there," said Detective Hunt, who was riding in an unmarked police car with his partner and Detectives Short and Wingert. In minutes, the team had John in their sights. They slipped behind his car, but didn't pull out their cop lights just yet. They wanted to observe him for a bit, making sure he was alone, and looking for a place to pull him over. Preferably somewhere not too public, with few places for him to run, if he tried.

But John had been around cops often enough in his life to know when he was being tailed. He knew those unmarked cop cars so well, they might as well have been driving around in good old-fashioned black-and-whites with big red lights on top. He slowed his car to a crawl, then made a U-turn.

"He's doing a little counter-surveillance," Detective Short said as John drove by their car, looking directly at them.

"Yep," Detective Hunt said. "No use pretending now."

John turned his car into a strip mall parking lot at the corner of Long Beach Boulevard and 23rd Street. He wasn't all that far from Grandma's house as he looked up into his rear-view mirror to check his tail. And as he did, police pounced. Cars surrounded him from all directions.

John stepped out of his car, hands raised, and demanded to know what was happening.

"What's up with this?" he said to his old friend, Detective Hunt. "Why are you hounding me now?"

"You're under arrest," the investigator told him.

"For what?" he said.

"Conspiracy to commit murder," Detective Short answered.

At that, John said not another word as police put on the cuffs and escorted him into the back of the cop car.

"He's probably not going to say much," Detective Hunt said. "He knows better."

Back at the Long Beach police station interview room, John said he never met some guy named Skylar. Said he had never even been to Newport Beach before. He may have been a lifelong street thug, but Detective Short was struck by how oddly polite John was as detectives bombarded him with questions. Usually, a gang member of his stature cursed out his interrogators. Told them to go to hell and drop dead. But not John. He patiently listened to them, simply waited for them to finish each query, and then told them with the utmost courtesy, "I have no idea what you are talking about."

"Where were you on the afternoon of November fifteenth?" Detective Short asked him.

"I was working," he said.

"Where?" Short asked.

"I'm a handyman," he said. "I was doing some repair work. Painting a fence."

But it didn't matter. With his connection to Myron, Alonso's identification, and Orlando's story, police had enough to throw John in jail on suspicion of murder. And phone records would reveal a flurry of calls between Skylar's cell, Myron's, and, on the afternoon of November 15, a third phone. The last was registered to John Fitzgerald Kennedy.

It was hard to tell who was more thrilled to see John behind bars—the Newport Beach detectives who had been toiling to find the mystery gang member. Or the Long Beach officers, sick of putting up with John's antics for so many years.

At the evening briefing, when the Long Beach watch commander announced John had been arrested on suspicion of murder earlier that day, the room erupted in applause. The officers stood up in a nod of appreciation to the Newport Beach detectives, for reeling in another one of the Hawkses' murderers, and for taking the notorious gangbanger off their streets, probably for good.

Meanwhile, as Reverend Wood learned of the arrest in his church across town, he scrambled to find his apprentice pastor an attorney. A fundraising effort had to get underway immediately. They'd need a lot of money to hire the lawyer he had in mind—Winston McKesson. Winston was an associate in the Law Offices of Johnnie L. Cochran, Jr., the firm started by the lawyer who'd earned O. J. Simpson his acquittal. Maybe, armed with an attorney from a firm like that, and a little prayer, John would be home soon, Reverend Wood thought.

"Whatever is happening right now," the minister said, "we've lost a young man who was a real agent of change for this city. He's a good man and I won't separate myself from him now."

In the weeks following John's arrest, the city's local paper, the Long Beach *Press-Telegram*, ran a series of articles critical of a gang intervention program that employed men still considered active gang members by the city's own police department. Shortly after, the city disbanded the program for good.

CHAPTER TWENTY-NINE

For months, Jennifer knew investigators were after her. Sergeant Byington, Detective Sailor, Detective Krallman—they all wanted her in jail. But she would do everything she could to remain a free woman. She wasn't on the boat that night. She wasn't in Mexico with Michael and Skylar when JP was killed. Building a case against her would be harder. But not impossible.

And so weeks ago, in early December, before Skylar was ever arrested, Jennifer hired an attorney to represent her. His name was Mike Molfetta. Charismatic, smart, cocky—he was everything a client in trouble could ask for in an attorney.

Mike remembered clearly the day Jennifer walked into his office, seven months pregnant, Skylar at her side. The couple had been referred to his office by another attorney, representing them in the civil case with Mo Beck.

Skylar did most of the talking, telling Mike and his partner, Ed Welbourn, about the couple who'd turned up missing after he bought their boat. And now, Skylar and Jennifer feared police were looking at them as suspects. They needed help, Skylar said.

After the meeting, Mike told Ed they should definitely take the case.

"But I want to take Jennifer," he said. "You handle Skylar . . . I don't want anything to do with him. I think the guy's either a hit man or a serial killer. Either way, my impression is he's a pathological bullshitter."

The meeting was, in fact, the last time Mike would ever have a civil conversation with Skylar.

As for Jennifer, she most certainly would be a suspect, Mike knew that much for sure. She'd already told investigators she had been on the boat, and that she waved good-bye as the Hawkses drove off in their car on November 15. That made her an accomplice, if Skylar did do anything bad to this couple. And if she was going to survive this investigation, she'd likely have to sever all ties with her husband. Eventually, Molfetta would have to convince her of that reality. But at the time, he simply called and told her he'd take her case. Ed would represent Skylar.

Jennifer couldn't know at the time what a lucky break she just caught. Mike was considered one of the best defense attorneys working in the annals of Orange County criminal law—and that was by the county's prosecutors. And they ought to know. Because Mike used to be one of them.

Actually, Mike never wanted to be an attorney at all. He wanted to be a pro football player. And he was, for one season. After playing ball for Occidental College in Los Angeles, he was drafted by a pro team in Europe. But when that ended, he landed back in the United States, and moved onto his dad's couch.

"What the hell are you doing?" his dad finally said after tiring of the sight of his son doing nothing day after day. "Get a job or go to school! I don't care what you do, just do something."

So, on a whim, Mike went to law school.

"Not because I wanted to be a lawyer," Mike said of his decision, "but because it was something to do."

Then, during his second year in school, he landed a job in the Orange County district attorney's office. And when a veteran prosecutor, one who'd handled many high-profile homicide cases, took Mike under his wing, "I was hooked," Mike said.

He soared as a prosecutor. And in 1994, one year before his dad—the man who had forced him off the couch and into law school—would pass away, Mike Molfetta was named Prosecutor of the Year.

The hot-shot prosecutor still had a penchant for athletics, of-

ten playing rugby in his off hours. And it was during one of
those games that he ended up with a fractured neck. With a
lightened caseload, to give him a chance to heal, Mike's bosses
handed him a new challenge—train the two young law clerks
who just came into the office. One was a young woman who
would later become his wife. The other was Matt Murphy. As
Mike prepared Matt to handle his first trial, a gun possession
case, a fast friendship grew between the men.

But that changed the moment Mike made the shocking decision to leave the district attorney's office.

"I was one of those guys that everybody said would never
become a defense attorney," Mike said. "I worked hard, I tried a
lot of cases. I was just one of those guys. But there's a lot of political bullshit you have to put up with when you're a prosecutor, because your boss is a politician. The district attorney is an
elected position. I got sick of the political bullshit."

Eventually, he opened his own law firm, this time representing the accused. And as good as he was at putting bad guys in
jail, he was just as adept at defending them. Suddenly, the
friendship between Matt and Mike turned into a healthy rivalry,
with each trying their damnedest to outdo the other.

"I'll always have a special place in my heart for Matt," Mike
said. "But over the years, I've had the pleasure of kicking his
ass, too." Matt still winces over the memory of Mike beating
him in a drunk-driving case nearly a decade ago. So, learning
Mike was now representing Jennifer, was not a great day. Matt
knew his job just became a lot harder.

"He is, truly, one of the most talented attorneys I've ever
seen," Matt says, begrudgingly. "And I know he thinks he'll get
Jennifer out of this. But he's wrong this time."

"We'll see about that," Mike would say later. "It's the teacher
against the student."

As the arrests began, Mike knew how the game worked well
enough to know Jennifer didn't have much longer. Her days of
freedom were definitely numbered. With that in mind, he called
his old friend to ask for a favor.

"Just call me before you do it," he asked Matt. "If you're going to arrest her, give me a heads-up first. Tell me and I'll turn her in."

"Okay," Matt promised. "You'll get the call before we do anything."

Mike did the best he could to prepare her for the moment. He had long conversations with her, advising her to cooperate, to stay calm. And most important, not to say one thing to the detectives until he was present. She told her attorney she was being watched. She could feel the investigators looking at her as she came and went from her house. He told her yes, they probably were watching—which is why it was more important than ever to stay calm.

And he gave her one other piece of advice: stop talking to Skylar. Since her husband's arrest, she was a frequent visitor to him at the jail, bringing in their children, too. She even insisted that her parents go to the jail, just so he'd never be without someone to see during visiting hours. It was the one piece of advice from her attorney she would not obey. She continued to see Skylar, every chance she could get. In fact, her visits were so frequent, investigators were reluctant to put her in jail too soon because every conversation she had with Skylar, they were listening. It was something Skylar and Jennifer were aware of, so they whispered into the phone a lot, tried mouthing things to each other. Skylar took to bringing a pencil and paper for the visits so he could write clues to what he wanted her to know and hold them up to the glass for her to see. It was often obvious they were discussing the Hawks case. So the investigators decided to give Jennifer enough rope, letting her have access to Skylar a little longer in hopes that she'd say something she'd later regret.

And there was one more reason to delay her arrest—her pregnancy. Of course, she could have given birth behind bars. But that meant the county jail would have to pick up the tab for her medical costs. So they were comfortable to wait it out, letting her have the baby and giving her time to heal, before making her a ward of the county.

On April 8, 2005, Jennifer checked into jail to visit her husband. Her father was there, too, helping her manage the kids. She was startled when she got the tap on her shoulder and looked up to see Mike.

"Hey," he told her. "They're here for you."

It shouldn't have been a surprise, but it was still a shocking moment. She fought tears before kissing her children and then handing them over to her father. Mike told him to take them out of the room. "So they don't have to see their mom being arrested," he said.

A caravan of reporters and photographers waited outside as Jennifer was led away in handcuffs.

"Obviously, someone tipped off the media," Mike said.

Jennifer did exactly as Mike instructed, refusing to speak to Detective Sailor or Sergeant Byington. She referred every question to her attorney. And when Mike finally met with Jennifer in the hours after her arrest, she had one question for him:

"Could I get the death penalty?" she asked. "Will they try to go for that?"

"No," Mike said. "I promise you, that's not going to happen."

"How can you be so sure?" she said.

"Look, of course, I can't predict the future," he said. "I could have a date with the Queen someday, but I'm pretty sure that's never going to happen. And that's what I'm saying here."

Still, no matter how much convincing he did, he knew she'd obsess over the possibility, as remote as it might be. All clients do. It's unavoidable. Mike's had clients throw up on his shoes over it. But Jennifer had so much going in her favor: she was a woman, and it was always hard to get a jury to put a woman to death; she was a mommy to young children; finally, as he saw it, Jennifer was a woman duped by an evil husband. In that regard, she was kind of a victim herself, he thought. Skylar lied to her, told her he inherited the boat, that the money for it came from his dad. She had no idea he murdered people to get it. That's what Mike would make a jury see. Jennifer was a woman not used to male attention. She wasn't very pretty, she wasn't very bright. And so, when Skylar came along, he swept her off her feet just by doing something no other man had done—paying attention to her. She became easy prey for her husband.

She was gullible. And now, he'd tell the jury, she was paying the price for that. Matt would be lucky to get any conviction here, let alone a death sentence.

But even as Mike reassured Jennifer the State of California would never put her to death, he left one thing out.

"There are three things in this world that will happen with a certainty," he would say later. "The sun will rise tomorrow, we'll all pay taxes on April 15, and Skylar Deleon will be put to death."

If looks could kill, no doubt Skylar Deleon would have died in a Santa Ana courtroom on the afternoon of April 15, 2005. On that day, all five defendants gathered before a judge for the first time. And it was the first time John laid eyes on Skylar since he dropped him off after his fateful boat ride back in November. In fact, it was five months to the day since John had taken his trip out on the *Well Deserved*. And now, his hands and feet shackled, as he was escorted into the glass-enclosed inmate box, all John could do was stare at Skylar. And he stared hard, squaring his jaw and squinting his eyes in a look that seemed to say, "If I weren't a bound man, I would destroy you."

It was also the first time Jennifer would make her appearance in court as one of the accused. Skylar avoided John's punishing eyes and instead looked pleadingly at his wife. Her face was emotionless, but they held each other's gaze for several seconds, until a deputy broke the moment and instructed Jennifer to sit on a bench behind her husband, out of his eyesight.

But if emotions ran high inside the defendant box, it was perhaps even more intense out in the courtroom's seating area. One side of the aisle was filled with over a dozen friends and family of the defendants. Reverend Wood was among them, seated with other parishoners from the Community Prayer Center.

On the other side, at least twenty of the Hawkses' loved ones crowded together. Beyond the immediate family, fellow boaters were there, people who volunteered in the early days of the search to post flyers and scour Newport Beach for signs of the much-loved couple. They all wanted to see, in person, the group responsible for taking the lives of their friends. Ryan would later call the experience "gut-wrenching." By now, Matt had shared enough details of Alonso's confession with Ryan that he was aware how his parents met their end. It killed him inside to think about it.

The proceeding itself took only a matter of minutes, as each defendant entered a "not guilty" plea to two charges of murder. Bail was denied for everyone.

The media mob gathered outside of court for a statement from Jennifer's attorney. For weeks, authorities hinted that Skylar was a ringleader in a plot to kill Tom and Jackie. But now to think his pregnant wife had been involved, too. It was a shocking detail that would make great headlines.

"There were some things that Jennifer did," Mike told reporters, "which, arguably, make her part of some sort of plan. To the extent she knew what was going on, that remains to be seen."

Mike announced he'd ask a judge to sever Jennifer's case from Skylar's and the remaining defendants'. He didn't say it, but he already knew to win this thing, Jennifer would simply have to turn on her husband.

As the post-court noise died down, Mike called out to his former co-worker. He had to know just one thing.

"John Fitzgerald Kennedy?" he said. "Is that really that guy's name?"

Matt broke out into a laugh. "Yeah," he said. "That's really the guy's name, if you can believe that. What was his momma thinking?"

Matt picked up his briefcase and walked briskly down the hall, only to realize he was being followed by a very angry black woman. He turned to look at her and recognized her from court—one of John's supporters. Immediately, Matt realized she must have heard him laugh at John's name, and wasn't pleased.

"Hey!" she shouted out to him, walking quickly to catch him. "Hey, you . . ."

Matt stood his ground for a moment, simply staring.

"What's your name?" she demanded. "I demand to know your name!"

Her hostile approach was meant to be intimidating. She was furious, ready to lash out. Matt, however, burst out laughing. He turned on his heel and continued down the hall. "Stick around, sweetheart," he shouted behind him. "You'll find out."

CHAPTER THIRTY

Sergeant Byington and Detective Sailor didn't expect Skylar to talk to them as he walked into the jail's interview room and saw them seated at the table before him. They thought he'd take one look at them, the investigators responsible for throwing him in jail, and tell them to go to hell. But he didn't.

"Now, what do you want?" he said in an exasperated-sounding voice, but settling into his seat anyway.

The detectives were stunned, and elated. They expected his reaction to come closer to every other defendant's they'd ever tried to interview after an arrest. It usually went something like, "Drop dead. And get my attorney."

Instead, Skylar looked positively eager to chat. But to understand Skylar was to understand that he was a man who has craved attention all of his life. He has always wanted to be the big shot, the man with all the answers. And that need was magnified now that he was behind bars, where he was alone, with few friends. And few visitors. His dad, a convicted felon, was forbidden from visiting. His main ally in life, his wife, was also now in jail. And he had no close friends to speak of.

Even his grandmother, the one he'd lived with after high school, had washed her hands of him once she learned the details of his case.

"I don't give one hoot in hell if Jon or Skylar or whatever he goes by now ends up on death row," Marlene Jacobson said after her grandson's arrest. "That's his fault. He had a better start than that and then he just turned around and married Jennifer. She wanted and wanted. And she got everything she wanted. If I have to go up and testify against them, then I will."

Skylar was totally isolated.

And so, in a way, Skylar probably welcomed this command performance from Byington and Sailor. He likely craved this attention, even if the attention came from detectives intent on putting him in prison for the rest of his life.

Skylar eagerly pulled up a chair and awaited their questioning.

"We'd like to talk to you about Jon Jarvi," Byington said.

"I didn't know him that well," Skylar began.

But the detectives made it clear they suspected he knew more than he let on about JP. They were especially curious about the extravagant purchases and large bank deposits Skylar made the day following JP's death. Then there were all those cell phone calls Skylar made near the Mexican border on the day of the murder. And wasn't it curious that he and Jennifer ended up with JP's van in front of their house, even though they supposedly didn't know the man very well?

Skylar backpedaled into familiar territory.

"My dad," he said. "He was working with my cousin, Michael Lewis, on some drug deal with JP."

According to Skylar, his father and cousin hatched the plan to kill JP. Skylar, of course, had nothing to do with it. He only found out JP was dead after the job was already done. And if he said anything about it, his father promised Skylar and his family would be next.

"That's the kind of guy he is," Skylar insisted. "I keep trying to tell you, he's dangerous. And he's connected to dangerous people. My family's life is at stake just by talking to you."

By now, the detectives had seen and heard Skylar's "Daddy did it" tale of woe so often, they had trouble even feigning interest in Skylar's lie.

"He certainly likes that story," Detective Sailor would say to

Sergeant Byington much later. "It's always Dad and it's always Dad's drug deal gone bad."

But neither one bought it this time around. They let him talk for a while. In fact, two hours later, he was still talking. And now, it was the detectives who were getting impatient to get out of there.

"Well, thanks for talking to us, Skylar," said Detective Sailor, trying to wrap up the interview. "If you think of anything else . . ."

An invitation that allowed Skylar to launch into another rant on his father.

"Damn," Detective Sailor told Sergeant Byington as they finally left Skylar that afternoon. "I thought he'd never stop talking. I kept trying to walk away, but he just went on and on."

"Well," Sergeant Byington realized, "we're probably the only people he knows still talking to him."

If the detectives expected the same greeting when they went calling on Jennifer, they would be sorely disappointed. As Jennifer was led into the interview room from her cell and scanned the same scene Skylar did just hours before, she stood still in her tracks.

"No way," she said as soon as she laid eyes on the investigative duo. "No way."

With that, she turned around, refusing even to hear why the detectives had come to see her, and demanded to return to her cell.

Jennifer's reaction to their visit was so drastically different from her husband's, it actually made the detectives laugh out loud. As Jennifer stood with her back turned to them, awaiting a guard to escort her from the room, the sounds of their amusement rang in her ears.

Jennifer's cooperation would have certainly been nice. But they had another ace to draw on—Michael Lewis. As detectives narrowed their investigation efforts, Michael realized his cousin's antics just landed him in a position to go to prison for the rest of his life.

But Michael, living in Oatman, Arizona, spent the months away from his cousin becoming a born-again Christian. And, much like Alonso, he felt deep remorse over what happened, even if Michael had nothing to do with the death himself. So, despite his earlier vow not to turn his cousin in, he changed his mind. He told the police everything about his trip across the border with Skylar and JP that December afternoon. "I don't know exactly what happened on that back road in Ensenada," Michael said. "But it was the last time I ever saw JP."

On August 18, 2005, Matt Murphy formally charged Skylar with murder for financial gain in the slaying of JP Jarvi. It was another charge that could bring him the death penalty.

Matt would have loved to charge Jennifer in that murder, too. But Michael, his key witness, couldn't say how involved Jennifer was in the plot. She did call Michael after the murder and asked him to lie, to say it was she, not Skylar, in Mexico with him, getting Tijuana ice cream that murderous afternoon. And Jennifer did help Skylar get rid of JP's van, riding behind him as he dropped the Astro at the auto lot, and giving him a ride home. That made her an accessory after the fact. And that's how she was charged.

Michael was also arrested in Arizona and extradited to California. Days later, he found himself in chains, sitting on a bus with a load of inmates, all bound for court. Among the crowd sat Skylar and Jennifer. They were separated, men on one section of the bus, women on the other. So Skylar shuffled in his chains until he jockeyed a position next to Michael.

"I don't want to talk to you," Michael told him. "You're the reason I'm in this mess."

"Just listen a minute," Skylar said. "All we have to do is stay together on our story. Just say we went down to Mexico with my dad for some drug deal he was doing and things didn't go so well. Say the guy didn't have enough money for my dad. So he killed him."

"I don't want to listen to you anymore," Michael said. "I just want out of this, I want to go home to my family."

"And you will," Skylar said. "If you stick to the story. And if you do, I'll take care of your family, no matter what happens, I promise. I'll look after them, even if you get convicted. But you won't, because as far as the cops will know, my dad did it."

But Skylar didn't sound like the cocky man who once likened himself to the devil. He sounded panicked. Even a little paranoid, rambling on about other people "narcing him out."

"I think Jennifer might even be talking," he confided. "But I tell you something, if I go down for this? Everyone goes down with me."

Michael was scared. And he had reason to be. In court, Matt didn't go easy on him, charging him with the same offense as Skylar—murder. Even if his version of events were true, even if he was duped into cooperating with the murder, Matt wanted Michael nervous. He wanted him to realize he could spend the rest of his life in prison if he decided to change his story again and cover for Skylar. It worked. Michael ignored Skylar's advice and cooperated with police. After 7 months behind bars, he was released on his own recognizance. If he continued to cooperate, and made good on a promise to testify against his cousin and Jennifer in court, he would likely be offered a plea bargain that would allow him to remain a free man.

CHAPTER THIRTY-ONE

"My dad's the reason I'm here," Skylar said into the phone from behind the glass partition. In the months since going to jail, his face grew gaunt, his cheeks caved inward. The orange jail jumpsuit he wore hung on him like an overcoat swallowing the wire frame of a hanger. His weight dipped from 165 pounds when he entered custody to a slight 115.

The small frame made him look dainty and vulnerable. He spoke in almost a whisper.

After months behind bars, Skylar agreed to a jail interview, the first time he would speak out since his arrest. Skylar knew the conversation would be against the wishes of his attorney, who advised him to keep his mouth shut, especially to police and reporters. But again, Skylar, hungry for the spotlight, didn't care.

"My dad," Skylar went on, "he was the one who knew the Hawkses. I only met them through him. My dad is a big drug runner. He said he was there for some drug deal with them."

According to Skylar, the Hawkses were major dealers themselves. The *Well Deserved*, he said, was for drug runs between Mexico and the United States.

"Methamphetamine," Skylar said. "They sold meth."

He soundlessly mouthed out most of his story, in an attempt

to keep the jail's recording system from picking up his conversation. Other times, he used a small pencil to jot down words and phrases, then pressing his note to the glass, out of sight from the guards behind him.

He picked up his pencil to jot out, "I was paying them for my dad. I last saw them alive after visiting them on that boat."

As far as Skylar saw it, he had been charged in the deaths of two people who were never murdered.

"As far as I know, they are still alive," he wrote. "I did go on that boat, but I left and they were still alive. Alonso stayed with them after I left. He was suppose to stay with them."

When challenged, told that his story sounded crazy, since nothing in the Hawkses' past indicated they were anything but honest, hard-working people, a crushed look crossed his face.

"I know," he mouthed, imploring with his eyes to be believed. "But it's true."

His dad was the one who should be arrested, he said.

"I know he's around, he's in the country still," he said. "He still calls my stepmom, threatens her all the time. But he's real sick. He has HIV."

And yet—despite going to great lengths to trash his father and pin the murders on him—Skylar still clearly had an emotional attachment to him. He was disappointed John hadn't found a way to pay him a visit.

"I thought maybe he was going to come see me today," Skylar said. "He told my stepmom he wanted to see me. He said he would try to see me today."

As he spoke, Skylar pushed a pair of adult diapers he was holding to the side.

"For my incontinence," he said.

He also held on to two photographs. He picked them both up and held them to the glass. One was of his children, both dressed in white and sitting against a white background, looking adorably innocent.

"I miss them so much," he said. "I just want to get out of here. I want to get back to my wife and my kids."

The other was of Skylar and Jennifer, dancing on their wedding day. The groom in that picture looked so dramatically different from the man today, holding the photo. He was heavier, even muscular, with his face round and full and happy.

"I don't know why I'm losing so much weight," he said. "I'm not getting what I need in here. Diapers, medical supplies, stuff like that. When I got down to a hundred and twenty-three pounds, they gave me double portions, took blood tests. But they couldn't find anything. So they put me back on single portions and now I'm down to a hundred and fifteen pounds. I don't know why I can't have double portions anymore."

Nerves, he said, had nothing to do with it. Despite knowing he could spend the rest of his life in prison, despite knowing he could even lose his life, Skylar claimed he was not the least bit scared.

"I just want this to be over so I can go home," he said. "Home to Jennifer."

Their marriage, he said, would of course survive the drama they were currently going through—though she had, he acknowledged, stopped writing to him.

"But that's just because of her attorney," he said. "He won't let her. But the last time we were in court, she was in the cell next to me, so we could talk. We just talked about how much we love each other. And miss each other. Yeah, when we get out, we'll be together. I know it."

Skylar's weight dropped to 99 pounds.

"I'm sick," he told guards at the jail. "I need to go to the hospital."

In fact, Skylar had been to the hospital many times during his incarceration. But the doctors never found anything wrong with him. Still, the weight continued to plummet.

The deputies who ran the Santa Ana jail housing should have been alarmed by his appearance. And they would have been—if they didn't know better. If they hadn't figured out exactly what Skylar was up to.

Skylar ate most of his food. Even scooped up most of the second helping he was given. Then he threw it all back up. Other inmates watched the routine, as Skylar thrust his finger down his throat to force up anything he'd ingested. He'd follow that with a round of jumping jacks, his cellmates said.

But that wasn't all. As his physique grew increasingly slender, he began growing out his hair and his fingernails. He spent the money Jennifer's parents sent him on ChapStick and colored pencils at the jail's commissary, which he mixed together to create lipstick. He shaved off his eyebrows and then drew them in with a brown pencil, etching out a thin and finely arched brow. When that wasn't enough, he wrote to Jennifer, asking her to send him some of her makeup.

"Just some of the Wet 'n' Wild stuff," he told her, referring to the cheap, bottom-of-the-barrel makeup line. "I need it because the guards are making me dress like a woman or they say they'll beat me up."

In truth, he simply wanted to turn himself into a transsexual.

Eventually, he had some shocking news for a doctor during one of his hospital visits.

"I used to have a uterus," he said. "I was born with one. And before I was arrested, I was even taking hormone injections to prepare for my gender reassignment surgery."

He claimed he was getting sick, now, because he needed to continue taking them.

But authorities were not buying his act.

"If I had a dollar every time some guy comes in claiming he's born with girl parts and needs an operation . . ." the jail psychologist told Sergeant Byington.

For most inmates, according to the psychologist, the claim is really a form of gender dysphoria, a condition in which a person of one sex better identifies with the other. But for Skylar, investigators believed he had a more simple motivation.

"His whole deal is to show the jury, 'Hey, how could I have possibly done these things?'" Sergeant Byington said. "He wants them to think, 'How could such a slight man like that kill three people?'"

There probably was a lot of truth in Sergeant Byington's interpretation of Skylar's feminization. But according to Mike Molfetta, it isn't the first time Skylar has pulled his "man trapped in the body of a woman" routine.

"He's told Jennifer before that he was born with a uterus," Mike Molfetta said. "He told her he needed an operation to have it removed. But I don't believe he's ever talked to her about a sex change operation. But he's just a freak, when you look at how wacky his lies are. The man's such a liar, how do you ever know what he's talking about? And you know what? What a great defense to use in his death penalty phase—he's a confused boy, anguished over this lifelong deformity. It'll be a great act! He'll do anything to garner sympathy."

Matt Murphy, however, rolled his eyes in disgust at Skylar's latest antics.

"I don't care if he shows up in court in a skirt and lipstick. I'm still going to prove he was sane the day he murdered those people," Matt said.

But there was at least one more motivation for Skylar's weight loss and gender confusion routine.

From jail, Skylar began laying the groundwork for his escape. And the hospital, where security would be the most lax, was his best chance at making a run for it. And so, his many trips to the doctor were nothing short of reconnaissance visits, a chance to scope out easy exits.

But Skylar didn't believe he could pull it off all on his own. He needed help. Again, he looked to gang members—white supremacists and black gang inmates, with connections to fellow bangers on the outside. Someone looking to make a lot of money.

"I'll pay them a hundred and fifty thousand dollars if they'll help me bust out of the hospital," he told an inmate with ties to the Crips.

But that wasn't all he'd ask of them—he also wanted someone who was willing to kill. Michael Lewis had to go. And so did his father, John Jacobson. With them dead, he figured, it would be a lot harder to disprove his fictional story, the one alleging his big, bad drug-dealing daddy was behind it all.

To fund his scheme, Skylar befriended a naïve but wealthy young man who landed in jail on suspicion of oral copulation on a minor. As the man awaited his day in court, Skylar learned his fellow inmate was sitting on a trust fund worth a few hundred thousand dollars. Within weeks, he conned his new friend into giving him the access code to his account at TD Water-house. Skylar didn't hesitate calling the Waterhouse company, arranging for a $200,000 check to come his way.

As Skylar saw his plan fall into place, he furiously wrote Jennifer a series of letters. "You'll see," he told her. "We'll get out of this. You'll see. I'll make it alright."

But as with everything Skylar planned, there were snags. An alert TD Waterhouse employee was suspicious over the transaction and reported it to the account holder's family. The check never arrived.

And Skylar didn't count on betrayal from his fellow inmates, either. Maybe he knew it was possible, but with not much else to lose, it was a gamble he was willing to take.

"Hey, your boy is in here asking us to kill people," came one call into Matt Murphy's office. "He wants witnesses in his case killed."

It wouldn't be the last call, either. And there were letters, too. All from inmates alleging Skylar offered them money for various things: to swear in court they were together in Mexico on the day of the Hawkses' murders, to help him bust out of the hospital, to help him murder his cousin, to murder his father. One guy reported Skylar was drawing out maps to Mike's house and giving detailed descriptions of John's converted U-Haul truck. Another wrote to say Skylar was walking around talking about his "buddies from the Marines" who were planning to bust him out. The inmates were all eager to talk, hoping to cut a deal for themselves in the process.

Matt decided to shut Skylar up for good, slapping him with two charges of solicitation to commit murder. Matt never expected he'd actually go to trial on the charge, he just wanted Skylar to know they were on to him. And to ensure he couldn't scheme anything else, Matt arranged it so Skylar would sit in isolation until trial.

"I don't want him talking to anyone," Matt said. "The guy's fucking mouth is dangerous."

Matt tried to use the opportunity to convince John Jacobson it was time to cooperate with investigators, and testify against his son.

"I know he did some bad things," John said. "I know he tried to have me killed. But you know what? He's still my kid, and I won't do it."

He even tried to make good on his promise to visit Skylar, though jailers wouldn't grant the former convict's request. Instead, he left behind $40 on his son's account in jail, just so Skylar would know his dad was thinking of him.

John did, however, vow to testify to anything when it came to Jennifer.

"That bitch," he said. "She's the one who got my son into all of this. My kid didn't do anything until she met him."

Matt nodded. It's nothing he hadn't thought about himself. Skylar was still a cold-blooded killer in his mind. But it's true he never broke a law until he met Jennifer. Once they got together—"Fire and gasoline," Matt said. "Fire and gasoline."

Mike Molfetta worried for his client. He spent a lot of time convincing her she needed to cut ties with Skylar, for her own sake. If Mike had it his way, she'd get right up on the stand and testify against her husband. And now was her chance. Matt didn't challenge Mike's request to sever Jennifer's case away from the other defendants. So she would be tried alone, without her husband and John and everyone else at her side. And now, her trial would begin in a few short months, on November 7, 2006.

Mike's strategy was simple—Jennifer would have to testify how she had been manipulated, deceived. She'd admit that maybe she was a little dumb and couldn't see that Skylar had been lying to her repeatedly. She couldn't see that because she loved him, probably a little too much. But she never thought the father of her children would betray her this way, making her an unwitting accomplice in his murder scheme. Maybe then she'd come off as sympathetic. Other women on the jury could maybe relate to her. They'd see her as another one of Skylar's victims.

But to make that believable, she'd have to turn on him. And that was hard for Jennifer. Even if it meant earning her freedom, going home to her kids, she still couldn't let go of him.

"You don't understand," Jennifer said. "I am angry at him. I'm pissed off. But my kids. How can I testify against their father?"

It sounded like an excuse. But Mike tried to understand her position. If Skylar were put to death, she'd forever carry the knowledge that she helped put him on death row. She'd be reminded of that fact every time she looked at their son and daughter.

But Mike bluntly told her to grow up.

"If ever a guy needed to be put down, Skylar does," he said. "As a man, I'd like to grab him by the neck and throttle him myself."

Jennifer claimed to get it. She knew she should probably divorce him. For now, she promised not to speak to him again.

"I hope so," Mike told her, "because there are only two choices here. Either you will go home. Or you will spend the rest of your life in prison."

She did stop writing her husband—though he continued writing her. Often. She kept every letter. And when he wrote that her parents had stopped visiting him, stopped bringing by the children, Jennifer should have turned a blind eye to his complaints. But she was there to defend him.

Lana and Steve admitted they didn't want to see him anymore. They were furious to learn he used the dollars they gave him each week to buy ChapStick and colored pencils to turn himself into a woman. Finally, Steve Henderson grew a backbone and stood up to his daughter. Despite what she wanted, he refused to take his grandkids to see their father. Jennifer, typically, blew up. She couldn't stand her loss of control. During a jail visit with her cousin, Danielle Dunning, Jennifer unleashed her temper.

"You know, my father was supposed to come visit me yesterday, but he didn't," Jennifer told Danielle. "So he's depriving me of my dad. And now he's going to deprive my kids of theirs?"

"Yeah," Danielle said, trying to placate Jennifer.

"My mom, she wants me to take it out on her and not my dad, but he's the one who made that decision . . . Whatever. He got his Father's Day card. And he doesn't even talk to me anymore."

"You have a right to be upset," Danielle offered.

"I love my dad, but he's an asshole," she told Danielle. "That's just the way it's always been. You know, and he likes to control everything. It makes you wonder why I ended up marrying somebody that doesn't make any decisions. That doesn't act like he cares, at least that I know of, you know? Somebody that seems so passive, because, it's like, I finally get to have my say."

CHAPTER THIRTY-TWO

It is a tragic irony that in those days, as Jen made demands ensuring her children would continue to know their parents, Matt and Ryan prepared a final good-bye to their own.

On July 29, 2005, Tom and Jackie would have celebrated sixteen years of marriage together. To mark the occasion, the pair, who spent so much time having fun in the sun, wanted to do something different—a trip exploring Alaska's wilderness.

Instead, friends and family planned a memorial service on the couple's anniversary date, at long last taking the time to publicly mourn their passing, and say good-bye. Ryan led the service in San Diego, California, where Tom's brother, Ryan's mom, and countless fellow boaters gathered to grieve. At the same moment, Matt and Tom's father led another ceremony in Prescott, Arizona, where Tom worked and Jackie raised her family. And in Cleveland, Ohio, Jackie's parents held a ceremony for 100 people in a state park near their home.

In a nod to the couple's Hawaiian-style wedding so many years ago, most of the mourners wore Hawaiian shirts and flip-flops.

Ryan addressed the 100 mourners at Mission Bay Park, telling them how, as a kid, he never quite understood his father's tough love method of raising his sons.

" 'You'll thank us when you turn out to be the man you will become,' " Ryan said his father would tell him. Tears filling his eyes, he said, "Well, I never got to thank them."

With no bodies to bury, the memorial was the formal act of good-bye to the couple their son described as having "an ambition for life."

"From a family standpoint, we want them to know we realize they've passed on to a better place," he said. "And they did it together."

In Ohio, Gayle O'Neill, a devout Catholic, read a passage from the Bible before kneeling with her husband, Jack, to toss a wreath of carnations into a nearby pond. Others joined them at the water's edge to toss in flowers and offer words of prayer.

Because they were planners, Tom and Jackie actually had wills drawn up before they set off on their ocean voyage. They left specific instructions on how they'd like their lives to be remembered should they meet an untimely demise. And what they wanted did not involve tears and words of regret. They wanted a party, full of laughter and Pacifico beers. They even set aside enough cash to pay for the celebration.

Relatives said they weren't ignoring the request. The memorial, they insisted, was just a placeholder for the big event to come. There will be a time to party, Ryan insisted, once justice is served.

"We can't celebrate their life yet," he told reporters that day. "Not until the people responsible for taking their lives are punished for everything they did."

Shortly after their disappearance, the family created a website, tomandjackiehawks.com. What began in the early days of the investigation as a tool for spreading word on the search evolved into something so much more. It became the go-to point for updates in the case, to share photos of the couple, and post messages of love, grief and anger.

As the months passed, and then a year came and left, the website still received hundreds of new messages from friends and strangers all over the country, touched by the tragic story.

"I met Tom & Jackie in October last year at Catalina Island," wrote one website guest. "They invited some friends and myself to [the] *Well Deserved* for dinner. In the few hours I was lucky to share with them I saw a couple that truly loved each other and life itself more than anyone I have ever met. I was a stranger and was treated like an old friend. . . . Happy anniversary, Tom and Jackie. You are in my heart."

"Tom and Jackie," read another entry, "we love and miss you very much, God keep you in his loving arms. Love, Captain Rich and Kelly and family."

"What a tragedy," began another, "Like Tom, I'm also 57 and have realized that life is just too short. I now intend to adopt Tom's fitness routine as part of my personal quest. May Tom and Jackie's spirits live on in all our lives."

Other messages were full of outrage.

"Hang the perpetrators of this heinous crime," said one. "Hang them now. Deal punishment swiftly and severely. I just this moment read about the Hawkses' death[s] and it chilled my soul."

"I don't know Tom and Jackie personally," came a January 2006 entry, "but I have been keeping up with the story. I know . . . that those murderers are where they should be. . . . I hope they rot in prison."

Eventually, the site became a place for messages of love from friends and family during the holidays, birthdays, or any time the family gathered.

"Happy B-Day to 'THE BEST FRIEND' anyone could ever ask for," Hal and wife Mary wrote on December 24, 2005. "We talk to Matt & Ryan and I am so impressed how much they are both like you, each in their own way. . . . I LOVE and MISS YOU, MY FRIEND. Remember, You WILL ALWAYS BE OLDER & SHORTER THEN ME."

Friends Mike and Kathy on April 8, 2006, added: "Tom and Jackie were our best friends. Our daughter and her husband gave birth to their son today. In loving memory of 'Uncle Tom' they named their son Jack Thomas."

"Another year has passed, darling daughter," Gayle wrote on April 22, 2006. "We miss you more and more each day. We all wanted to wish you a Happy Birthday. We will all get together again this year to celebrate for you and to remember what a wonderful Daughter, Sister, and Aunt you were. We know that you are with Tom and happy in the arms of our Lord. Love you so much."

"Happy Birthday MOM," Ryan wrote. "I Can't stop thinking of you, take care of DAD."

"We love and miss you," Matt added.

But one anonymous entry will always stand out for Ryan and Matt.

"I am a sister to one of those accused," began the message, "and I do want to say that I am very sorry for the losses. Your family is always in my prayers and I hope for the best. Although I do not ever think that my brother would ever do a thing like that. . . . God Bless You All and may justice be done for the Hawkses', to those who deserve it."

CHAPTER THIRTY-THREE

Dear Friends and Family,

The time has come for justice to be served for the murder of my parents on November 15th 2004. This Monday, November 6th trial will be held for Jennifer Henderson. Deputy District Attorney Matt Murphy will be giving his opening argument to the jury this day. This is one of the most important days to show support for Tom and Jackie Hawks because the jury needs to see how many lives they touched and the kind of people they really were.

I understand that some of you have responsibilities (job, children, etc.), and people show their support in different ways. This is a painful process so please don't feel obligated to come on my behalf, or my parents, because we know you have already shown a great amount of respect and support for our family. But if you can make it, the trial will be held at 700 Civic Center Drive West, in Santa Anna, California. It will be in Court Room C35 at 9:00 am.

Ryan Hawks
Nov. 2, 2006

Ryan's email announcement was effective. On day one of the trial, the courtroom was packed with supporters. And the media. Jennifer's mother, Lana, was there, too, looking on as her daughter entered the courtroom in a demure, soft pink sweater and gray slacks, her long brown hair pulled into a low ponytail, tied at the nape of her neck. She looked more schoolmarm than murderer. Mike Molfetta sat confidently at her side.

Matt knew he had his work cut out for him.

He had to somehow convince jurors that the doe-eyed young lady before them was a cold-blooded woman who helped mastermind two murders, and conspired to cover up a third. And he had to beat Mike Molfetta to do it.

But Matt had some powerful images on his side of the courtroom, too. Betty Jarvi, Jon's elderly mother, was there. So was Tom's brother, James, next to his loving wife. And in the front row sat Dixie, next to her son, Matt. And then there was Ryan.

In a tragic twist, Ryan was in a devastating dirt-biking accident just weeks before the trial began. His bike took a twenty-five-foot plunge over a cliff, going 35 mph. The fall knocked him unconscious. He came to in an intensive care unit, ironically, the very same hospital Jackie awoke in years ago following her nearly fatal motorcycle accident. Now, her stepson wearily opened his eyes to learn he was suffering from two broken femurs and a sprained neck. His doctors didn't know if he'd make it to the trial. But they didn't know Ryan.

"I've got to be there," he told them. "If I have to walk into that courtroom with a damn morphine drip attached to my arm, then that's what I'll do."

And so, he was there, his muscular frame now terribly thin, metal rods surgically implanted into his legs. He wore a neck brace. He was temporarily wheelchair-bound, and the right wheel of his chair cut slightly into the court aisleway. As a result, as jurors approached the jury box every day, they had to pass that chair, stepping around Ryan. They couldn't begin, or end, their daily service without inching by the victims' son.

Matt began, speaking to jurors for over two hours, methodically laying out his case against Jennifer. He painted her as a co-conspirator with her husband, who actively plotted the murder against the Hawkses. Even going onto their boat to meet them, holding her pregnant tummy and the hand of toddler Hailey, just to earn the trust of the people she knew her husband was going to kill.

"As we go through the evidence, keep asking yourself," Matt said, pausing a moment to point at the defendant, " 'What did she know?' "

Jennifer sat motionless, refusing to meet the prosecutor's gaze. She looked like a frightened girl. But Matt reminded his audience, "Jackie and Thomas Hawks were fooled by Jennifer Deleon. But you folks will not be fooled by her. You will not let this woman get away with what she did."

But Mike had an uglier villain to show the jury. He showed them Skylar. And blamed it all on him.

"He's more than what goes bump in the night," he told jurors. "He's more than the bogeyman. He is evil."

And Jennifer? Why, she was just a naïve wife, and mere putty in this master manipulator's hands, he said.

Early on in the trial, it was anybody's guess which version of the facts jurors would believe. It's true, she wasn't on the boat when Tom and Jackie died. It's true, Alonso, Matt's star witness, never saw her throughout any part of the planning.

But Alonso was with Skylar when he called his wife, telling her to come "put these people at ease." It was, however, Alonso's firsthand account of the Hawkses' death that riveted the courtroom. Especially his memory of Jackie, begging for her life.

From the stand, Alonso told of it all.

"She kept saying, 'Skylar, why are you doing this? We trusted you! You brought your wife and daughter here. We trusted you.' "

Alonso paused then, trying to hold in his own tears.

"She was just crying. She was just saying, 'I don't want to die.' "

Ryan never before shed a tear in court. It was that vow he made, not to let his parents' murderers see him break. But now, listening to those last moments, it was too much. He dipped his head and silently wept.

Matt painstakingly laid out the pattern of calls Skylar made to Jennifer's cell phone that night—and in the hours before and after JP's death. He put the real estate agent on the stand, who talked of Jennifer's orders to find a house with a 55-foot boat slip. He put Skylar's aunt on, Colleen Francisco, who testified to hearing her niece confess, "We needed the money." Even Jennifer's father testified against her, describing her as "happy" and "excited" the first day she brought him onboard her new yacht.

And Matt pointed out that if Jennifer was so frightened of her husband, then why did she pay him thirty-four visits while he was in jail—every day she could, until her own arrest?

Still, by the time Matt Murphy prepared to deliver his closing arguments, he wasn't sure he had the jury sold. He still worried they would buy Mike's tale of Jennifer as a loving wife kept in the dark and scared of an evil husband. Everything might ride on these last words delivered to jurors. What he said had to ring in their ears as they entered that deliberation room. It would be the closing statement of his career, he thought.

It was November 15, 2006, as he stood in front of the jurors.

"Today is the two-year anniversary of the Hawkses' death," Matt told them. "Just a quirk of the calendar that I'm offering you my closing argument today. But just think, Jennifer had all that time to say something. And she never did. And she didn't because she wasn't some scared, confused, manipulated housewife. She didn't because she was a co-conspirator in this. Her whole goal was to get their money. She wanted it. Every bit as much as Skylar did."

Matt spoke for most of the morning, summarizing every detail, convincing jurors Jennifer knew exactly who Skylar was, because she was just like him.

"Remember, she had a reminder of what her husband was all about every moment she was on the boat, charming the Hawkses," he told them. "Because the entire time she was on the *Well Deserved* that day, befriending Tom and Jackie, think about the ring she had on her finger. The one bought after Jon Jarvi was murdered. She was wearing a ring bought with Jon Jarvi's blood money. And she put it on her finger, and she wore it on the boat to meet the people she knew her husband was going to kill next.

"Every piece of evidence you've seen is consistent with one thing, and one thing only—she helped murder these people. Don't let her get away with it."

It was a powerful close, one that left even Mike Molfetta saying to jurors, "Wow. I've just gotta say, 'Wow.'"

But he hammered home that Jennifer was never on that boat. She wasn't in Mexico when Jon Jarvi was killed. And there was no physical evidence linking her to either scene. "There is no smoking gun," Molfetta said. "There is nothing. Zippo. This case boils down to one thing: Skylar.

"And nobody could control Skylar. Not his father. Not the Seal Beach jail, where he killed someone while in their custody. Not the Santa Ana Jail guards, where he solicited two murders and embezzled two hundred thousand dollars in their custody. But somehow, you are supposed to believe this woman, the schoolmarm, the churchgoer, she could control him? This vile bag of you-know-what? No way."

Both arguments were expertly presented. Mike fought hard to conjure up reasonable doubt for a willing juror. And, as Matt knew all too well, "You just never know what can go through a juror's mind," he said. "I think O. J. Simpson taught us all that."

But if the jurors were ever caonfused by the two very different presentations of Jennifer Deleon, there was no sign of it. It took just over a day before they returned their verdict.

As they pronounced her guilty, Jennifer's traditionally stoic face broke. In all the time investigators spent with her, they'd never seen her show any emotion other than the occasional outburst of anger. She didn't cry when her husband was arrested. She didn't cry when she was put into handcuffs. But now, as she listened to jurors pronounce her guilty on all counts, tears slid down her face. She never turned around to look at her parents, who burst into the courtroom late, moments after the verdict was read. Jennifer simply stood, allowing deputies to lead her away.

And as the jurors made their way out of the courtroom, the last juror to leave stepped around Ryan's chair once again, and this time, he briefly gripped the young man's shoulder and squeezed it tightly.

In a back conference room at the courthouse, the Hawks family gathered, waiting for Matt. When he finally entered, having given his last interview to the team of reporters in the hall, the Hawks family broke away from their chairs to give the prosecutor a standing ovation.

Matt could only smile. He had to admit—winning never felt so good.

In the hours before Jennifer was supposed to be sentenced for her role in the murders, she sent a letter to Superior Court Judge Frank Fasel, demanding a new attorney. Some thought it was just a stall tactic. But she insisted she wanted her current attorney, Mike Molfetta—a man considered one of the most talented defense attorneys in the county—fired. She accused him of being unprepared and inadequately representing her in court.

In truth, Mike had spent hundreds of hours preparing Jennifer's case. And more of those hours than he cared to remember were spent begging her to cut ties with Skylar. But she refused, continuing to write love letter after love letter to her husband. The fact of the matter was, by the time she heeded his advice, it was way too late. Not until nearly the eve of her trial, when she was finally scared for her own fate, did she cut him out.

The sad truth for Jennifer was, in fact, had she listened to her attorney a long time ago, she could have walked away a free woman.

Shortly after Mike agreed to represent Jennifer, Matt Murphy threw out what could have been a life-saver.

Back then, in the heat of the investigation, detectives still weren't sure what to think of Jennifer. She could have been, they conceded, the naïve church-going woman she presented herself to be. Or, well, if not that, then at least not a fellow mastermind in a plot to murder an innocent couple for a new boat. It was rare to run across a woman with a heart that cold.

So, Matt made the offer.

"If she cooperates," he said, "if she tells us everything she knows about Skylar, and everything she's overheard about the Hawkses' disappearance, we'll give her immunity."

As Mike laid out the offer to Jennifer, he knew what a sweetheart of a deal it was. He urged her to snap it up.

Still, days ticked by before Matt's phone rang with a response from Mike.

"She won't do it," he said. "We're turning it down."

Later, Mike would lament to an *Orange County Register* reporter, "Why pay good money for a lawyer if you're not going to listen to him? But I know what I do for a living. And I know that eventually, the lawyer is going to be blamed."

So, Judge Fasel granted Jennifer's request for a new lawyer and appointed her a public defender. A public defender would handle her appeal motions and stand next to her in court when her sentencing finally arrived.

Even Matt could only shake his head at the stupidity of her decision to let Mike go.

"It's just the final bad decision Jennifer has made in a long line of bad decisions for herself," he said.

Jennifer's conviction had an interesting effect on Skylar. He began showing up to court hearings looking, for all intents and purposes, like a woman.

During a pre-trial hearing, Skylar sat next to his attorney appearing needle-thin. His bony frame left his cheekbones so pronounced, some in the courtroom could have sworn he was wearing blush. He wore his eyebrows plucked and finely arched, while his fingernails had grown long and been neatly filed.

He looked absurd sitting next to his co-defendant, John Kennedy, whose muscles had grown even more hulking in jail. His shaved head and long, thin beard gave him a menacing look.

When the judge asked Skylar if he agreed to waive his right to a speedy trial so his defense attorney could have more time to prepare, he answered in a voice so soft and breathy, he could have been channeling Marilyn Monroe.

"Yes, sir," he daintily whispered.

And as Skylar sashayed his way back to the holding cell, Matt Murphy realized the gold-colored jail jumpsuit Skylar wore bore the words "Women's Jail" on the back.

Only later would Matt learn from jail deputies that from time to time, clothing from the women's facility gets mixed in with clothing from the men's. And somehow, some way, Skylar got his hands on a woman's jail jumpsuit, and decided to wear that to court.

Matt couldn't have cared less what Skylar wore to any pre-trial hearings. But he'd put his foot down when the trial began. The prosecutor was pretty sure he was on to Skylar's game.

"He wants the jury to look at him and say, 'Oh, that frail little guy couldn't have killed those people,'" Matt said. "And his lawyer can argue, 'Don't put Skylar to death. He's such a timid man, he'll never hurt anyone.'"

But Matt wasn't too concerned. He'd make them see the monster lurking within that feminine frame. He'd make them see beyond the arched eyebrows, into the murderer raging within.

CHAPTER THIRTY-FOUR

As the days of 2006 wound to a close, the wheels of justice rolled in full force for the Hawks family.

Jennifer was convicted on first-degree murder charges. By Oct. 5, 2007, she would be sentenced to two life sentences without the possibility of parole. She would spend the rest of her life in behind bars.

Alonso and Myron sat in jail, awaiting trial. They were both cooperating with police now, agreeing to testify against their co-conspirators. In doing so, they would save their lives, but not escape prison. Alonso would probably serve 15 years. Myron, even less, only because he wasn't stupid enough to be on the boat that tragic night.

Even Skylar's father had decided to stop protecting his son. He was now willing to testify against Skylar, if the prosecutor needed him, John admitted in a *Los Angeles Times* interview.

"If he has any heart left in him at all, he'll confess," John told the paper.

But it's doubtful a confession would make much of a difference now. Skylar Deleon and John Kennedy—scheduled for trial in early 2008—were about to face the ultimate penalty.

On September 5, 2006, Orange County District Attorney Tony Rackauckas held a press conference to make an announcement. His office, he told the press, would ask a jury to hand down the death penalty for Skylar Deleon and his muscleman, John Fitzgerald Kennedy. The callous way in which the Hawkses were murdered, coupled with Skylar's additonal murder charge, and John's long-time gang affiliation, all played a part in their decision, the DA said.

"The decision to seek the death penalty is the most serious responsibility I have as the district attorney," said Tony, standing at a podium before rows of camera crews, photographers, and journalists from all over Southern California. "But there are some murders that are committed with such a malignant heart, such callousness, that the only just penalty is death. This was a clear case. These two joined in this cruel and callous murder. Deleon the brain, Kennedy the brawn. Now they will face the same penalty and their fate will be decided by the People of Orange County."

It's an announcement Ryan and his family had been waiting almost two years to hear.

"I'm all for it," Ryan said. "But true justice would be to take them out on a boat, tied to a sixty-pound anchor, and let them sweat it out. Let them know it's coming as the boat rides out to sea. Then throw them over. That would be justice."

His family does take comfort, however, in knowing those responsible are now being forced to pay for their crime. The vow Ryan made to see every person in the plot punished will be fulfilled. He takes solace in remembering how hard the investigators and the prosecutor worked to give his family that. And he is grateful.

But the tragedy has forever changed him. It's hard to look at the world with unbridled optimism, the way he did before. It's hard to see only the good in people, the way he did before. And it's hard to fall into a sound sleep, the way he did before, without their final moments drifting into his mind.

"When I think of how my mom cried, how she breathed in her first breath of water when that anchor dropped, how my dad fought back even when he was blinded and handcuffed . . . That tension will forever be in my shoulders. It's a burden," Ryan said. "And I will always live with that."